Anguished Hope

Anguished Hope

Holocaust Scholars Confront the Palestinian-Israeli Conflict

Edited and Introduced by

Leonard Grob and John K. Roth

WILLIAM B. EERDMANS PUBLISHING COMPANY

GRAND RAPIDS, MICHIGAN / CAMBRIDGE, U.K.

Published 2008 by

Wm. B. Eerdmans Publishing Co.

2140 Oak Industrial Drive N.E., Grand Rapids, Michigan 49505 /

P.O. Box 163, Cambridge CB3 9PU U.K.

Printed in the United States of America

13 12 11 10 09 08   7 6 5 4 3 2 1

Library of Congress Cataloging-in-Publication Data

Anguished hope: Holocaust scholars confront the Palestinian-Israeli conflict /
    edited and introduced by Leonard Grob and John K. Roth.
        p.   cm.
    Includes bibliographical references and index.
    ISBN 978-0-8028-3329-7 (pbk.: alk. paper)
    1. Arab-Israeli conflict.   2. Holocaust, Jewish (1939-1945) — Influence.
    3. Holocaust, Jewish (1939-1945) — Moral and ethical aspects.
    4. Arab-Israeli conflict — Moral and ethical aspects.
    I. Grob, Leonard.   II. Roth, John K.

    DS119.7.A66596   2008
    956.04072 — dc22

                                                    2008012000

www.eerdmans.com

To Stephen and Nancy Weinstein
  who so generously support the Holocaust Symposium
    at Wroxton College

The highest form of wisdom is kindness.

Talmud Berakhot 17a

Yours is not to complete the task,
yet neither are you free to desist from it.

Ethics of the Fathers 2.20

Contents

PROLOGUE: *Haunted by the Holocaust*

Leonard Grob and John K. Roth

The opposite of life is not death, it's indifference.

Elie Wiesel

Having survived the Holocaust, Elie Wiesel has dedicated his life to fighting against indifference, against silence in the face of injustice. For Wiesel, indifference is not morally neutral: "When truth is in danger, silence equals guilt."[1] Addressing the question of what kind of response can break the silence of indifference, Wiesel notes that "there are no sufficient literary, psychological, or historical answers to human tragedy, only moral ones."[2]

The thirteen contributors to this volume — all scholars of the Holocaust — are at one in the endeavor to combat silence with a *moral* response to the human tragedy that is the Palestinian-Israeli conflict. Although no comparison is intended between the systematic destruction of European Jewry during the Holocaust and the ongoing strife in the Middle East, the essayists in this volume try to remain faithful to Wiesel's assertion that "wherever men or women are persecuted because of their race, religion, or political views, that place must — at that moment — become the center of

1. Elie Wiesel, *And the Sea Is Never Full: Memoirs, 1969-*, trans. Marion Wiesel (New York: Schocken Books, 1999), p. 136.
2. Elie Wiesel, "The Nobel Lecture," delivered December 11, 1986, in *From the Kingdom of Memory: Reminiscences* (New York: Summit Books, 1990), p. 249.

1

the universe."[3] The contributors to *Anguished Hope* thus refuse to avert their eyes from the often lethal acts of hostility carried out on a daily basis in that region of the world. They choose not to be bystanders in the face of a seemingly intractable conflict, one that has been termed nothing short of a new Hundred Years' War. While addressing the current suffering of both Palestinians and Israelis, each contributor endeavors to attend to the silent screams of the victims of the Holocaust; each feels the heavy weight of speaking before the faces of the murdered ones. Aspiring to honor the memory of the Holocaust's six million dead, each contributor addresses the dilemmas and prospects that produce "anguished hope" for a just resolution of the struggle in the Middle East.

Never before, to our knowledge, has a group of Holocaust scholars *writing as such* collaborated on a volume dedicated solely to the Middle East conflict. The contributors to this book are convinced that those who possess expertise in Holocaust studies have a distinctive responsibility to address the Palestinian-Israeli conflict. What is the source of this conviction?

The specter of the Holocaust haunts the turmoil in the Middle East. What the Holocaust scholar Zygmunt Bauman calls "the Holocaust's life as a ghost" is never far from the Middle East arena,[4] contaminating the air breathed by both Israelis and Palestinians. Israeli Jews, like their Jewish counterparts everywhere in the world, have been traumatized by the memory of centuries of antisemitism, which culminated in the Holocaust. Given the murder of one out of every three Jews alive just seven decades ago, how could the Jews of Israel and elsewhere *not* suffer trauma? As a people, Jews have become "hereditary victims,"[5] whether or not someone in their immediate family or even an acquaintance had been slaughtered at the hands of the Nazis. Jews worldwide — and most especially Israeli Jews living in a state whose very existence and legitimacy are questioned by some of its Palestinian and other Arab neighbors — view the world in terms of actual or potential victimizers and victims, paradoxically drawing "a sense-giving reassurance from every sign of hostility toward them."[6]

3. Elie Wiesel, "The Nobel Address," delivered December 10, 1986, in *From the Kingdom of Memory*, p. 233.

4. Zygmunt Bauman, "The Holocaust's Life as a Ghost," *Tikkun: A Bimonthly Jewish Critique of Politics, Culture, and Society* 13, no. 4 (July–August 1998): 33-39.

5. Ibid., p. 36.

6. Ibid., p. 37.

What some have termed an Israeli "siege mentality" is but one manifestation of the workings of the Holocaust's life as a ghost.

This is not to say that ghosts must be conjured up to account for wariness on the part of Jews living in many nations who currently suffer from a resurgence of age-old antisemitism and the advent of newer forms of antisemitism. Nor must ghosts be posited to explain the fear of Israeli Jews who, as of this writing in the summer of 2006, faced the danger of Hezbollah's rocket attacks and continued suicide bombings and explicit threats of the eradication of their state emanating not only from Hezbollah but also from other extremist groups, such as Hamas and Islamic Jihad, as well as from the governments of Iran and Syria. The blend of threats — perceived and real — to Israel's existence has produced a toxic brew.

The very establishment of the State of Israel is linked inextricably to the fate of six million Jews during the Holocaust. Although Zionism has millennia-old roots in the yearnings of the Jewish people to return to the land of their forbears, the birth of the State of Israel and the ongoing Palestinian-Israeli conflict have emerged in significant ways from the events of 1933-45. Memory of the Holocaust pervades the consciousness of Israelis. Explicit allusions to the necessity that Israel remain strong in the face of the Palestinians — the current "Amalek," or inveterate foe — abound in the Hebrew press. Today's "tough" Israeli Jews are contrasted with those (alleged) Diaspora weaklings who are criticized — inaccurately and unfairly — for allowing themselves to be victimized during the two millennia of antisemitism, which reached its climax during the Holocaust. "Never again!" became the mantra both of successive Israeli governments and of the ordinary Israeli on the street; Jewish blood would never again be shed with impunity. The State of Israel was to change the direction of a history that had culminated in the destruction of two-thirds of European Jewry.

Memory of traumatic events in both the distant past and, especially, the more recent past haunts Palestinians as well. Although Muslims have constituted a majority in historic Palestine for more than thirteen centuries, the indigenous people of the region have seldom been treated justly by a succession of ruling powers. During the late nineteenth century and first half of the twentieth, Jews fleeing the pogroms — and later the gas chambers — of eastern Europe brought about the dispossession of large numbers of these indigenous people. Escaping the burning buildings of

Europe, Jews "landed on the backs of the Palestinians."[7] With great frequency do Palestinians allude to the 1948 establishment of the State of Israel and the expulsion of hundreds of thousands of inhabitants of the land as their Naqba, or catastrophe. Just as Israeli Jews halt all activity and observe a moment of silence on Yom Hashoah (Holocaust Remembrance Day), so do Palestinians observe a silence on Israeli Independence Day — the day of the Great Catastrophe. "My Holocaust is as traumatic for me as yours is for you," is a commonplace saying among Palestinians as they address claims that Israelis alone are true victims.

Many Palestinians argue that the U.N. partition plan of 1947 was largely, or even solely, the product of European guilt: Palestinians were to pay the price for the actions of European perpetrators and bystanders during the Holocaust. Jewish suffering during the Holocaust is said to be a mere pretext for what is in reality little more than acts of raw Western imperialism. In the Muslim Middle East and notably from Iran's president, Mahmoud Ahmadinejad, resentment and rage against Israel are fueled — with the contradiction ignored or the irony unintended — both by denial that the Holocaust ever happened and by invidious comparisons that equate Israeli policies toward Palestinians with Nazi Germany's genocide against the Jews of Europe. In sum, both Palestinians and Israelis perceive themselves as victims in a seemingly interminable conflict that is incessantly haunted by the ghost of the Holocaust.

For the contributors to this book, then, those who study the Holocaust have a duty to speak out about the Palestinian-Israeli conflict. Jewish and Christian essayists, represented in roughly equal numbers in this volume, share the commitment to honoring the Holocaust's dead in the course of addressing the conflagration in the Middle East. Each recognizes that the Holocaust is a watershed event in human history, one that calls for a reexamination of the ethical and religious traditions in the West that proved themselves unable to stem the tide of Nazi Germany's genocidal acts. Both Jewish and Christian contributors acknowledge (explicitly or tacitly) that traditional paradigms of moral conduct or of theological understandings cannot provide reliable lenses through which to view the Middle East conflict.

Jewish contributors speak against the backdrop of a world that has

7. Michael Lerner, *Jewish Renewal: A Path to Healing and Transformation* (New York: G. P. Putnam's Sons, 1994), p. 219.

given ample cause for total despair. They address the Palestinian-Israeli conflict in the context of refusing such despair, identifying *challenges* (Part I of this book), noting *risks* (Part II), and, finally, working toward *tikkun olam,* the "repair of the world," in the course of setting forth *possibilities* (Part III). Christian contributors, mindful of their tradition's two millennia of anti-Jewish thought, which seeded the ground for the coming of a Holocaust, refuse their own forms of despair. Haunted by the memory of a genocide carried out on the Christian watch, and therefore questioning and reconfiguring elements of their faith traditions, the Christian essayists identify challenges, risks, and possibilities pertinent to an ongoing conflict involving the welfare of both their Jewish and Muslim brothers and sisters. Although *Anguished Hope* does not presume to provide "solutions" for the Palestinian-Israeli conflict, both Jewish and Christian contributors agree that post-Holocaust reflection about the conflict can contribute perspective, vision, and sensitivity, without which the chances for just solutions are diminished.

None of the contributors to this volume lays claim to special expertise in Middle East studies. Their scholarly experience and expertise are not in the disciplines — most especially history and political science — from which Middle East scholarship has traditionally emerged. Instead, these writers study and teach literature, philosophy, education, religion, and theology. These disciplines and perspectives also have important and even fresh insights regarding the Middle East conflict. The contributors, moreover, utilize the fact that they are somewhat removed from expertise in Middle East studies to make the case for a sensitive humility with regard to the dilemmas at hand. The volume's organization, style, and texture underscore its commitment to a spirit that combines passion and modesty, strong argument and the thoughtful listening that dialogue entails and enjoins.

This collection of essays is first and foremost conceived as a conversation among concerned colleagues who share a focus on the Holocaust as a common point of departure for discussing the Palestinian-Israeli conflict. Each essay in this volume is followed by a series of questions distilled from queries raised by the twelve other essayists. These constellations of questions are then addressed by the original contributor in a second essay, entitled simply "Response." The volume's format thus illustrates the claim — implicit or explicit in each essay — that dialogue between the warring parties must replace the ongoing violence in the region.

A commitment to speak from a common base in Holocaust studies does not imply that the contributors to this book reach anything resembling consensus with regard to the specific nature of the challenges, risks, and possibilities identified throughout the work. Responses to the conflict run the gamut from a suggestion that fidelity to memory of the victims demands that the Holocaust, in some sense, be "forgotten" so that a just two-state solution can be forged, all the way to the assertion that the lessons of the Holocaust demand some hard questioning as to whether a solution of that kind is truly realizable — or even desirable. As the writing of these essays unfolded, priority was given not to consensus among the contributors but to the hope that each contributor would listen well to the others: In the words of the German Jewish philosopher Martin Buber, "In a genuine dialogue each of the partners, even when he stands in opposition to the other, heeds, affirms, and confirms his opponent as an existing other."[8] The contributors to this volume tried to honor the essence of Buber's declaration.

The contributors to *Anguished Hope* come from four nations: Belgium, Germany, the United Kingdom, and the United States. This international makeup helps to promote the book's dialogical thrust, for several of the essayists pointedly address prevailing (and often conflicting) perspectives on the Palestinian-Israeli conflict that exist in their home countries. In particular, many European perspectives have challenged and enriched those of American contributors; some American understandings of the conflict have done the same for those of the European contributors.

The intent to speak to one another dialogically is expedited by the fact that all thirteen contributors are part of a group that meets biennially in Oxfordshire, England, at the Wroxton College campus of Fairleigh Dickinson University. The Wroxton Holocaust Symposium, led since 1996 by Leonard Grob and Henry Knight, is devoted to international, interfaith, intergenerational, and interdisciplinary dialogue. Committed to returning to Wroxton every two years and to working with one another in the intervening months, the group's thirty-six members share a concern to use their base in Holocaust studies as a means to work toward "the repair of the world." Few of the minefields that threaten to explode in the face of partners-in-dialogue are more dangerous than the Palestinian-Israeli conflict. Addressing this conflict has tested the mettle of the contributors to *Anguished Hope.* How were we to remain committed to dialogue in the face of that conflict, which has served as a lightening rod, igniting the passions

8. Martin Buber, *Pointing the Way* (New York: Harper & Row, 1958), p. 238.

of Holocaust scholars everywhere? How could these scholars best honor Wiesel's claim that "when human lives are endangered, when human dignity is in jeopardy, national borders and sensitivities become irrelevant"?[9]

In the endeavor to be faithful to Wiesel's injunction, we were blessed with two extraordinary opportunities. First, in June 2004 all thirteen of us gathered around a seminar room table at Wroxton to review and comment on the initial abstracts for our respective essays. Then, in July 2005, as the writing process moved toward completion, the generous hospitality of the Samuel Rosenthal Center for Judaic Studies and its director, Peter Haas, permitted nine of us to meet at Case Western Reserve University, in Cleveland, Ohio, to review the first draft of the entire volume. Those who were unable to make the journey to Cleveland were kept abreast of our discussions through extensive e-mail contact. In the end, despite having endured some tense moments, we tamed our most unruly passions and engaged one another in constructive dialogue. The reader will have to be the judge, but we hope that our reflections on the Palestinian-Israeli conflict — generously supported by Bill Eerdmans and Roger Van Harn, and clarified and enhanced by Linda Bieze and Craig Noll, our fine editors — embody another of Martin Buber's observations: "When a man is singing and cannot lift his voice, and another comes and sings with him, another who can lift his voice, the first will be able to lift his voice too."[10]

Our project is ongoing, even as our work as contributors to an edited volume is at an end. We have learned — and must continue to relearn — to listen to one another. Not only in these pages and in their aftereffects but also in the Middle East itself, the voice of the other must continue to be heard even in his or her physical absence as we proceed, in the words of Theodore Adorno, to "think against ourselves." In one fundamental respect, however, we leave the volume as we began it: We leave in *anguish* before the seemingly unending cycles of violence in the Middle East. And we leave in *hope* that, despite a century of unrelenting enmity, a just reconciliation can ultimately result from the Palestinian-Israeli conflict. Even as the conflict continues to rage, we refuse despair, heeding the words of the sages who remind us that we are never free to desist from contributing to the work of *tikkun olam.*

9. Wiesel, "The Nobel Address," p. 233.
10. Martin Buber, *Ten Rungs: Hasidic Sayings* (New York: Schocken Books, 1947), p. 84.

I. CHALLENGES

If we who study the Holocaust are to have hope — albeit "*anguished* hope" — for Israeli-Palestinian reconciliation, we must not avert our eyes from the many challenges that lie before us as we address the Middle East conflict. Part I of this volume presents responses to a series of such challenges by five of our contributors. From their study of the Holocaust, these authors identify issues that they believe must confront all those who would reflect on resolution of the Israeli-Palestinian conflict. All endeavor to face these challenges head-on, arguing that the lessons of Holocaust may yield some fresh insights into possibilities for peace in the Middle East.

In the opening chapter Peter J. Haas addresses a fundamental challenge to all observers of the Israeli-Palestinian conflict: If no answers regarding a satisfactory resolution of the conflict have thus far emerged, perhaps, Haas suggests, the wrong questions are being asked. Israelis and Palestinians have each created what Haas terms a Grand Narrative, a tale of possession and dispossession in the ongoing conflict. Both narratives make claim to exclusive possession of Truth and Justice. In the course of telling what is deemed to be "the" story of the conflict, each people demonizes the other, regarding that other as ultimately incapable of understanding anything but brute force. Haas's understanding of mutually exclusive and absolutist moral accounts owes much to his study of the monolithic narrative constructed by the Nazis during the 1930s and 1940s. That narrative depicted Aryans as the only true humans, allowing Jews, in particular, to be regarded as subhuman and thus to occupy a space outside the bounds of a moral universe. Haas explores the dangers inherent in Israeli and Palestinian absolutist versions of what is right, just, and true. Employing as a case study the mutually exclusive interpretations of the cause of the reported death in 2000 of Muhammad al-Dura, a twelve-year-old Palestinian, Haas lays bare the dangers of allowing one allegedly objective narrative to define what constitutes a moral universe. Haas concludes his chapter by arguing that hope resides in the possibility that each party may be willing to alter its Grand Narrative so as to allow for the legitimation of at least some elements of the Grand Narrative of the other.

Echoing Haas's theme that what is deemed moral may well endanger prospects for the peaceful resolution of conflicts, John K. Roth cites the Holocaust as a prime example of the possibility that we humans can be "duped by morality": Both pre- and post-Holocaust Western ethico-religious imperatives failed to prevent genocide. Indeed, beliefs in "the just" or "the good" have proved, and continue to prove, deceptively reassuring. The reader is challenged by Roth to rethink whether or not we are the dupes of what is commonly understood as the moral high ground. Roth uses as a case study what he believes to be the well-intentioned, but most certainly misguided, actions of the Presbyterian Church U.S.A., which in 2004 endorsed a policy of selective divestment from multinational corporations operating in Israel. Although couched in stirring moral terms, this divestment initiative, according to Roth, unjustly characterized Israel as the more culpable of the two parties to the Middle East conflict. Forgotten in the course of Presbyterian advocacy of divestment was Jewish memory of the boycotts that preceded the Holocaust and that served as a harbinger of what was to come. Forgotten as well, Roth argues, is the fact that Israel, for all its military might, remains at present an imperiled people. Rather than allowing questionable, often facile moral judgments to support policies of *divestment,* the Presbyterians, according to Roth, might act more in accordance with the prophetic injunction to pursue justice if they were to *invest* more fully in peacemaking initiatives in the region. Financial resources could be employed to support those forms of economic development that would benefit both parties to the conflict. Such development might well serve to bring Israelis and Palestinians together in the course of bolstering economic interests held in common. Such a proactive investment policy might well further a resolution of the Middle East conflict, while at the same time healing the rifts between Presbyterians and Jews worldwide. As Roth goes on to mention in his brief response, the Presbyterians' 2004 divestment initiative was halted by thoughtful reconsideration that took place in June 2006, only a few weeks before Hezbollah militia units in Lebanon and Israeli military forces ramped up the violence in the Middle East. While that escalation dealt a blow to Palestinian-Israeli reconciliation, it also made creative plans for economic investment in the region more important than ever, for without them, the hopes for a lasting peaceful settlement will be even more forlorn.

David Blumenthal agrees with Haas and Roth that important challenges to peace in the Middle East have roots in lessons learned from the Holocaust. For Blumenthal, we must attend to one crucial lesson to be gleaned from the Holocaust: We must, in his terms, "beware of our beliefs." Jews in particular must question some key beliefs prevalent in the Western world of today if their very survival is to be ensured. Jews did not take seriously enough the pronouncements of the Nazis during the 1930s. "We cannot afford to be wrong yet again," Blumenthal declares. The bulk of his chapter consists of an analysis and attempted refutation of six such views, views deemed to be commonly held in the twenty-first-century Western world. Blumenthal endeavors to "unpack" and then to repudiate beliefs ranging from the assumption that the Israeli-Palestinian conflict is at the heart of problems in the Middle East to the claim that reason and law are fundamental to all societies. The notion that poverty is at the root of Israeli-Palestinian conflict is examined, as are the claims that most Palestinians desire a two-state solution and that Islam is essentially a religion of tolerance, with only occasional aberrations of fanaticism. All these beliefs, Blumenthal asserts, must be resisted. We cannot be blinded by what he deems to be merely naive assumptions. Allowing them to direct public policy with regard to the Israeli-Palestinian conflict, Blumenthal concludes, may well pose dangers to Jewish existence — something that cannot be risked in a post-Holocaust world.

It seems at first glance that Leonard Grob's chapter, entitled " 'Forgetting' the Holocaust," takes exception to fundamental claims made by those whose contributions to Part I have thus far been discussed. Haas, Roth, and Blumenthal all speak of challenges posed by *memory* of the Holocaust to a resolution of the Israeli-Palestinian conflict. What does Grob mean by *forgetting* the Holocaust? We must forget, according to Grob, in order to better remember, in order to better memorialize the six million dead. Remembrance has all too often been reductive in nature, admitting one and only one lesson to be learned from the Holocaust: Never again will Jewish blood be shed with impunity. Focusing on this one lesson

alone, he claims, has promoted a culture of victimhood that prevents Israel
— in Grob's judgment, the stronger of the two warring parties — from
taking necessary initiatives to resolve the conflict. Post-Holocaust Zionism, Grob argues, has most often offered a totalizing account, or
metanarrative, of Jewish suffering and redemption, a narrative in which
Palestinians are reduced to being incidental or "bit" players. True remembrance involves a measure of forgetfulness of the image of eternal
victimhood seemingly burned into the consciousness of Israeli Jews. All
metanarratives are suspect, Grob argues, recalling the destruction wrought
by a Nazi metanarrative that radically repudiated human solidarity. In the
Middle East conflict, metanarratives must be replaced by an "internarrative," one forged by Israelis in ongoing dialogue with their Palestinian
neighbors. Israelis, according to Grob, must refuse to create any narrative
other than one that sees Palestinians as full partners in the process of creating two viable states. Only by freeing themselves of a victim identity will
Israelis be able to take the initiative in breaking the cycle in which victims
inevitably become victimizers in order to prevent further — and sometimes merely perceived — suffering.

Britta Frede-Wenger begins the final chapter in Part I of this volume
by speaking directly about the special challenges that the Holocaust poses
to a German who wishes to address the Palestinian-Israeli conflict. When
Germans talk about the conflict, Frede-Wenger asserts, they are talking
(between the lines) about themselves, about their self-image in a post-
Holocaust world. Often this self-image includes guilt feelings. Frede-
Wenger argues that, although guilt is perceived to haunt contemporary
German society, she herself feels more anger than guilt, anger at the legacy
bequeathed to her by her grandparents' generation. There are dangers in
dwelling on guilt, for guilt feelings can lead to moral paralysis. Furthermore, seeing oneself as guilty can make the other — in this case, the Jewish
other — "innocent." Innocence, Frede-Wenger argues, is a problematic
term. If Israeli Jews appear to be not so innocent in their encounters with
Palestinians, then perhaps Germans do not need to be so guilty! Frede-
Wenger concludes her chapter by noting that guilt must be replaced by responsibility — for prosecuting those who committed crimes during the
Holocaust, for the well-being of the Jewish people, and for remembering
what human beings are capable of doing to one another. Solidarity with
the victims of oppression is called for. "There must be an end to suffering."
This, Frede-Wenger concludes, is the foremost lesson of the Holocaust.

Both sides of the Middle East conflict must reflect on the causes of suffering in the region. Each people must realize that, even when acting toward what they perceive as the "good," they risk contributing to the suffering of others. Frede-Wenger does not want to engage in the weighing of one people's suffering against another's. Rather — in an appropriate closing both to her chapter and to Part I of this volume — she challenges the parties to the conflict to see not only the suffering among their own people but also the suffering that each party has inflicted upon the other.

1. *Moral Visions in Conflict:*
Israeli and Palestinian Ethics

Peter J. Haas

I

A rule of academia is that if you are getting unhelpful answers, you are asking the wrong questions. As regards the Israeli-Palestinian conflict, much of public discourse has reached this impasse. Rather than leading to a resolution, public rhetoric from both sides has created mutually exclusive claims to Truth and Justice while depicting the other side as understanding only force and deserving subjugation or annihilation. The result of such rhetoric is to greatly decrease the possibility of accommodation. If this has become the answer, I submit, then we must, and can, reformulate the question.

In the following, I shall try to show that the question of who owns the Truth in the Middle East is dysfunctional because it presupposes that there is an answer owned by one side and that the other side is therefore wrong or even demonic. This logic, in turn, justifies all sorts of extreme physical behavior in the name of Truth and Justice. The ultimate tragedy of such a presupposition is that it masks the deeper complexities of the situation and supports an ethic that leads us away from, rather than toward, resolution.

My approach in what follows is informed by my academic study of moral discourse, especially on how an advanced, educated, Western country like Germany could perpetrate the Holocaust. My answer to that question has been that the rhetoric used by the Nazis was simple, monolithic, and radical. It coherently (given its presuppositions) cast non-Aryans as inhuman and, through the deployment of various theological and scientific warrants, fashioned an ethic that, taken to its logical conclusion, justified the elimination of Jews (and other non-Aryans) as being in the service of the Good.[1] To be sure, matters in Nazi Germany were more complex in that this ethic was backed up by a ruthless totalitarian regime. Nonetheless, many people who should have known better participated in the dehumanization and eventual slaughter of others. My conclusion has been that any totalizing rhetoric that is uncritically accepted and that includes demonization of the other carries within it the seed of disaster.

For this reason, in what follows I reexamine the discourse that has come to characterize the Israeli-Palestinian crisis. The standard public rhetoric of both sides has been shifting to the Right at least since the outbreak of the "al-Aqsa intifada" in 2000. In the process, the more radical discourses of each side (using such phrases as the biblical "Amalek" or the qur'anic "sons of monkeys and pigs") have made it impossible to find a place for the legitimate grievances of the other to be heard and understood. In fact, the other side is now often regarded as having no legitimate grievances at all. My contention is that only by breaking such mutually exclusive rhetoric, and so making the voice of the other hearable, can some sort of peaceful coexistence be possible in the Middle East.

Before proceeding, I acknowledge that I am fully aware that there are many points of view on each side. Part of the problem in the Israel-Palestine conflict is that the struggle is not only between "the Palestinians" (or "the Arabs" or "the Muslims") on the one side and "the Israelis" (or "the Jews" or "the West") on the other, but also among various groups, factions, and perspectives within each side. One dynamic of the escalation of rhetoric has been not only the demonization of the other but the marginalization and delegitimation of less radical narratives on the same side. Allowing the other to be heard is thus not limited to the other side but includes learning to tolerate dissenting voices within one's own side.

I begin my analysis by looking at the Western tradition of moral discourse. This tradition, it is important to note, stands behind not only Judaism and Christianity but Islam as well. All three religions, after all, draw their theological and philosophical roots from the Greco-Roman world. In fact, it could well be that it is precisely the closeness of the basic assumptions on the part of all three religious traditions that has made possible the

---

1. See Peter J. Haas, *Morality after Auschwitz: The Radical Challenge of the Nazi Ethic* (Philadelphia: Fortress Press, 1988).

Manichaeistic tendency on each side to demonstrate the total falsity of the other side. Each sees the other in the exact same terms, only with the poles reversed.

II

To grasp the basic semiotics of the rhetoric at hand, it will be helpful to look at the assumptions shared by each side. It has been a given in Western moral philosophy, from Plato and Aristotle onward, that there is an objective Good and Just out there, which humans have the innate capacity to know. A virtual sea of ink has been spilled in the West during the last two and a half millennia over exactly how we might know what this Good is (i.e., by intuition, insight, observation of nature, or revelation), what its content might be, how we measure it (e.g., by outcome or by intention), and how free we are to act upon it in the first place.[2] I think it is fair to say that over the last 2,500 years or so, just about every possible combination of the above views has been vigorously championed by one or another Great Thinker. But whatever side one took, the common conviction remained firmly in place for nearly two millennia that the Good and the Just exist and are knowable and in fact demonstrable. It follows that those who failed to recognize this belief were either unable or, more damning, unwilling to do so.

By the end of the nineteenth century, this central conviction was being seriously questioned, giving way to what we might call a postmodern view of multiple truths depending on place, time, and perspective. Just as developments in astronomy and biology decentered the earth as the stable and known heart of the cosmos, so philosophy began to show us that notions of the Good or the Just were only artifacts of human thinking. "Truth," as Einstein would help us see, is nothing but some perspective of events from a particular point in time and space. It is crucial to note at this point that this insight does not mean that all truth claims are entirely relative and contentless, as is sometimes mistakenly assumed. Einstein's own theory of relativity notes, for example, that while there may be no absolute way to measure movement in the cosmos, there can still be wrong mea-

2. Even for the ancient Greeks, moral teachers could just as well be poets or playwrights as philosophers or scholars.

surements. The same holds true for postmodern philosophical and moral argumentation. The morality of a claim might be argued from several perspectives, all true, given their frames of reference, but this does not mean that all are equally valid. What the postmodern perspective does preclude is our claiming that only *one* such point of view is right and that *all* others are ipso facto wrong and not even deserving of a hearing. It is precisely this postmodern notion that other perspectives can legitimately be given a hearing that I hope to build on in what follows.

I build on the premise that ethical discourses in our postmodern world are embedded in particular narratives that themselves are anchored in particular social, political, and philosophical settings. It is through such narrative structures that words and events take on meaning and so moral valence. The result, as the French philosopher Emmanuel Levinas tells us in his several discussions of "the meaning of meaning,"[3] is that moral decisions are something other than the outcome of thinking or knowledge itself but rather are an extension of our own linguistic situation. For this reason there is such interest today in narrative theology, narrative ethics, and even narrative bioethics.[4] Moral analysis in the postmodern world is not about identifying the absolute metaphysical Truth that governs a situation but rather about constructing a metanarrative that takes account of the complex subnarratives that describe the situation as a moral problem to begin with. Darrell Fasching, in his *Narrative Theology after Auschwitz*, puts it succinctly: "Theology is not so much a matter of metaphysics as it is a task of reflecting on our encounter with the 'other' as the occasion for understanding our relationship to the Wholly Other."[5] Let me hasten to reiterate that Fasching and others still aver, in full sincerity, that there is still good and bad, right and wrong, appropriate and inappropriate. Their claim, rather, is that the resort to narrative tells us that whatever truth we

---

3. See, for example, Emmanuel Levinas, *Totality and Infinity: An Essay in Exteriority,* trans. Alphonso Lingus (Pittsburgh: Duquesne University Press, 1969), pp. 287-307.

4. The distinction I am making here is between what is often referred to as a *principalist* approach to moral warranting as opposed to a *narrative* approach. See Rita Charon and Martha M. Montello, eds., *Stories Matter: The Role of Narrative in Medical Ethics* (New York: Routledge, 2002), esp. the essays by Walter M. Robinson, "The Narrative of Rescue in Pediatric Practice," pp. 97-108, and Howard Brody, "Narrative Ethics and Institutional Impact," pp. 149-53.

5. Darrell J. Fasching, *Narrative Theology after Auschwitz* (Minneapolis: Fortress Press, 1992), p. 2.

find will emerge from the details and meaning of each particular situation, a situation that is itself already constructed by the intersection of a variety of earlier narratives. This is the operative methodological assumption of what follows as we turn attention to the moral rhetoric of the Middle East.[6]

Sorting through the rhetorics of the Middle East is made more complex by the fact that there are a plethora of mutually exclusive narratives, often about the same event. This complexity increases the temptation to settle on one narrative as being the right one and thus define all the others as wrong. For any one incident, for example, there might well be a liberal Jewish narrative, a right-wing Israeli narrative, a liberal Israeli narrative, a Muslim narrative, an Islamic Jihad/Hamas narrative, a family narrative, a Christian narrative, a secular narrative, an American narrative, a British narrative, a French narrative, an Israeli "settler" narrative, a "Fox News" narrative, a victim's narrative, a soldier's narrative, a terrorist's narrative, and so on. All freely use the language of right and wrong, good and evil, justified killing, unjustified victimization, and demonization of the other. To repeat, I am not claiming that all the above narratives are necessarily equally valid or useful, but rather that no one of them should be regarded a priori as the *only* valid narrative, to the complete exclusion of all the others.

Let me proceed with a concrete example that has generated a variety of narratives. I focus on the reported death of Muhammad al-Dura, a twelve-year-old Palestinian who, according to the original news reports, was caught with his father between rioting Palestinians and Israeli soldiers on September 30, 2000, and, while crouching behind a concrete barrel, was fatally shot. What makes the story interesting for our purposes is that the event was caught on film and widely broadcast. The incident consequently became so famous that stamps were issued in Muhammad al-Dura's honor. A street was named after him in Baghdad, and Osama bin Laden even referred to him as an icon of Israeli viciousness and Western immorality. The Israeli and Jewish responses, in contrast, claimed that the shooting, if it even occurred, was the foreseeable consequence of the Palestinian-instigated intifada. In short, a complete array of well-documented, tightly argued, and mutually exclusive moral narratives sprouted up around the affair. In fact, the whole incident is an interesting example of what Arthur

6. See, for example, Tod Chambers and Kathryn Montgomery, "Plot: Framing Contingency and Choice in Bioethics," in Charon and Montello, *Stories Matter*, pp. 77-84.

Kleinman has called the commercialization of victims, that is, the use of graphic images of victims and victimization as part of a marketing strategy.[7] In this case, the incident was appropriated and narrativized by both sides as an iconic representation of the moral degeneracy of the other side. My point in using this story is to demonstrate the dangers of letting one, and only one, "objective" narrative define one's moral universe.

Although the incident as it appears on the taped version seems clear, other relevant facts need to be taken into account. Subsequent investigations have established three important facts. One was that shooting in the area had been going on for some time before Muhammad al-Dura appeared on the scene. This raises the question as to what this young boy and his father were even doing there at all: did they wander recklessly into a violent confrontation, for example, or were they perhaps part of the rioting mob? The second fact established by the subsequent investigation was that the bullets hitting the concrete barrel behind which the boy and his father were couching were coming not from the direction of the Israeli forces but from the direction of the Palestinian rioters and the cameraman. Again, a number of questions arise: Was the boy in fact shot directly by Israelis, or was he perhaps the victim of a ricochet? Was he maybe hit by a Palestinian bullet, and, if so, was it by accident or on purpose? We might even ask whether the presence of a French cameraman right there at the crucial place at the crucial moment was nothing more than a fortuitous coincidence. This last question opens the door to the biggest question of all, namely, whether the whole event was staged and whether in fact Muhammad al-Dura was even shot at all. I pose these questions simply to illustrate that at the very outset a number of narrative possibilities exist, each entailing its own particular moral lesson.

The third fact is that we now know that the shooting of Muhammad al-Dura, as recorded, never happened; it was a staged piece of propaganda. Outtakes of the videotape, for example, show Muhammad al-Dura fidgeting and looking around after he was supposedly dead. It also turns out that the death certificate of the "dead" Muhammad al-Dura predates the incident by about three hours.[8] Confronted with these and other pieces of evi-

---

7. See Arthur Kleinman and Joan Kleinman, "The Appeal of Experience: The Dismay of Images; Cultural Appropriations of Suffering in Our Times," in *Social Suffering*, ed. Arthur Kleinman, Veena Das, and Margaret Lock (Berkeley: University of California Press, 1997), pp. 1-24.

8. James Fallows prepared a well-researched and well-written report on the entire epi-

dence, some of the French and Arab media people involved in editing and airing the tape have now admitted that the incident was not literally true but was meant to be only representative of Israeli brutality. But curiously, the fictitiousness of the incident has become largely irrelevant. For the Israelis, the airing of the video itself only proves the right-wing narrative that the Palestinians cynically exploit their own children for political ends and are willing to promote the most outrageous lies against Israel and the Jews to a gullible Christian West. Alternatively, for the right-wing Palestinian narrative, the video is true, even if it did not happen, because Palestinian children are indeed being shot by Israelis all the time when no cameraman is around. These claims and counterclaims demonstrate, I submit, that the moral narrative and its lesson are much more important than "the facts" and that, in some sense, the larger narrative *produces* the facts. I want to explore this last proposition a bit further. I end this section, though, by quoting from the Fallows article cited earlier in this paragraph. The author concludes that "the images intensify the self-righteous determination of each side. If anything, modern technology has aggravated the problem of mutually exclusive realities. With the Internet and TV, each culture now has a more elaborate apparatus for 'proving,' dramatizing, and disseminating its particular truth."[9]

III

I dwell on Fallows's phrase "mutually exclusive realities." The story I just told cannot be interpreted at all unless it is placed in a larger narrative. On the most basic level, one has to know who Israelis are, who Palestinians are, what their conflict is about, and something about the symbolic meaning of the Israeli village of Netzarim, which is where the incident

---

sode and its various aftermaths, "Who Shot Mohammed al-Dura?" *Atlantic Monthly,* June 2003 (see http://www.theatlantic.com/issues/2003/06/fallows.htm). There was also an in-depth report on Hessische Rundfunk by Esther Shapiro entitled "Three Bullets and a Dead Child," coming to the conclusion that the incident was staged. For another report on this incident, see Amnon Lord, "Who Killed Muhammad Al-Dura? Blood Libel — Model 2000," Jerusalem Center for Public Affairs, no. 482, Av 6, 5762/July 15, 2002, available at http://www.jcpa.org/jl/vp482.htm. Richard Landes has produced a brief documentary film, *Pollywood* (2005), about this episode.

9. Fallows, "Who Shot Mohammed al-Dura?" p. 56.

took place.[10] Such knowledge is part of more complex Israeli, Jewish, Zionist, Palestinian, Arab, and Muslim universes of discourse. None of the events I have so briefly sketched, I submit, has any real meaning, any moral valence, outside of these Grand Narrative structures. What gives the particular case of Muhammad al-Dura so much purchase is that the story (or stories) built around it corroborate and validate much larger metanarratives.

But what are these metanarratives? On a simple level, the Grand Narrative, of which the story of Muhammad al-Dura is a part, tells of the struggle of a people who are defending their land against those who wish to take it away. Furthermore, those defending their land are threatened by an enemy with alien values, an enemy who understands only the use of force and who does not regard the death of a child on the other side as important. In short, the enemy is godless and inhuman in its immorality. Furthermore, this struggle is being fought not only on behalf of those presently alive but on behalf of all those generations yet to come. It is a struggle to preserve a cultural or religious legacy that the current generation is commanded by history or God or justice to carry forward. This struggle over land around Netzarim is then part of a larger struggle — a larger narrative, if you will — that has to do with the self-definition, self-understanding, survival, and destiny of the people involved, one that is rooted in deep historical, emotional, and psychological soil, and that also has an impressive and compelling internal coherence and self-evidence. Note that the above synopsis can be read as articulated either by an Israeli or by a Palestinian.

With this common synopsis in mind, we can now see why what "really" happened is irrelevant in light of whatever larger "truth" the story of Muhammad al-Dura illustrates. As Fasching puts it, we are talking here about "a central thesis of contemporary narrative ethics theory: namely, that the story we understand ourselves to be in defines the meaning of good and evil for us and shapes our ethical behavior."[11] In other words, in some sense both the Israeli and the Palestinian readings of this video are true: it was a staged event to be used as a propaganda tool, as the Israelis say; but it is also representative of what the Palestinians experience to be

10. Netzarim was one of the first Israeli settlements in the Gaza Strip. It is located just south of Gaza City and thus is situated between the Palestinian areas in the northern Gaza Strip and those in the southern part.

11. Fasching, *Narrative Theology after Auschwitz*, p. 187.

what is actually happening to their children during Israeli military raids. While we can acknowledge the truth of both simultaneously, just as two different readings of the speed of the moon can be true, depending on where the measuring instrument is located, the Grand Narrative of each side declares that only its reading is true and the other is false. The result is a validation, even a normalization, of a certain kind of violent death.[12] The reason is that the deaths caused by a suicide bombing or an Israeli targeted assassination fit into a much larger narrative of national survival than does the loss of life by other causes, even if just as tragic. Thus deaths due to revenge killings, criminal activity, traffic accidents, corruption in the delivery of medical care, and so forth are not given the status of the deaths caused by terror or the self-sacrifice of the Shahid (martyr). The reason should now be clear: A death due to the intifada fits into a master national narrative and so has a broader resonance, whereas other deaths do not.[13]

This mutually exclusivistic reading brings me back to the thesis of this essay. Postmodernism tells us that when we take only one narrative into account, we not only misunderstand the fullness of the situation but are in fact perpetuating a moral injustice, since we are privileging one narrative over all others, thereby affording recognition to some suffering and discounting or dismissing other suffering as of no moral consequence. To repeat, this does not mean that every narrative is worthy, but it is to say that more than just one deserves a hearing. This is precisely the problem that the Holocaust brings out. In the Nazi worldview, there was but one authorized metanarrative determining all moral reasoning. This metanarrative declared Aryans to be the only true humans, relegating all others to some level of nonhuman status. The logical conclusion followed.

IV

I conclude by noting that no Grand Narrative is a monolithic and immutable construct. Rather, all metanarratives are works in progress, constantly

12. On the problem of making suffering ordinary, see Veena Das, Arthur Kleinman, Mamphela Ramphele, and Pamela Reynolds, eds., *Violence and Subjectivity* (Berkeley: University of California Press, 2000), esp. the introduction.

13. On this distinction, see Arthur Kleinman, "Pain and Resistance: The Delegitimation and Relegitimation of Local Worlds," in *Writing at the Margin: Discourse between Anthropology and Medicine* (Berkeley: University of California Press, 1995), pp. 120-46.

being re-formed by lived experience. As Susan B. Rubin points out, there is no view from nowhere, and in fact I want to argue that since no moral narrative ever exists apart from the people who are thinking it, such a narrative can always change as the people who think it undergo change.[14] Narratives can and do change as individuals talk about and allow themselves to rethink their narratives. The Israeli and the Palestinian stories have changed over time and are undergoing change as we speak. New metanarratives can and do emerge, if we are willing to let them.

V

Does my reframing of the question in the end help in finding an answer? I think in some ways it does. The issue is not who is "right" in the Middle Eastern conflict. To assert an answer to that question is already to presuppose a narrative that cannot be accepted by the other side. Hope resides in the possibility that each side will be able to change its Grand Narrative to allow at least some legitimacy to the Grand Narrative of the other. There are signs that this movement is happening, although the extent to which this change will develop is entirely unknowable. It is the possibility of each Grand Narrative to remain cohesive and yet allow for the legitimacy of the narrative of the other that offers the hope for some mutual acceptance in the Middle East. It is not a question of who is right and who is wrong, but of whether each Grand Narrative can finally make a place for the Grand Narrative of the other.

14. Susan B. Rubin, "Beyond the Authoritative Voice: Casting a Wide Net in Ethics Consultation," in Charon and Montello, *Stories Matter*, p. 111.

Contributors' Questions for Peter J. Haas

You claim that what really happened (regarding the al-Dura issue) is "irrelevant." But for whom is actual historical fact irrelevant? Are not all narratives equally privileged? If narratives construct their own truths, their "facts," what criteria do we have to evaluate a given narrative from an external point of view? Or are there no "external points of view"? Why, as you claim, should narratives be open to other narratives if there is no external good — the objective of a peaceful resolution to the conflict — driving this process of opening? Must one not care about something?

You argue that each people's narrative must remain "cohesive," while at the same time allowing for the legitimation of the narrative of the other. But does not "cohesiveness" belong to a concept of narrative that will disallow the mutual acceptance you embrace? To achieve your goal, must not radically new narratives arise that foster mutual acceptance precisely because they are fragmented, disjointed, and discontinuous? How, concretely, do you envision beginning steps in the Middle East that will allow the Gordian knot to be cut? What will allow for the cessation of violence that will create a space in which multiple "broken" narratives can coexist?

Response by Peter J. Haas

Leopold von Ranke once famously announced that we must tell everything "the way it really happened" *(wie es eigentlich gewesen war)*.[1] Historians today recognize how simplistic this description of the historian's work is. It is not to say that "facts" are unimportant, but it is to say that a simple fact in and of itself is meaningless. A so-called fact needs context and interpretation in that context. It is in light of this elemental notion of modern historiography that I made my comment about what really happened being irrelevant. What is relevant, however, is how one selects, describes, and understands what really happened. To take the example at hand, the demonstration that Muhammad al-Dura really was not shot in the way depicted in the video does not fundamentally change anything about anyone's understanding of the Israeli-Palestinian problem. The "fact" of the event simply becomes absorbed into the prevailing rhetoric. In other words, the meaning of the video persists despite the facts; hence the irrelevance of the facts.

By calling the facts irrelevant, then, I was trying to say that that simply citing "facts" so as to use them to toss accusations back and forth serves no helpful function. It is like two siblings fighting. Sally hit Bill because, according to Sally, Bill started it by hitting Sally first; but Bill self-righteously claims to have hit Sally only because Sally did Y; Y happened,

---

1. For a discussion of Ranke's well-known quotation (from the introduction to his *History of the Latin and Teutonic Nations*), see Hajo Holborn, "The Science of History," in *History and the Humanities* (Garden City, N.Y.: Doubleday Books, 1972), pp. 81-97.

of course, as a perfectly fair response to Bill's doing X, itself a result of Sally's prior act of W, growing out of Bill's anger at Sally's doing V, and so on into an infinite regress. All the cited facts in the dispute may or may not be accurate, but as any parent who has tried to sort out this pattern of point/counterpoint knows, there is no way to figure out finally what "really" happened. Nor does "what really happened" really matter. The need is to move beyond pinning down who did what to whom when and where and out of what motives and to establish a new relationship. It is important to teach siblings that there is not only a past but a present and a future.

In the Israeli-Palestinian conflict we have a similar rhetorical structure. Both sides have file cabinets full of facts and accusations ready to be deployed against the other side, accusations that may be true or false or partially true to some unknowable degree. Many of these concrete accusations and "facts" go back to the 1920s and earlier — that is, before any living memory. So many of the "facts" that are invoked to justify this, that, or the other event are part of each side's mythic inheritance. Proving one such fact as accurate, inaccurate, partially accurate, or whatever is, as I have said, irrelevant. Does it really make a difference as to why anti-French Arab irregulars attacked Tel Hai in 1920? My assertion is that the actual description of what happened at Tel Hai (today an Israeli memorial site of early self-defense forces) is of no more than academic importance. The same question applies to my more recent example of Muhammad al-Dura. As I tried to stress in the article, the story (whatever it is) of Muhammad al-Dura is "true" for each side in the sense that knowing what "really" happened and why is moot (except maybe among academics); it will not change anybody's mind.

But to say that facts are irrelevant does not mean that narratives are therefore fixed and thus impervious to change. Just like "facts," narratives do not exist in monolithic, self-evident isolation. Turning again to the al-Dura affair, we can see, for example, that just as there are now multiple stories about what "really" happened, so there are many interpretations growing out of these stories (including the choice of which story is the real one). It should not be forgotten that neither the Israelis nor the Palestinians (nor the Jews, nor the Arabs, nor the Muslims) operate with a single narrative. While any particular narrative must have enough coherence to be plausible, I at no point meant to exclude the possibility of there being a variety of possible alternative narratives out there competing with each other in the marketplace of ideas. I hardly need to say that, on the Israeli side, Labor is operating out of a different narrative than Likud, that the Israeli human rights organization B'tselem has a different reading of the facts than does Yesha (the council representing Jews living in Judea, Samaria, and Gaza), that the Women in Green (pro-Settlement) see the same events differently than do the Women in Black (anti-Settlement), and so forth. On the Palestinian side, there are not only differences between "indigenous" Gazans and "indigenous" West Bankers and refugees, but clear differences between Fatah, Hamas, Hezbollah, and Islamic Jihad. To take one example: there is no doubt (as far as I am aware) that a Qassam rocket was fired from Bet Hanun in the Gaza Strip into the Israeli border town of Sderot on Friday, May 6, 2005. It would not be hard to show in just a few minutes how this agreed upon fact can generate a whole host of different meanings, depending on whether you integrate it into the narrative of right-wing Likudniks, human rights activists in B'tselem, members of Islamic Jihad, officials in Fatah, and so on. In short, a fact in isolation means nothing. But by that same token, any one fact can have at any one time a variety of meanings and interpretations.

My point in all this is to stress that any narrative, while it must have some internal coherence, must also always be plastic and flexible. A narrative is always a work in progress, struggling to absorb and give meaning to new events as they occur. Failure to do so will eventually render the narrative irrelevant. By the same token, narratives also have to take other, competing narratives into account (unless such other narratives are forcibly repressed). In this situation, narratives gain purchase among a population if they seem to be functional, that is, if they seem to account for events better than their rival narratives and they are able to produce desired results. Conversely, narratives lose purchase if they appear to be implausible, incoherent, or dysfunctional. To be sure, function and dysfunction can themselves be issues of debate and diverse interpretations. One person's utopia might well be someone else's dystopia. Nazism may have seemed functional in 1935 when it provided meaning, jobs, food, and pride; and dysfunctional in 1945 amid death camps, ruins, starvation, and utter defeat. That is not to deny that there were anti-Nazis in 1935 and pro-Nazis in 1945, but it is not hard to say that popular consensus, based on lived experience, could very plausibly have changed during those ten years. My claim as regards the Israeli-Palestinian situation is no different: what appeared to be a functional narrative at one point could become discredited (among some at least) at a later point, while a rival narrative, once dismissed as dysfunctional or dangerous, could come to be seen (among some at least) as having something to offer after all. This can be the result of a sudden "conversion experience" (like Paul on the road to Damascus), or it can be a gradual shift in perspective. In other words, to say a narrative is coherent does not mean it is unchanging or unchangeable.

Let me offer a concrete example of how this might apply to the current Middle East ("current" being the summer of 2005). It seems that governing narrative structures on both the Israeli and the Palestinian sides are undergoing change. On the Palestinian side, the crucial event was the passing of Yasser Arafat. His death allowed a different governing narrative, that of the pragmatic Abu Mazen (Mahmoud Abbas), to emerge within Fatah itself and so achieve public articulation. This narrative, that armed struggle is not helpful and that what is needed is the construction of a civil society in the Palestinian territories, must now demonstrate to the "Palestinian street" that it can deliver important goods (jobs, security, peace, justice, whatever). It must do so in competition with other narratives (those of Arafatists, Hamas, Islamic Jihad, etc.). The process will likely be long and gradual. On the Israeli side, the tipping point was a conversion experience in the mind of Prime Minister Ariel Sharon. For whatever reason or set of reasons (economic, security, demographic), he determined that Israel must withdraw unilaterally from the Gaza Strip and most of the West Bank. In this decision he aligned himself with some (but not all) moderate narratives on the Israeli political scene, while alienating the more right-wing narratives of his own Likud party. His policy will survive if he can persuade enough people on the "Israeli street" that his approach will deliver important goods (security, economic prosperity, preservation of the Jewish character of the state, whatever). There is no guarantee that either of these narratives will achieve rootage, but what makes the summer of 2005 different from the summer of 2004 is that different narratives were for the time being in the driver's seat. I do not say that the prior narratives have evaporated. They are still out there with their staunch adherents, but a narrative and rhetorical shift is occurring, with observable results on the ground, at least for now.

I return to my original point. The facts about Muhammad al-Dura have not changed. What have changed are the narratives. After all, narratives are not just about the past but also about the present and (maybe primarily) about the envisioned future. If we think of the present differently, we can then begin to think of the future differently as well, and vice versa.

The past does not factually change, but its meaning and influence do. In some real and significant way, then, the future really does remain open, and our choice of narrative remains a choice, based on life experience, personal psychology, and a host of other influences. My point is that the "facts" do not predetermine the narrative; rather, the narrative defines and gives meaning to facts. There is no *eigentlich* (authentic or objective) meaning, only human perceptions of where we are, how we got here, and where we would like to go. The rest is commentary.

2. Duped by Morality? Defusing Minefields in the Israeli-Palestinian Struggle

John K. Roth

Everyone will readily agree that it is of the highest importance to know whether we are not duped by morality.

Emmanuel Levinas, *Totality and Infinity*

We human beings are often deceived or fooled. Our own plans, dispositions, and actions account for much of that result. Typically, however, we do not think that morality dupes us. At least if we consider ethical reasoning, we tend to think that it is not misleading but trustworthy instead. Such reasoning provides the guidelines and insights that can keep us on track or warn us that we have gone in wrong directions. As this line of thought would have it, we will sooner or later be duped if we fail to follow where ethical reasoning leads, but ethical reasoning itself is not deceptive. If it were deceptive, that condition would exist only to the extent that ethical reasoning had not been done well or carried out sufficiently. Unfortunately, the thought with which Emmanuel Levinas began *Totality and Infinity* suggests a more radical and tragic alternative, namely, that deception may be inseparable from ethical reasoning.

No event did more than the Holocaust to show that humanity has been duped by morality. The fact that we can identify what Peter Haas has called the Nazi ethic and what Claudia Koonz has more recently named the Nazi conscience scarcely gives comfort regarding the nondeceptive quality of ethical reasoning.[1] Instead, their studies show how reasoning

---

1. See Peter J. Haas, *Morality after Auschwitz: The Radical Challenge of the Nazi Ethic*

can produce lethal rivalries that undercut confidence about the philosophical and religious foundations, as well as the actual content, of moral traditions that were at odds with Nazism and yet apparently unable to check Nazi power until millions had been slaughtered. After that catastrophe, the Holocaust has been called a "negative absolute," to use Michael Berenbaum's phrase, but that status, warranted as it is, may also be deceptive, for the threat and practice of genocide — to name only one of the evils besieging the world — has not abated and may grow worse.

With the Holocaust reverberating within it, the Israeli-Palestinian struggle adds to the dilemmas that characterize our being duped by morality. Consider four ways in which that claim has validity. First, the post-Holocaust cry "Never again!" is an ethical imperative whose meaning is problematic and whose credibility is lacking. On the one hand, it expresses determination to resist the destruction of one's people, including the destruction of the State of Israel. On the other hand, no people has exclusive claim to that imperative; Palestinians can have a version of it, too. Embedded within ethical reasoning, "Never again!" is deceptively reassuring.

Second, "the killing will stop," it is sometimes said, "when people have had enough of it." This claim contains an ethical hope, namely, that human beings will not keep killing because we value life too much for that. The Israeli-Palestinian struggle, whose latest tragic chapter has been going on for more than five years at the time of this writing in 2006, reveals that we may be duped twice if we place too much hope in our valuing of human life: weariness about killing is not identical with "enough of it," and even the early 2005 breakthroughs of hope, which included handshakes between Israeli prime minister Ariel Sharon and Mahmoud Abbas, the Palestinian leader who was elected to succeed the late Yasser Arafat as president of the Palestinian Authority, did not offer much empirical reassurance that all would turn out well, even before deadly warfare between Israel and Hezbollah broke out in July 2006. Whatever the prospects for new and ultimately successful Israeli-Palestinian negotiations, a history of broken agreements; dead-ended road maps to peace; terror unleashed repeatedly by Islamic Jihad, Hamas, and Hezbollah; the Israel Defense Force's retaliations; and the Israeli government's construction of a con-

---

(Philadelphia: Fortress Press, 1988); and Claudia Koonz, *The Nazi Conscience* (Cambridge, Mass.: Harvard University Press, 2003).

troversial security barrier to prevent terrorist acts all leave the hopes for justice fragile and the chances for lasting peace unsettled.

Third, ethical realism requires one to recognize that retribution is as important as it is unavoidable. Here the assumption is that inflicting harm in return for harm will eliminate a problem, if not by "teaching people a lesson," then by weakening or destroying others to such an extent that they can do serious harm no more. The dupery in this case is likely to be that winning the war is not the same as winning the peace.

Fourth, the realism, ethical or not, that drives the Israeli-Palestinian struggle reaffirms that a higher ethic is needed. That ethic would be one that stresses the shared humanity of those sustaining and feeling the conflict's impact, one that underscores how people should respect, if not love, each other, one that can help people to transcend differences of nationality and religion. Such an ethic may well be needed, but here, too, deception is not far to find. Its extent depends on how easily or thoroughly one thinks the gap between *is* and *ought* can be closed.

Dupery about how easily or thoroughly the gap between *is* and *ought* may be closed is illustrated by the arguably well-meaning but misguided actions that were initiated by the Presbyterian Church, U.S.A. (PCUSA) at the meeting of its 216th General Assembly (June 26–July 3, 2004) in Richmond, Virginia. I have written the preceding sentence with regret, for I am a life-long Presbyterian whose father spent his life as a pastor in that denomination. I am also a Holocaust scholar who has tried to improve Jewish-Christian relations, but a PCUSA decision to "initiate a process of phased selective divestment in multinational corporations operating in Israel" was taken at a huge price that was not worth the cost.[2] Presbyterian-Jewish relations deteriorated badly in 2004-5. It will be some time before they can be restored, let alone improved, although the rejection of the divestment initiative in June 2006 — see the Postscript below — took needed steps to mend relations that had turned very sour indeed. The 2004 Presbyterian initiative was always unlikely to affect Israeli-Palestinian relations for the better. It is to be hoped that its rejection by the PCUSA leads to a better outcome by turning the PCUSA stance in a substantially different direction.

---

2. The quotation is from the Resolution on Israel and Palestine (2004), which was approved by a vote of 431 to 62 at the 216th General Assembly of the PCUSA. The complete text of the resolution, plus discussion pertaining to it, is available through the Internet at http://www.pcusa.org/worldwide/israelpalestine/israelpalestineresolution.htm#1.

To clarify those claims and to eliminate misunderstandings that may surround them, a brief account of the PCUSA's history and structure, as well as of the ill-timed 2004 divestment initiative, will be helpful. Tracing its heritage to the Protestant Reformation in sixteenth-century Europe and to the early leadership of the French lawyer John Calvin (1509-64), the PCUSA has about 2.3 million members. They belong to 11,000 congregations that are led by some 14,000 clergy. The church's governance, which takes place primarily at the congregational level and in regional jurisdictions called presbyteries, emphasizes the role of elected representatives. Biennially, clergy and laypersons, the latter group consisting of elders who are elected in their home congregations to handle local church affairs, are commissioned from the presbyteries to convene the church's General Assembly, which has responsibility "for matters of common concern for the whole church," including the setting of priorities regarding the church's "witness for truth and justice."[3] The PCUSA has financial assets of approximately $8 billion, including the investment portfolio of its Board of Pensions, which was valued at $6.4 billion at the end of 2004.

In its 1987 document "A Theological Understanding of the Relationship between Christians and Jews," the PCUSA affirmed that its identity is "intimately related" to the ongoing identity of the Jewish people, acknowledged "in repentance" Christian complicity in "anti-Jewish attitudes and actions," and expressed determination to end "the teaching of contempt for Jews."[4] Both before and after that 1987 statement, the PCUSA affirmed the State of Israel's right to exist within borders that are permanent, recognized, and secure. Such language can be found in the General Assembly's action at Richmond in June 2004, but at the same time a General Assembly Resolution on Israel and Palestine ignited a Presbyterian-Jewish firestorm. Acting on a proposal from the Presbytery of St. Augustine, Florida, the General Assembly started a process that could have resulted in the church's divestment in multinational corporations operating in Israel.

As pointed out by Vernon S. Broyles III, a member of the PCUSA Social Justice Ministries staff, various Christian churches have frequently used corporate divestment to protest against environmental abuses and

3. For the source of the quoted passages and for more information about the General Assembly, go to http://www.pcusa.org/generalassembly.

4. This document is available through the Internet at http://www.pcusa.org/oga/publications/christians-jews.pdf.

human rights violations.[5] The apartheid situation in South Africa in the 1980s remains a prominent example. Furthermore, the PCUSA's divestment process requires careful deliberation before any stock is sold. The PCUSA's Mission Responsibility through Investment Committee (MRTI) is responsible for those evaluations. In the controversial case of possible divestment in certain multinational companies doing business with Israel, the key criteria focused on whether a corporation provided products, technologies, or services (including financial ones) supporting (1) Israel's occupation of Palestinian territory as borders were defined by the Green Line of 1948, (2) violence that targets innocent civilians, and/or (3) the separation barrier, or protective wall, that the Israeli government erected for security reasons in 2003-4.[6]

Both the General Assembly resolution and the rhetoric used by its defenders made clear that, however nuanced its language, the steps toward divestment tilted decisively in the Palestinians' favor. It did not follow, however, that the tilt actually favored the Palestinians as much as the advocates of divestment assumed, for the Israeli and Palestinian economies are intertwined and overlapping. Divestment might not affect Palestinians as negatively as it affects Israelis, but those consequences would not fall on Israelis alone. Meanwhile, as the 2004 Resolution on Israel and Palestine sized up the situation, "prospects for a negotiated just peace have so deteriorated that people in the region generally, and particularly the Palestinians, have been driven to the edge of despair and hopelessness."[7] Among other things, that language expressed deep concern for Palestinian Christians, including Palestinian Presbyterians, with whom the PCUSA has close ties. Presbyterians should stand in solidarity with them, just as they should also stand in solidarity with the Jewish people.

5. See Vernon S. Broyles III, "The Presbyterian Case for Divesting from Israel," *Christian Century*, February 8, 2005. Broyles's article was part of an important symposium, "Money, Morals, and Israel: An Exchange," in the *Christian Century*, a leading Protestant weekly. Responses from Barbara Wheeler, president of Auburn Theological Seminary, and Ira Youdovin, executive vice president of the Chicago Board of Rabbis and president of the Council of Religious Leaders of Metropolitan Chicago, disagreed with Broyles, whose rebuttal is also part of the exchange. See *Christian Century* 122 (February 8, 2005): 30-38.

6. See the MRTI's "Guidelines for the Implementation of Phased, Selective Divestment Related to Israel and Palestine," adopted November 6, 2004, which can be found at http://www.pcusa.org/worldwide/israelpalestine/resources/20guidelinesdivestment.pdf.

7. The text of the resolution is available through the Internet. See n. 2 above.

Much of the time the Israeli-Palestinian conflict seems to defy resolution, but events in that region are as unpredictable as they are mercurial,
as surprising as they are volatile. Less than a year after the General Assembly's bleak prognosis and the very pro-Palestinian resolution that followed
from it, circumstances seemed to change in ways that made the divestment
overture not only lopsided and morally wrong but also embarrassing for
its clumsy ill-timing. Although Arafat was not well in June 2004, he was
alive and still in enough control that windows of opportunity for a just
and peaceful settlement were much harder to discern than they were a year
further on. Nothing guaranteed that the hopeful notes of 2005 would be
amplified, but it is unlikely that the PCUSA divestment initiative could
have done much to correct the Israeli-Palestinian causes of hopelessness
and despair that the Presbyterian proponents of divestment insisted they
wanted to relieve. Nevertheless, coupled with Presbyterian proclivities for
careful deliberation, which can produce good decisions but not necessarily
expeditious responses, the General Assembly's pro-Palestinian tilt left the
divestment card on table too long. As long as it was in play, Presbyterian-
Jewish relations were in decline.

The Holocaust should not put the Israeli government above fair criticism by Christians (Presbyterians or otherwise), Jews, Palestinians, or anyone else. But that catastrophe should make post-Holocaust Christians, and
recently Presbyterians in particular, pause before unfair steps are taken that
jar Jewish sensibilities and trust, as the Presbyterian divestment initiative was
bound to do. Even more specifically, awareness of the Holocaust should
warn Christians against using inflaming or defaming language of the kind
that Broyles employed when his accusation that the government of Israel is
guilty of "gross injustice" was followed by the invidious allegation that "Jewish victimhood makes it impossible for our Jewish sisters and brothers to
connect their suffering with that of the Palestinians at the hands of Israelis."[8]

Christianity and Christians have a special relationship and obligation to Judaism and Jews, which is constituted in large part because we
Christians owe them a debt that can never be fully repaid. That debt exists
especially because the Holocaust would not and could not have happened
without many centuries of Christian hostility toward the Jewish people.
Such a judgment does not mean that Christianity caused the Holocaust.

8. Vernon S. Broyles III, "Occupation Is the Issue: A Rebuttal," *Christian Century,*
February 8, 2005.

Christian hostility toward Jews was not sufficient by itself to produce such horror, but Christianity's animosity toward Jews was a necessary condition for that disaster.

Gas chambers and crematoria did not begin the Holocaust. It started with steps that isolated and separated Jews. Those Nazi policies included economic measures. One can understand that the Presbyterian advocates of divestment felt that they were defending the rights of Palestinians who have been seriously harmed by the Israeli-Palestinian conflict, but that advocacy was largely tone-deaf and amnesiac with regard to Holocaust history and Jewish memory. In February 2005, when Jay Rock, the PCUSA's coordinator of interfaith relations, tried to explain the church's divestment policy to leaders of the Anti-Defamation League, Rabbi Gary Bretton-Granatoor, the ADL's interfaith director, cut to the chase: "When they said 'divestment,' we heard 'boycott.'"[9] Presbyterian disclaimers to the contrary

9. Rabbi Gary Bretton-Granatoor was quoted in James D. Davis, "Church Plans Roil Jewish Leaders," *South Florida Sun-Sentinel,* February 13, 2005. From the time that the PCUSA divestment initiative was first announced, Jewish reaction was sharply critical, as illustrated by the following examples. One Jewish critic was U.S. Congressman Howard L. Berman (D-CA). His letter of protest (dated September 14, 2004) to Clifton Kirkpatrick, stated clerk of the General Assembly, charged that "the Presbyterian Church has knowingly gone on record calling for jeopardizing the existence of the State of Israel." His letter contained signatures from thirteen other members of Congress, four of them Jewish, three of them Presbyterian. The letter is available through the Internet at http://www.house.gov/list/press/ca28_berman/presbyletter.shtml. Rabbi Eric H. Yoffe, president of the Union for Reform Judaism, stated that the PCUSA's action "has caused utter dismay in the Jewish community." See Alan Cooperman, "Israel Divestiture Spurs Clash," *Washington Post,* September 29, 2004, p. A8. Dennis Prager, a respected Los Angeles commentator on religious affairs, was even more direct. "Incredibly," he wrote on July 20, 2004, "the General Assembly of the Presbyterian Church (USA) joins the list of religious groups committing evil." Calling the PCUSA action "immoral, sinful and bigoted denigration of the Jewish state," Alan Dershowitz's essay in the *Los Angeles Times* (August 8, 2004) went on to find the divestment initiative "so one-sided, so anti-Zionist in its rhetoric and so ignorant of the realities on the ground that it can only be explained by the kind of bigotry that the Presbyterian Church itself condemned in 1987 when it promised 'never again to participate in, to contribute to, or (insofar as we are able) to allow the persecution or denigration of Jews.'" These examples of criticism, and others like them, did not always grasp correctly all the details of the Presbyterian divestment initiative, but they made clear how deeply the church's position wounded Presbyterian-Jewish relations. Those relations were harmed further when two PCUSA officials, Kathy Lueckert and Peter Sulyok, members of an October 2004 fact-finding trip to the Middle East, met with officials from Hezbollah, a recognized terrorist organization that went on to wreak havoc in its war with Israel in 2006. They eventually left their PCUSA jobs,

notwithstanding, Bretton-Granatoor did not miss the target, for beyond its symbolic gesture, the PCUSA divestment initiative could not have been effective as an economic sanction unless many other institutions took similar decisions.

Presbyterian wealth is considerable, but it is insufficient by itself to influence economic policy substantially, let alone dictate it decisively. Jewish leaders, however, were rightly concerned that the Presbyterian initiative could encourage what came for a time to be called "divestment creep" or even "divestment envy," which might have led other Christian denominations to take related steps that singled out and isolated Israel at the very time when a disturbing upsurge of antisemitism, much of it fueled by anti-Israeli sentiment, has become widespread.

Steps in that direction were in the making internationally, for in late February 2005 the 150-member Central Committee of the World Council of Churches (the WCC consists of some 349 Protestant and Orthodox Christian churches) commended the PCUSA's unmistakably pro-Palestinian and anti-Israeli divestment action. Citing Luke 19:42, a New Testament passage that speaks about "the things that make for peace," a WCC document released on February 21, 2005, "reminds churches with investment funds that they have an opportunity to use those funds responsibly in support of peaceful solutions to conflict. Economic pressure, appropriately and openly applied, is one such means of action."[10]

but not before more needless damage had been done. Jewish unhappiness with Presbyterians was also deepened by the church's establishment and support of Congregation Avodat Yisrael, a church for Messianic Jews in the Philadelphia area.

10. See the WCC Central Committee's news release "WCC Central Committee Encourages Consideration of Economic Measures for Peace in Israel/Palestine," February 21, 2005 (http://www2.wcc-coe.org/pressreleasesen.nsf/index/pr-cc-05-08.html; see also http://www.oikoumene.org/GEN_PUB_5_Second_report.o.779.o.html#1573). Noting a growing desire for "a just, equitable and lasting peace in both Israel and Palestine," the WCC reiterated its 1992 position that "criticism of the policies of the Israeli government is not in itself anti-Jewish," which is a viable distinction but also one that may contain dupery. The WCC approached that line because its statement was couched in ways that accuse Israel of decades of illegal occupation and "illegal activities in occupied territory [that] continue as if a viable peace for both peoples is not a possibility." The WCC places the fault for the Israeli-Palestinian conflict primarily and emphatically on the doorstep of every Israeli administration since 1967, if not before. Christians as well as Jews should therefore think carefully about the most credible responses to the following question: At what point does the distinction between criticism of Israeli policy and anti-Jewish sentiment collapse and/or legitimate, however unintentionally, postures and policies contrary to the interests of the Jewish people

Presbyterians and WCC members who advocate divestment may be seeking comfort in the hope that they are defending the oppressed and thus occupying high moral ground, but a consequence of their action, unintended though it may be, is to give aid and comfort to antisemitism, thus adding further to the sorry Christian record that has accumulated over the centuries and that culminated in the Holocaust's near-destruction of the Jewish people. That tragedy is compounded by the fact that the divisive Presbyterian-Jewish confrontation and its unfortunate spin-offs could have been avoided without compromising Christian ethics, defense of Palestinian rights, or appropriate and needed post-Holocaust Christian solidarity with the Jewish people.

Much of Christian ethics is shaped by the voices of Hebrew prophets such as Amos and Micah, whose calls for justice and righteousness were echoed by Jesus. Presbyterians are faithful to that tradition when they speak and act against murder and injustice and when they do so fairly. The Presbyterian divestment initiative was couched in language that not only protested against current Israeli policies but also condemned terrorism and suicide bombings from the Palestinian side. Nevertheless, Jews were right when they said that the Presbyterian initiative emphasized the former disproportionately and thus gave less than fully justified attention to the latter.

Despite their protests to the contrary, the advocates of divestment took the Palestinian side in ways that treated Israel unfairly at the very time — and not for the first time, either — when Israel was making major strides toward a peaceful settlement. In particular, whether the Presbyterian advocates of divestment acknowledged it or not, their actions tended to isolate Israel and drive a deep wedge between Presbyterians and Jews. In this context, it is important to remember that while Israel is a strong country, even one possessing impressive military might, it continues to be surrounded by nations that can scarcely be said to wish it well. A two-state solution to the Israeli-Palestinian conflict is desirable; most Presbyterians, including me, affirm it. One would be duped, however, to assume simply that a two-state solution will bring peace and security to Israel forever.

precisely because those stances are anti-Israeli? Probably most Jews will answer that question very differently from the WCC. They will be right to do so because their realistic sensibilities about the importance of the State of Israel, its significance for the vitality of the Jewish people, and its precarious situation in the Middle East, which pronouncements from Christian groups can do little to improve but much to worsen, will run deeper and stronger than any Christian's are likely to do.

Much depends on the nature of the Palestinian state, as well as on the policies of Israeli administrations.

At the February 16, 2005, meeting of the Church Relations Committee of the U.S. Holocaust Memorial Museum, my colleague David Blumenthal — a contributor to this volume — reminded me that when the previously mentioned 1987 document "A Theological Understanding of the Relationship between Christians and Jews" was written, Presbyterians invited Jewish representatives (Blumenthal included) to deliberate with them. Little, if any, consultation of that kind took place before the PCUSA launched its 2004 divestment rocket. One wonders what would have happened if Presbyterians had consulted more widely, bringing to the table not only Palestinian Christian voices but also those of concerned Israelis and American Jews.

The context for such deliberations might have been shaped as follows: To the point of anger, Presbyterians could have said, we are deeply concerned about the suffering of Palestinians during the Israeli-Palestinian conflict. We are equally determined to respect and honor the existence of the State of Israel, whose security has been undermined by Palestinian terrorism. Help us to formulate peacemaking policies, including those pertaining to Presbyterian economic resources, so that we can do more to "let justice roll down like waters, and righteousness like an everflowing stream" (Amos 5:24).

If such consultations had been held, I doubt that the Presbyterian divestment policy would have been put into play. Perhaps — I am cautious so as not to be duped — a much more creative *investment* policy could have emerged instead. Especially after the warfare of 2006, such policies are needed more than ever, and Presbyterian financial resources need to be better deployed and more wisely used to support developments, industries, and projects of mutual benefit and interest that would bring Palestinians and Israelis together in ways that create the conditions needed for a viable two-state solution. Such an investment policy would give priority to enterprises that bolster and connect both Palestinian and Israeli economic interests, for the chances for peace will be enhanced if economic interests between the two peoples and eventual states are interlocking, interdependent, and structured for mutual well-being. To assist such development, even in the relatively small ways that PCUSA resources could advance them, would provide steps in the right direction that others could emulate. Such planning might mean that some PCUSA economic resources would be reapportioned and reallocated, but instead of divestment that pressures by punishment, the emphasis would be on creative investment planned through consultation and dialogue.

Such a position is akin to that held by Presbyterians Concerned for Jewish and Christian Relations (PCJCR), a group of PCUSA clergy and laypersons to which I belong. Supporting a two-state solution to the Israeli-Palestinian conflict, PCJCR opposed the General Assembly's divestment posture, called early on for postponement of any further action toward divestment, and worked successfully to reverse the 2004 divestment decision at the 2006 General Assembly. Concurrently, the PCJCR has supported "proactive engagement and selective investment of time, talent, and financial resources in companies, not-for-profits, NGOs and diplomatic efforts that are likely to promote a just and lasting peace in the region."[11]

The PCJCR's position may also turn out to be yet another instance of being duped by morality, a phenomenon that has been rife in the Israeli-Palestinian struggle and the world's reaction to it. Be that as it may, the possibility that morality may dupe us does not, must not, mean the demise of ethical reasoning. Where the Israeli-Palestinian conflict is concerned, that possibility entails instead that moral reflection and the policies that emerge from it need to proceed as far as possible with undeceived lucidity about both the threats that Israel continues to face and the needs of Palestinians for an economically and politically viable state of their own. The PCUSA's 2004 divestment policy did not pass that test, but a wise investment policy could do so. If the window for peace that opened unexpectedly in 2005 is not to be closed by subsequent events, such investment policies, which the PCUSA and other Christian churches might help to underwrite, could play important parts, ones that help Palestinians and Israelis alike, ones that heal relations between Jews and Presbyterians, whose recent sorry state, at least for me, was nothing less than heartbreaking.

11. The quotation is from the PCJCR media release "Presbyterians Challenge PCUSA Divestment Decision," December 8, 2004.

Contributors' Questions for John K. Roth

Should symbolic actions toward the Jewish people by Christians always be prohibited because of the debt — one "that can never be fully repaid" — owed to Jews by Christians? Might this argument not encourage inaction in the face of new injustices? You say that Christian antisemitism is guilty of providing the necessary (though not sufficient) conditions for the Holocaust to have occurred. But are there not dangers in alluding to any guilt that might be construed as eternal and collective? Might such guilt lead to too easy a condemnation of such actions as those of the PCUSA? Might such a carefully limited divestment strategy constitute a call to remember the Holocaust?

You claim that the Presbyterian divestment strategy tilted toward the Palestinians. Might divestment, targeted solely toward corporations supporting what to most of the world community is an immoral and self-defeating occupation, be tilted as much toward Israel as it is toward the Palestinians? (Prime Minister Sharon himself employed the term "occupation.") Is it not, paradoxically, in Israel's interest to have corporations be pressured to end their support of occupation? Would divesting from Caterpillar, Inc. — makers of bulldozers that demolish homes and help build others — endanger or enhance Israel's security? Although limited divestment is one small tactic to be located amid a much-needed greater investment in fostering mutual understanding in the region, might "divestment," in this context, constitute a form of "investment"? Are we post-Holocaust individuals not obligated to engage in acts of resistance whenever "occupation" is named as such by the world community?

Response by John K. Roth

When Emmanuel Levinas said that "it is of the highest importance to know whether we are not duped by morality," he was not thinking about bulldozers.[1] Nevertheless, these powerful earthmovers, especially the ones built by Caterpillar, the American heavy-equipment giant, deserve consideration in relation to Levinas's remark and the questions about my essay.

Bulldozers serve human intentions. However constructive those intentions, they always include destruction of one kind or another. Economically driven and politically calculated, bulldozing raises ethical issues. Specifically, bulldozers have played a significant part in the Israeli-Palestinian conflict.[2] They will likely have a role in its resolution as well.

On April 13, 2005, Caterpillar, Inc., held its annual shareholder meeting in Chicago.[3] About 150 representatives of a protesting coalition, in-

1. Emmanuel Levinas, *Totality and Infinity: An Essay on Exteriority,* trans. Alphonso Lingis (Pittsburgh: Duquesne University Press, 1969), p. 21.

2. Caterpillar's D9 bulldozer has been especially controversial. According to a November 2004 report in *OneWorld,* reprinted by the Presbyterian News Service (http://www.pcusa.org/pcnews/2004/04524.htm), Caterpillar has produced the D9 to Israeli military specifications and sold it to Israel through the U.S. Foreign Military Sales Program. Armored by Israel, the D9 weighs 64 tons, stands 13 feet tall and 26 feet long, and its razing blade is called "the ripper." Human Rights Watch and Amnesty International are among the critics of Israel's use of such Caterpillar equipment in security actions that have allegedly damaged, if not demolished, Palestinian homes and roads, as well as water and sewage pipes.

3. The following account relies on an article by Toya Richards Hill, "150 Rally outside Caterpillar Meeting," which was carried by the Presbyterian News Service (http://www.pcusa.org/pcnews/2005/05204.htm).

cluding the Presbyterian Church (PCUSA), urged Caterpillar to consider whether the sale of bulldozers to Israel violated the company's policies about corporate responsibility. Caterpillar's shareholders trounced the protesters' initiative, which received only 3 percent of the vote. Far from cooling Presbyterian heat, however, that defeat still left Caterpillar high on PCUSA's list in the "phased selective divestment" plan that remained in effect, at least for a time, after the denomination initiated it in 2004.

Governed by the belief that the Holocaust should not put the Israeli government or any corporation above fair criticism by Christians and also by the conviction that the Holocaust should make post-Holocaust Christians pause before unfair steps are taken that jar Jewish sensibilities and trust as the Presbyterian divestment initiative has done, my essay argued that Presbyterian divestment from companies such as Caterpillar would be unlikely to change corporate policy or to improve the conditions of needy Palestinians, but such sanctions would mean that Presbyterian-Jewish relations would remain in decline. Instead of *divestment,* I contended, the Presbyterian emphasis should be placed on a creative *investment* policy, one that would bring Palestinians and Israelis together in ways that create the conditions needed for a viable two-state solution. My tracking of the situation since the time of my original writing and in light of my colleagues' questions does not lead me to change those judgments substantially. To see why, consider some 2005 events.

Jack Marcum conducts and studies surveys for PCUSA's Research Services. In November 2004 a representative sample of Presbyterians — members, ruling elders, and clergy, the last category including pastors of congregations and other ordained ministers — was asked, "Do you favor or oppose the PCUSA undertaking a phased, selective sale (divestment) of the stock it owns in multinational corporations whose dealings in Israel support the Israeli occupation of Palestinian territories?" The responses, summarized and analyzed in Marcum's report "The PCUSA, Divestment, and Israel" (June 2005), revealed numerous splits.[4]

Among members and ruling elders, 42 and 46 percent, respectively, were opposed to the divestment initiative; 28 and 30 percent were in favor; 30 and 23 percent reported no opinion. Among pastors and other ordained ministers, 43 and 24 percent were opposed; 48 and 64 percent were in fa-

4. Much of Marcum's research is summarized online at http://www.pcusa.org/research/panel/summaries/1104sum.pdf.

vor; 9 and 12 percent expressed no opinion. These findings showed a relatively low level of support for divestment among Presbyterian laypersons and a relatively high level of support for divestment among Presbyterian leaders who are not pastors of congregations. The pressure for divestment and the strain it produced between the PCUSA, Israel, and other Jewish communities did not come primarily from Presbyterian grassroots but from leadership that was not fully in touch with its chief constituencies.

Marcum also found a theological divide. Among Presbyterians describing themselves as theologically conservative, a perspective that frequently includes strong support for Israel, 55 and 58 percent of members and ruling elders and 75 and 58 percent of pastors and other ministers opposed divestment. Presbyterians who self-identified as theological liberals had a different profile. They favored divestment: 50 and 46 percent of members and ruling elders, and 77 and 79 percent of pastors and other ministers. Presbyterians who characterized themselves as theological moderates split more evenly, but split nonetheless, between those who favored and those who opposed divestment.

Marcum's findings revealed anything but a broad-based Presbyterian mandate for the PCUSA's divestment plan regarding Israel. That news was good, but I did not take much comfort from it because Marcum rightly stated that the percentages cited above did not contain the survey's most surprising result. It resided in the fact that a majority of Presbyterian laypersons were "not at all aware of the 2004 Assembly action to explore possible divestment." Among Presbyterian members and ruling elders, a majority — 61 and 51 percent, respectively — reported that they were not aware of the PCUSA divestment initiative, while just 14 and 19 percent indicated that they were very aware of their church's action. Here another gap revealed itself, for among pastors and other ministers, 65 and 50 percent, respectively, indicated that they were very aware of the PCUSA divestment initiative, while only 5 and 15 percent stated that they were not aware of it. Fortunately, in 2006 many Presbyterian laypersons, as well as clergy, became better informed and acted on their convictions to change Presbyterian-Jewish relations for the better by taking action to negate the divestment initiative at the 2006 General Assembly meeting in Birmingham, Alabama. Yet a question lingered: What about Caterpillar and its bulldozers?

Before considering that question in more detail, notice that Presbyterians have been represented in a Christian-Jewish working group that has met since May 2004. Facilitated by the American Jewish Committee and the National Council of the Churches of Christ, the group's activities included plans for investigative travel to Israel and the Palestinian territories in September 2005. Meanwhile, an exchange of letters in the spring of 2005 indicated the intensity of divestment-related tensions.[5] On April 22, 2005, Jewish partners in the working group wrote to their Protestant colleagues, including the Presbyterian Jay Rock.[6] Affirming a commitment to dialogue and to a just and lasting peace in the Middle East, the Jewish letter also expressed ongoing disappointment and distress that "any Protestant denomination . . . would consider the weapon of economic sanctions to be unilaterally and prejudicially used against the State of Israel." Noting that holding Israel to "a standard different from any other sovereign state" produces "an environment which makes constructive dialogue almost impossible," the letter concluded by calling "our Christian colleagues to reject all negative economic and political sanctions, for they undermine peace, foster prejudice and give hope to extremists on every side." While making no mention of Caterpillar and its bulldozers, this letter implied condemnation of Presbyterian considerations about divestment from that corporation.

The April letter drew two important responses. On May 10, 2005, the Protestant members of the working group replied on letterhead from the Office of Interfaith Relations, National Council of Churches USA. Observing that various Protestant denominations, not only the PCUSA, were at different stages — and will be for some time — in considering "economic leverage as one part of a strategy to end violence and support justice in the creation of lasting Palestinian-Israeli peace," the Protestants cautioned that it would be unwise for their Jewish colleagues "to picture the

5. The letters are available online through links accessible at http://www.pcusa.org/interfaith/dialogue.htm. My quotations from these letters come from this Web site.

6. The Jewish signatories were Rabbi Gary Bretton-Granatoor (Anti-Defamation League), Betty Ehrenberg (Orthodox Union), Dr. David Elcott (American Jewish Committee), Ethan Felson (Jewish Council for Public Affairs), Rabbi Eugene Korn (American Jewish Congress), Mark Pelavin (Union for Reform Judaism), and Mark Waldman (United Synagogue of Conservative Judaism). In addition to Rock, the Protestant members of the working group were Rt. Rev. Christopher Epting (Episcopal Church, USA), Rev. Brian Grieves (Episcopal Church, USA), Dr. Darryl Jodock (Evangelical Lutheran Church in America), Dr. Peter Makari (United Church of Christ/Disciples of Christ), Rev. Dr. Larry Pickens (United Methodist Church), Dr. Shanta Premawardhana (National Council of Churches, USA), Dr. Franklin Sherman (Evangelical Church in America), and Jim Winkler (United Methodist Church).

situation in 'make or break' terms," a point made by the Protestants in re-
ply to the Jewish suggestion that constructive dialogue would be "almost
impossible" so long as "negative economic and political sanctions" remained on the table. While making no mention of Caterpillar and its bulldozers, this letter left the door wide open for Presbyterian divestment from
that corporation.

On June 3, 2005, Jay Rock sent his Presbyterian response to the April
letter. It contended that Jewish characterizations of Presbyterian intentions, not only in the April letter but elsewhere, used "inexact and emo-
tionally loaded language" that "perpetuates the chilling, and false, image of
a church calling for the economic undermining of the State of Israel." Rock
stated that the PCUSA, following direction from the General Assembly, its
highest governing body, "has as its goal engagement with selected corporations to ask them to reconsider and cease business activities that support
the violence of the current situation in which Israelis and Palestinians live."
Divestment was not ruled out, Rock added, but would be a last step. While
this letter made no mention of Caterpillar and its bulldozers, they were
certainly present between the lines.

My reading of this exchange inspired little hope that prospects for a
just and lasting peace between Palestinians and Israelis would be advanced
within the parameters of the discussion carried on by Jewish-Christian
working groups where wrangles about divestment and economic sanctions are so much in the spotlight. The Holocaust and its aftermath influence my judgment. The involvement of Christianity and Christians in the
Holocaust, if only as bystanders, produced a debt to Jews that Christians
can never fully repay. However, far from encouraging inaction in the face
of the multiple injustices in the Israeli-Palestinian conflict, honesty about
that debt should concentrate Christian attention, including Presbyterian
policy, on the most constructive steps that can be taken to secure a just and
lasting peace in a two-state resolution of that conflict. The "tilt," if there is
one, should be governed by that goal, and what that proposition means,
economically, is that Christian denominations should concentrate on using *investment* more smartly, more ethically, than the emphasis on divestment and debates about it have done.

Within the focus I have in mind, "divestment" might constitute a
form of "investment," but that formulation does not put the priorities in
their best order. Christians and Presbyterians in particular need to think
long and hard about where their economic plans and resources can do the

most good in response to the Israeli-Palestinian conflict. An emphasis on investment, not divestment, should follow those insights. If that planning entails reallocation of stock portfolios toward some companies and away from others, so be it, but the emphasis ought to be on wise investment, not on punishing divestment. Such savvy investment will be not only prudent economically but also proper ethically and theologically.

A good place to begin in that regard would be for Christian denominations and the PCUSA in particular to consider carefully the plans developed in 2005 by the RAND Corporation.[7] RAND's forward-looking studies rightly recognize that a peace settlement is only one step in a much longer Israeli-Palestinian journey. A just and lasting peace cannot be achieved unless the anticipated Palestinian state is viable economically. By building a better Palestinian economy, which is not only a long-term need but also essential if the current conflict is to be resolved, Israel's best interests for security and regional stability can be served as well. The actions that RAND proposes, moreover, could begin with salutary effects *now*.

Central to RAND's vision is a corridor called the Arc. Emphasizing the need for safe and secure movement of people and goods in a Palestinian state that will be split between the West Bank and Gaza, the Arc involves what RAND describes as "a high-speed 140 mile interurban rail line, highway, aqueduct, energy network and fiber optic cable linking Palestine's major towns and cities." To the best of my knowledge, the RAND plans for the Arc do not mention Caterpillar and its bulldozers. It is not far-fetched, however, to imagine that the Arc's construction could use them, employing even the D9 more benignly than has sometimes been the case. If PCUSA thinking about the Israeli-Palestinian conflict put its stockholding priorities in sync with visions such as RAND's, good steps in the mending of the world enjoined by sound memory of the Holocaust — far better than those envisioned by divestment emphases, including those that might target Caterpillar — would be under way, and not a moment too soon.

---

7. Released on April 27, 2005, two RAND reports are especially significant: *Building a Successful Palestinian State,* produced by RAND Health, and *The Arc: A Formal Structure for a Palestinian State,* the result of work by the RAND Center for Middle East Public Policy. Information and commentary about these studies can be found online at http://www.rand .org/news/press.05/04.27.html and http://www.rand.org/commentary/052205BS.html. My account draws on these online sources.

A Postscript

By no means does this chapter about the Israeli-Palestinian conflict have anything approaching a happy ending. Nevertheless, a postscript is in order because action taken at the 217th General Assembly of the PCUSA, which met in Birmingham, Alabama (June 15-22, 2006), replaced the General Assembly's 2004 decision "to initiate a process of phased selective divestment in multinational corporations operating in Israel." Overwhelmingly (483 in favor, 28 opposed, 1 abstention), the Assembly determined instead that "financial investments of the Presbyterian Church (U.S.A.), as they pertain to Israel, Gaza, East Jerusalem, and the West Bank, be invested in only peaceful pursuits." The new action acknowledged that the 2004 initiative had caused "hurt and misunderstanding among many members of the Jewish community and within our Presbyterian communion." Referring again to the action taken in 2004, the 2006 policy statement went on to say, "We are grieved by the pain that this has caused, accept responsibility for the flaws in our process, and ask for a new season of mutual understanding and dialogue."[8]

Despite the apologizing tone of the 2006 statement, some of those who had favored the earlier policy noted that the replacement language did not officially repeal and rescind the 2004 initiative. They did not confirm that their agenda was completely off the table, but practically speaking, it seems unlikely that there is much life left in the 2004 plan that caused so many strained relations between Jews and the PCUSA. One reason for that judgment is that soon after the General Assembly finished its business in June 2006, violence in the Middle East escalated precipitously when Israel defended itself against Hezbollah's recurring rocket attacks. As fierce and bloody warfare ensued in July, letters signed by Clifton Kirkpatrick, the stated clerk of the PCUSA General Assembly, referred to "the repeated harsh and disproportionate retaliatory attacks on the country of Lebanon" and called on "the United States, acting in concert with the international community, . . . to achieve an immediate cease-fire and to launch an intensive diplomatic initiative for the cessation of hostilities."[9]

8. For more information, see Toya Richards Hill's article "GA Overwhelmingly Approves Israel/Palestine Recommendation," which is available through the PCUSA Web site at http://www.pcusa.org/ga217/newsandphotos/ga06124.htm.

9. I refer to letters dated July 19 and 21, 2006. The former was written to the PCUSA's

What good such Presbyterian rhetoric would do remained doubtful, perhaps indicating that dupery by morality knows no end. It seems certain, however, that creative investment — whether along the lines of RAND's proposal or some other — will sooner or later be needed more than ever in Gaza, the West Bank, and Israel.

church partners in Lebanon; the latter was from Churches for Middle East Peace, which includes PCUSA among its members, and was addressed to President George W. Bush. The texts of the letters are available online at http://www.pcusa.org/pcnews/2006/06371.htm and http://www.cmep.org/letters/7-21-06_Heads_Letter_Hezbollah-Israel.pdf.

3. *Beware of Your Beliefs*

David Blumenthal

When I first sat down to write this essay, Yasser Arafat lay sick, probably dead, in a Paris hospital. After his death, Arafat was replaced by Mahmoud Abbas, one of the few democratically elected leaders in the Arab world. That event and others, such as the Israeli pullout from Gaza, led to soaring hopes that peace between Israelis and Palestinians might be around the corner. Unfortunately, subsequent events, including but not limited to the war between Israel and Hezbollah in 2006, showed that these hopes were premature. No one actually knows what will happen next; the best guess for the future, however, depends on how one reads the past. Thus, in the interest of self-disclosure, I begin by noting that I am a Jew who has been a conscious Zionist for as long as I can remember. I recall the vote in the United Nations to establish the Jewish state and the switch in religious school to the Israeli pronunciation of Hebrew when the state was proclaimed. I was an active member of a Zionist youth movement, and my first trip to Israel was very much a Zionist pilgrimage.

I am also a religious Jew who takes seriously the presence of God and the truth of God's promises to the Jewish people of seed, land, and blessing. I therefore justify the Jewish claim to a homeland in Israel on both secular-historical and religious-spiritual grounds.

I am also an experienced rabbi and professor of Jewish studies, one who has taught Jewish civilization for some time and has been active in Jewish and Israeli causes, locally and nationally. I was also one of the organizers of the first trialogue group of Jewish, Christian, and Muslim scholars and was a consultant to the Presbyterian Church on some of its important documents concerning the Jews and Israel. I initiated courses and research on the Shoah at my university, have been a member of various committees of the U.S. Holocaust Memorial Museum and of the biennial international symposium of Holocaust scholars at Wroxton College in the United Kingdom, have written two books on the Shoah, and have edited the memoirs of a survivor and two volumes of essays on the Shoah.[1]

On the subject of the Israeli-Palestinian conflict, I was among the early speakers for Palestinian rights and have consistently supported the efforts of Israeli and Palestinian peace organizations. I vividly remember visiting a fellow student in an Israeli Arab village in 1959. It was then under curfew, and I saw their humiliation. I remember, too, sitting with them as they listed excitedly to Nasser preach about pushing the Jews into the sea. I recall being asked to address a large synagogue gathering together with a Palestinian in the early 1980s. I took a firm stand in favor of a Palestinian state alongside the State of Israel, much to the admitted astonishment of the Palestinian speaker. At about the same time, I was quietly dropped from the list of speakers to the young leadership group of the Atlanta Jewish Federation because of my espousal of Palestinian sovereignty and not just autonomy. Long ago I joined Oz ve-Shalom, the religious peace group, and, over the years, hosted at my university speakers from that group and related organizations. I have also encouraged speakers from the Israeli Right as part of the educational thrust of my work. During the course of my consultations with the Presbyterian Church, I visited Palestinians in Israel and in the West Bank, as well as Christians in Egypt.

Over the years, however, my position has changed because I found that my Palestinian and Muslim interlocutors embodied three characteristics that I found counterproductive. First, they totally politicized all discussions. All my attempts to discuss theology, peace, and a justice that would include Jews and the State of Israel, as well as Palestinians and a Palestinian state, were completely rejected. My "partners" wanted only to present the Palestinian side, not to dialogue. Second, my Palestinian and Muslim interlocutors refused to acknowledge any coresponsibility for the

1. David R. Blumenthal, *Facing the Abusing God: A Theology of Protest* (Louisville, Ky.: Westminster John Knox Press, 1993) and *The Banality of Good and Evil* (Washington, D.C.: Georgetown University Press, 1999); Alex Gross, *Yankele: A Holocaust Survivor's Bittersweet Memoir* (Lanham, Md.: University Press of America, 2001); and David R. Blumenthal, ed., *Emory Studies on the Holocaust*, 2 vols. (Atlanta: Emory University, 1985-88).

conflicted situation. They candidly approved terrorism, even when directed at innocent Israeli civilians. Occasionally, I would find individual Palestinians and Muslims who would realize the futility of terrorism, though not necessarily its inherent evil. But even for such rare individuals, the open expression of such opinions was regarded as national treason, and they simply would not make such statements in public.[2] Third, even though there were uneven attempts at political and religious dialogue with an elite, Palestinians and Muslims in general — ordinary people engaged in conversation, as well as the Palestinian and Arab media — have openly manifested a relentless wish to destroy the Jewish state and to drive out the Jews who have chosen to settle there.[3]

It has made no difference whether I have engaged in dialogue in the United States, Europe, or Israel. Nor have the auspices been a factor: Presbyterian, leftist, rightist, religious, secular, political, interfaith. Nothing has helped. While Jewish and Israeli interlocutors are also varied in their opinions and even in their prejudices, I have increasingly found Palestinians and Muslims to be very difficult dialogue partners. Frankly, they do not share a concern for Jewish existence. Nor do they share a sense of the inherent right of the Jewish people to exist in its homeland, granted that there must be some dignified, mutual accommodation that would make this possible. Perhaps in some ideal religious or ideological sense, they should not need to think such thoughts. But in the concrete situation in which we all find ourselves, I have found their refusal to want to deal with us Jews to be irresponsible, and I have found their hostility to us to be relentless. Furthermore, in the context of post-Shoah Jewish life, I have increasingly realized that I cannot dismiss that hostility as simply a negotiating position or as merely a cultural custom or a verbal convention. Instead, I must deal with the hostility as forthrightly as I can.[4]

2. During this period, I conceived an exemplary textbook in Jewish, Christian, and Muslim trialogue. I have never succeeded in finding a Muslim, Palestinian or otherwise, who would write the section on Islam. Every Muslim I have met has been afraid of any kind of "cooperation" — that is, collaboration — with me.

3. I once interviewed a well-educated Muslim from the United Arab Emirates for the masters in Jewish studies at Emory University. His interest was in modern Hebrew literature. He plainly told me that only literature written by Jews from Islamic lands was legitimate; the rest of modern Hebrew literature had too much *Yiddishkeit* (his word) and hence was simply not properly Hebrew literature.

4. For more on this topic, see my Response below.

In spite of my commitments and experiences, I recognize that I am not an expert on the Middle East or on the Israeli-Palestinian conflict. I do consider myself, however, an educated layperson with commitments who is not afraid to confront realities wherever they lie. It is with that background and in that spirit that I address the problem of the Israeli-Palestinian conflict in the context of post-Shoah experience.

In the 1980s I published "The Seven Commandments for Jewish Survival in a Post-Holocaust World."[5] It is worthwhile to list them yet again: "Be a little paranoid; Get organized and stay organized; Educate; Support the institutions of freedom; Reproduce; Confront your opposition; and Be prepared." I also offered pieces of advice: keep a good amount of cash and a valid passport at home, belong to a political lobby as part of your responsibility as a citizen, always vote, support peace movements, and be prepared to use political violence if necessary. Looking back, I still think the article contains many valid points. However, I would now add another injunction: "Beware of your beliefs." We live life based on certain convictions about human nature and society, and the most difficult part of cross-cultural communication centers on the beliefs each party brings to the table.

The Shoah took place, in part, because of the beliefs of those involved: that the world would not care about the Jews, since it had not cared about the Armenians; that the Germans were too civilized to carry out a plan of actual extermination; that the Allies would act out of humanitarian motives and bomb nonessential targets such as the Nazi camps; that ordinary people would not murder innocent others; that governments would admit people who were obviously refugees; and so on. One of the important lessons of the Shoah is that we must beware of our beliefs; we must aggressively question what we believe and what others believe, and furthermore, as Jews we must do so with an eye to the problem of Jewish survival. Had the Jews of the Shoah period been more realistic concerning their beliefs about human nature and society, perhaps many more would have been saved.

In this vein, I present six beliefs about the Israeli-Palestinian conflict that are not only widespread but also highly dangerous to Jewish survival.

---

5. "In the Shadow of the Holocaust," *Jewish Spectator,* Winter 1981, pp. 11-14; reprinted in expanded form as "Memory and Meaning in the Shadow of the Holocaust," in Blumenthal, *Emory Studies on the Holocaust,* 1:114-22; available on my Web site, http://www.js.emory.edu/blumenthal.

We need to examine these beliefs carefully because we Jews cannot afford to be wrong yet again about the world in which we live. It is our watch, our time for responsibility.

1. *The Israeli-Palestinian conflict is at the heart of the problems in the Middle East.* This belief is very widely held in the Arab world — to wit, that the State of Israel was imposed on the Arab world by the Christian nations of Europe and America as a response to their guilt for the Shoah. As more than one Arab has said, "If the Christians persecuted and killed the Jews, why should we have to pay by having them in our land?" In this analysis, it seems to follow that if only the Israeli-Palestinian conflict could be resolved, then there would be peace in the Middle East.

This belief seems to me to be very naive. As Haim Harari and many others have pointed out, the following serious events in the Middle East were not the result of the Israeli-Palestinian conflict:[6] the Iran-Iraq war (in which casualties reached as many as 1.5 million), the Taliban takeover of Afghanistan, the Iraqi invasion of Kuwait, the destruction of the city of Hamāh by the Syrians, the occupation of Lebanon by Syria, the al-Qaeda attacks against Saudi Arabia and Egypt, the 9/11 attacks on the Twin Towers in New York and on the Pentagon, the attack on the Spanish railroads and on the London underground, both American invasions of Iraq, and the Algerian revolution. None of these events was the product of the Israeli-Palestinian conflict. They were the result of struggles for power, oil, and influence, as well as many other factors. Yet the belief persists that the Israeli-Palestinian conflict is at the heart of the world's problems in the Middle East — and not only in the Arabic media and public statements but also in the European press and statements by European leaders. The popularity of this belief has led to many violent incidents that are anti-Israel, anti-Zionist, and anti-Jewish. The Israeli-Palestinian conflict is one part of the Middle East dilemma. Israel/Palestine, however, is not geopolitically significant. There is no oil to dispute, the land is not particularly arable, and there are few resources or industries to covet. In short, no one's national interest, except that of the Palestinians and the Israelis, is at stake. The belief in the centrality of the Israeli-Palestinian conflict must be resisted.

6. Haim Harari, "A View from the Eye of the Storm," in a speech given in April 2004 and widely distributed on the Internet (http://www.freeman.org/m_online/jul04/harari.htm).

2. *Poverty is at the root of the Israeli-Palestinian conflict and indeed at the core of the Middle East crisis; furthermore, poverty justifies the use of terrorism.* This belief is widely heard in leftist circles around the world. It is an outgrowth of Marxist analysis that understands all conflict to be class conflict and further teaches that class conflict can be resolved only by violent means. Some Western intellectuals are particularly taken with this argument, partly because it expresses their sense of guilt for the blessings they have. Some even try to justify terrorism as an expression of resentment at poverty.

This belief also strikes me as very naive. As Haim Harari has pointed out, there is much, much greater poverty in Africa, where people are really starving (as in the Sudan), but terrorism of the kind found in the Middle East is not widespread. There is greater poverty in India, but again, terrorism of the kind found in the Middle East is not widespread there either. Poverty indeed is an issue in the Middle East and also on both sides of the Israeli-Palestinian conflict, but poverty is not the central issue, and solving the problem of poverty would not resolve the tensions in either the local conflict or in the region. Poverty relief is important, but the belief that it holds the key to resolving the Israeli-Palestinian conflict must also be resisted.

3. *Reason and law are basic to all human societies. Hence, diplomatic activity to bring about the rule of reason and law is appropriate.* This belief is perhaps the most widely held philosophical and political principle in the Western world, especially in the United States. We Americans tend to think that people are reasonable and that law and respect for it provide the proper and ultimate place for the resolution of disputes. We further believe that humans of diverse origins and aspirations can, with reason and goodwill, settle their conflicts justly and live together peacefully.

Unfortunately, this belief, too, seems to me to be very naive. The world is not a place where there is liberty and justice for all. It is not a place of cooperation and good will, where the rule of law is the ultimate judge. To a considerable degree, the world includes terrorism. In that world, where murderers are called martyrs and museums are built to their memory, the ends justify the means. Whether the terrorists are Palestinian or Cambodian, the world of terror is not a world where reason and law prevail. Regimes that support terror are not entities to which one can appeal on the basis of law and reason. The Palestinian leadership has endorsed a life of terror. It would be very irresponsible to history, especially to Jewish history, not to recognize that Western belief in reason and law is only that — a belief, one that many Palestinians do not share.[7]

Furthermore, the world of Jew-hatred — and let us not sanitize it by calling it antisemitism — is also a world in which reason and law do not apply. All racial hatreds defy law and reason. The widespread teaching of Jew-hatred in Palestinian textbooks,[8] political statements, media,[9] mosques, and so on is testimony to a world that must be faced, not denied. Yasser Arafat was a Holocaust denier. Mahmoud Abbas, his successor, wrote a book on Holocaust denial.[10] The Egyptian media have released films based on Jew-hatred. The July 2005 Pew Global Attitudes Project report entitled "Islamic Extremism: Common Concern for Muslim and Western Publics" found "unfavorable" views of Jews at the following percentage rates in six of the countries surveyed: 60, 74, 76, 88, 99, and 100.[11] One might also add the well-documented reports of Palestinians standing on the rooftops celebrating the falling of Scud missiles on Israeli towns during the first Iraq war, or the cruelty with which an Israeli soldier was publicly executed in a Palestinian town, an event that was recorded by European television. No amount of denial of Jew-hatred in the Arab world will erase these facts. The Realpolitik that acknowledges them is better.

7. The very prestigious Palestinian public opinion survey PSR Survey Research Unit, in its Public Opinion Poll #13, taken September 23-26, 2004, indicated that, while 83 percent of all Palestinians want "mutual cessation of violence," fully 77 percent support the then-recent Beer Sheva bombing attack, that fully 48 percent "view armed attacks against Israelis as effective," and that there was widespread support for "firing of rockets into Israeli settlements in the Gaza Strip, firing of rockets from Beit Hanoun into Israel, and the 'liquidation' of Palestinians accused of being Israeli spies." See the PSR Web site, http://www.pcpsr.org/index.html.

8. On Palestinian and Arab textbooks, see http://www.edume.org. See also the discussion by Margaret Brearley in chap. 6 in this volume. Friends report to me that there has been an effort to eliminate some stereotypes in Palestinian textbooks, but even so, the story of Zionism is still not presented as a legitimate Jewish nationalist movement.

9. On Palestinian media, see http://www.pmwatch.org/pmw/index.asp. See also chap. 6.

10. On Holocaust denial, see Deborah Lipstadt, *History on Trial* (San Francisco: HarperCollins, 2005), pp. 299-300. See also Meir Litvak and Esther Webman, "The Representation of the Holocaust in the Arab World," *Journal of Israeli History* 23, no. 1 (Spring 2004): 100-115.

11. The countries surveyed were, in order of the percentages, Turkey, Pakistan, Indonesia, Morocco, Lebanon, and Jordan (the last two having a very high number of Palestinians). See the Pew Web site http://pewglobal.org/reports/display.php?ReportID=248.

It should also be emphasized that the United Nations has surely not been the embodiment of the ideals of reason and law. The 1975 "Zionism is racism" vote, the 2001 Durban conference, and a host of other votes and policies pursued by the United Nations are proof of this claim.[12] Blindness to these outcomes is a repetition of the blindness of the Shoah generations.

4. *Most Palestinians want a state that will exist side by side with the Israeli state.* This belief, reinforced by occasional statements by the Palestinian leadership, including Mahmoud Abbas, is widely believed in Israel and the West. Indeed, the "two-state solution" would seem to be the reasonable solution — indeed, even the only solution.

It seems to me that this belief, too, is very naive. There are certainly some Palestinians, including Mahmoud Abbas, who want a Palestinian state, even if that means recognizing a Jewish state alongside it, for there cannot be a Palestinian state without a Jewish state. However, it must also be remembered that, over the past half century, the official Palestinian representatives have rejected every offer to create a Palestinian state precisely because acceptance would also recognize the Jewish state.

The reason for this refusal is that, in Islamic thought, land once conquered by Islam always remains Islamic; it can never be ceded to a non-Islamic entity.[13] The classic instance of this policy is the Crusader conquest of the Holy Land. From an Arab point of view, the Crusaders were invaders who ruled the land temporarily and were justifiably expelled by force. Arguably, Saladin, the Islamic leader who expelled the Crusaders, is the only

12. See Anne Bayefsky, "One Small Step: Is the U.N. Finally Ready to Get Serious about Anti-Semitism?" a speech given at a U.N. conference on June 21, 2004. It was copyrighted by Dow Jones and Company and has been widely circulated on the Internet (http://www.opinionjournal.com/extra/?id=110005245).

13. This principle is known as *dar al-Islam* and has, as its counterpart, *dar al-harb,* the domain of the sword. A Google search for "dar al-harb" yielded 46,800 hits, among them Ahmed Khalil, "Dar Al-Islam and Dar Al-Harb: Its Definition and Significance," which states: "Dar al-Harb (Domain of War) refers to the territory under the hegemony of unbelievers, which is on terms of active or potential belligerency with the Domain of Islam, and presumably hostile to the Muslims living in its domain" (http://english.islamway.com/bindex.php?section=article&id=211). I call readers' attention to the expanded definition of *dar al-harb,* which includes all land that is under non-Islamic control but contains a Muslim population. I further note that, in the pronouncements on the underground bombings in London (July 2005), the term *dar al-harb* was explicitly used as an Islamic term justifying such bombings as part of the larger mission of Islam to the world. See also Brearley's contribution in chap. 6.

man in Islamic history generally known to Westerners. Every Arab leader aspires to be the modern-day Saladin who will expel the foreigners, the Jews, from the Islamic land of Palestine. The converse is also true: No Palestinian leader can recognize the moral right of the Jews to a homeland anywhere in Palestine — from the Jordan River to the Mediterranean Sea — without being a traitor to Arab history.

For these reasons and others,[14] there has been no real Palestinian peace movement, no popular political base for making peace with Israel, although there have been a few members of the elite, including Mahmoud Abbas, who have thought it useful to pursue peacemaking policies. For the most part, however, advocates of peace with Israel have been intimidated, persecuted, and even killed.[15] While this situation has created sympathy for the silence of such persons, it also has contributed to a double standard that demands Western civic courage from Israelis but not from Palestinians.

Finally, Palestinian belief in a "demographic time bomb" — that the population growth of the Palestinians will make them a majority of the Israeli population by 2010 or 2020 — means that many Palestinians neither need nor want a Palestinian state. They simply need to wait and let majority rule do the work that is necessary. The purpose of this strategy is to erase the Jewish presence in the Holy Land, to do away with the Jewish state. Certainly, one must give peace a chance, but it must also be remembered that the belief that most Palestinians want a two-state solution is only that — a belief.

5. *Islam is a religion of tolerance, with occasional aberrations of fanaticism.* The West wants very much to believe that this proposition is true, and thus this belief — that Islam must be, like all religions, basically humanistic — has become a fundamental premise in Western culture. Westerners point to the scientific achievements of the early Islamic period and to the tolerance often found in Muslims who are in the Muslim diaspora, while Jews point to the "golden age" of the medieval Islamic-Jewish symbiosis as evidence for the "true" Islam.

This belief, however, is another that I find to be very naive. Through-

14. For example: There is no prima facie reason why Palestinians should recognize the Jewish claim to the Holy Land at all. Also, there is a violently anti-Western, anti-imperialist ideology in the Arab world, and Israel is seen as an integral part of the imperialist, Western world. And so on.

15. See the PSR survey cited above in n. 7 on approval ratings for killing of "collaborators." I am not aware of statistics on intimidation of opponents, but such intimidation is widely reported.

out Islamic history, the phenomenon of dhimmitude has existed; that is, Jews and Christians were awarded protected status, but as minorities they were subject to special taxes and regular humiliation.[16] Such treatment is not tolerance, and its actual practice was worse than its theory. Furthermore, as Joel Kraemer has shown, even at its intellectual height, Islam sought to persecute its own philosophers, who were often accused of heresy, punished, and sometimes executed for their teachings.[17] The principle that land once conquered by Islam must always remain Islamic is indicative of intolerance too.

The reasons for this Islamic intolerance are many and complicated. Perhaps the most crucial, however, is a very long tradition of the lack of self-criticism. As Hava Lazarus-Yafeh has demonstrated, even the biblical stories retold in the Qur'an are distorted to eliminate the prophetic critique of society that is so crucial to biblical religion.[18] This lack of self-criticism generates the widely observed phenomenon that Arabs never blame themselves for anything that happens to them; it is always the Zionists, the Americans, the other who is to blame.[19] The lack of civic courage in Arab society is clearly seen in the following case: On March 11, 2005, the Muslim Council of Spain condemned Osama bin Laden as an apostate. In July 2005, at a conference entitled "The Reality of Islam and Its Role in the Contemporary Society," 170 Muslim scholars from forty countries issued a final communiqué that repudiated the decision of the Spanish Muslim Council: "It is not possible to declare as apostates any group of Muslims who believes in Allah, the Mighty and Sublime, and in His Messenger (may Peace and Blessing be upon him) and the pillars of the faith, and respects the pillars of Islam and does not deny any necessary article of religion."[20]

16. See Bat Ye'or, *Islam and Dhimmitude: Where Civilizations Collide* (Madison, N.J.: Fairleigh Dickinson University Press, 2002).

17. Joel Kraemer, "The Islamic Context of Medieval Jewish Philosophy," in *Cambridge Companion to Medieval Jewish Philosophy,* ed. Daniel Frank and Oliver Leaman (Cambridge: Cambridge University Press, 2003), pp. 38-68.

18. Hava Lazarus-Yafeh, "Self-Dialogue Partners in Jewish and Islamic Traditions," in *Judaism and Islam: Boundaries, Communication, and Interaction,* ed. Benjamin Hary et al. (Leiden: E. J. Brill, 2000), pp. 303-20.

19. See, for instance: http://groups.msn.com/MiddleEastAbrahamicForum/ debates.msnw?action=get_message&mview=0&ID_Message=67084&LastModified =4675500932346677344.

20. Reported by J. Pearl, "Islam Struggles to Stake Out Its Position," *International Herald Tribune,* July 20, 2005, p. 8.

The lack of self-criticism in Islamic society, including Palestinian society, stems also from the irreducible patriarchy of Islamic society. Disempowered economically and politically, Arab men are left with only one source of personal power — power over women, a power so absolute that, in most Arab societies, including Palestinian society, men are permitted to kill women in their family who defy the sexual taboos of the society. These "honor killings" are not considered crimes.[21] Such a deeply patriarchal society must do two things: It must honor the whole patriarchal hierarchy, suppressing all resistance, and it must at all costs avoid liberty and freedom for all. The assumption that Arab Islamic society is tolerant, or will be any time in the foreseeable future, is delusional and must be resisted.[22]

6. *A government is "legitimate" only when it derives from the participation of the governed.* This belief, one that I share, should also be watched closely because trust in its authority and credibility can be dangerously naive. Consider, for example, the position of Dennis Ross, the U.S. representative in the Israeli-Palestinian peace process from the Oslo talks to the second intifada. In the well-informed analysis of his 2004 book *The Missing Peace,* Ross maintains that the primary obstacle to peace was Arafat himself.[23] With Arafat's death, it seemed, peace should have followed in a reasonable period of time. Ross, however, points to other factors that prevented peace. Primary among them is that Arab leaders lack legitimacy. According to Ross, this lack accounted for the failure of Arab leaders to criticize Arafat and also for Arafat's inability to "take historic decisions." This same lack of legitimacy is also the basis for the inability of almost all Palestinians and the Arab world to recognize the moral legiti-

21. For a sharp view of Arabic patriarchalism, see Hisham Sharabi, *Neopatriarchy: A Theory of Distorted Change in Arab Society* (Oxford: Oxford University Press, 1988).

22. See, for example, the statement of Ibn Warraq of the Institute for the Secularisation of Islamic Society: "We are confronted with *Islamic* terrorists and must take seriously the *Islamic* component. Westerners in general, and Americans in particular, do not understand the passionate, religious, and anti-Western convictions of Islamic terrorists" (italics original). See the Web site http://socialissues.wiseto.com/Articles/EJ3010393206/. See also Robert Spencer, *The Myth of Islamic Tolerance: How Islamic Law Treats Non-Muslims* (New York: Prometheus Press, 2005).

23. Dennis Ross, *The Missing Peace: The Inside Story of the Fight for Middle East Peace* (New York: Farrar, Straus & Giroux, 2004), esp. pp. 13, 757. For a counterview, see C. Swisher, *The Truth about Camp David* (New York: Nation Books, 2004); and articles by R. Malley and H. Agha in the *New York Review of Books,* August 9, 2001, and June 13 and 27, 2002.

macy of the State of Israel, whose existence is seen as only an unwanted necessity.[24]

As a result of this lack of legitimacy and the consequent inability to recognize the moral legitimacy of the State of Israel, there has been no transformation of the Palestinian and Arab world, no change in the underlying attitudes of the Palestinian and Arab world toward Israel and Jews. The basic Palestinian narrative of victimhood and entitlement remains. It is taught in the schools, the media, youth camps, the mosques, public statements by leaders, and elsewhere. Violence is enshrined instead of being denounced. There is no "conditioning" of the Palestinian and Arab public to peace.[25] Ross also faults the United States, and himself as an integral part of the peace process, for not enforcing accountability.[26] He also holds Israelis accountable, but because Israel is a democratic society and hence its government has legitimacy, a majority of Israelis do question their own myths of victimhood and entitlement, hold their leaders responsible, vote them out of office if needed, and are ready to take historic decisions.

Detailed, learned, and at times perceptive though it is, Ross's analysis is naive because of the trust it places in the belief that a government is legitimate only when it derives from the participation of the governed. As one brought up in America, I agree that government should be "of the people, by the people, and for the people." Indeed, I firmly believe that the blessings of technology, prosperity, freedom, liberty, and the protection of human rights all derive from the democratic process. In addition, I believe it is laudable that the American government wants to export freedom and democracy to others. But that idea will work only in some contexts and not in others. Government in Islamic society has never derived its legitimacy from the people. One must grant Ross the chance to be right about legitimacy, but at the same time, one must beware of putting too much trust in a political philosophy that counts on arguments about legitimacy to set things right. Ross's belief about legitimacy is only that — a belief.

We Jews want peace. We want the acceptance of our moral legitimacy by Arabs, Palestinians, and the West. Culminating in the Shoah, so many centuries of persecution, so many years of fighting for our survival, have

24. Ross, *The Missing Peace*, pp. 762-63.
25. Ibid., pp. 42, 770-73, 766, 769.
26. Ibid., p. 770.

formed our psyches. But our yearning cannot be allowed to blind us as it did during the Shoah. We must resist our own yearnings and question the beliefs that are generated by those longings while, at the same time, maintain an intelligent and critical view of the workings and policies of all governments and political entities involved. We must resist the six beliefs listed above, each of which seems to me to be very naive. Allowing our policy to be guided by them endangers Jewish existence, a danger that Jews cannot risk in the post-Shoah period.

Contributors' Questions for David Blumenthal

You speak about a fundamental intolerance in Islamic society, and you imply that fanaticism is not aberrational but rather something inherent in the nature of this religious tradition. You speak of "Islamic thought" and "*an* Arab point of view." But is there *one* Islam (or *one* Arab perspective) with the fixed characteristics you attribute to it? Are there not many Islams? Are you not in danger of putting forward a specious *essentialist* claim? Might this be one instance of your failure to apply the same measure of critical acumen regarding your own assumptions that you have attempted to apply to the assumptions you are challenging?

On the one hand you claim that there *is* no Palestinian peace movement, and on the other you assert that there *can be no* such movement because rejectionism is inherent in Arab/Muslim society. How, then, is it logically possible for Palestinians to serve as partners for peace? You claim that failing to examine the six beliefs you articulate in your chapter endangers Jewish existence in a post-Shoah world. But what kind of policy derives from your rejection of these beliefs? How would your own beliefs allow for any possibility of peace in the region?

Response by David Blumenthal

My dialogue partners have focused their comments around two points. The first is my view that Islamic fanaticism is not aberrational but inherent in the nature of Islam. They maintain that this is a "specious essentialist claim" about Islam — "But is there *one* Islam (or *one* Arab perspective) with the fixed characteristics you attribute to it?" — and that, in so characterizing Islam, I myself am not being sufficiently critical.

I could not disagree more with my dialogue partners. Every religion, indeed every culture, does have a set of "essential" claims. Authorities within the religion may differ on the exact meaning of these claims, but it is precisely those claims that define the religion, that give it its identity. To point to those claims is, indeed, to do honest scholarship. It is to focus the attention of the reader on doctrines or practices that are definitive of the religion or culture under study. Thus, it is hard to talk about Christianity without some interpretation of Christ, or of Judaism without some interpretation of Torah, or of Islam without some appreciation of the centrality of the Qur'an. Furthermore, the "essential" identity of these traditions is not limited to the three parameters I have listed. One could add crucifixion, resurrection, and salvation to the definition of Christianity; or halakha, teshuva, and peoplehood to the definition of Judaism; or Shari'a, Muhammad, and worship to that of Islam. To do so is not to distort in a "specious essentialist" way the religion or culture under study; it is to attempt to delineate a series of parameters that define it, that enable a discussion of it. While one must be aware of the differences of opinion within each tradition, that awareness and those differences do not deny that each tradition really requires an "essentialist claim" to describe it.

There are two kinds of essentialist claims: the intellectual and the sociological. The intellectual essentialist claim would have to argue that certain ideas are "essential" to the proper definition of the religion or culture under study, allowing for some variations in interpretation. The sociological essentialist claim would have to argue that, independent of the formal teaching of the duly constituted authorities, the actual populace believes certain claims and practices them accordingly. In all cultures and religions, it is surely the case that the intellectual and the sociological claims overlap in some areas and differ in others.

Intellectually, it is the case in Islam that territory once under Islamic rule always remains Islamic, even if it is temporarily in the hands of others, called infidels. This is classic Islamic doctrine, and it is still taught as such.[1] Furthermore, and perhaps more important, this idea is the center of all popular Islamic claims to territory that was once Islamic, beginning with the claim to the Holy Land that was once redeemed from the Christian Crusader infidels and now needs to be redeemed from the Jewish infidels who occupy it. This essential claim also includes the liberation of Iraq (where this idea has particular force) from the American "occupation," as well as the reconquest of the Balkans and Spain. While talk of reconquering Spain and the Balkans is not taken seriously by the West, it is taken very seriously by Muslims, even if that goal is not on the top of their current political-military agenda. Meanwhile, Muslim talk about reconquest of the Holy Land and Iraq should be taken very seriously indeed.[2] From the point of view held by many Muslims, recovery of territory that is properly Islamic is precisely an essentialist claim of Islam, as well as of popular Islamic culture. Such territorial ambition is even a part of nationalist secular Arab culture, where calls for the reconquest of the whole of Palestine are common in the media, including Web sites, the press, and textbooks, as I have indicated.[3]

Politically correct, prior beliefs about the goodwill and tolerance of Islamic religion and Islamic peoples should not allow scholars to shrink from pointing to the reconquest of the whole of Palestine as a central element in popular and intellectual Islam. A failure of that kind points to false scholarship that is especially dangerous in the post-Shoah world.

---

1. See above, n. 13.
2. See the quotation from Ibn Warraq above, in n. 22.
3. See above, nn. 8 and 9.

The second critique of my position points out that, given the lack of an actual Palestinian peace movement and given the lack of a possible Palestinian peace movement because of the deep popular and intellectual roots of Palestinian nationalism in Islam, how can I believe at all in peace between Israelis and Palestinians? "How, then, is it logically possible for Palestinians to serve as partners for peace?" And again: "How would your own beliefs allow for any possibility of peace in the region?"

Given my early history, I have come reluctantly to the conclusion that almost all Palestinians are not partners for a real peace, at least not in the sense in which the word "peace" is used in the West. In the West, we usually use that word to refer to a state of ceased hostilities followed by a state of developed commercial, political, social, and other interpersonal and intergovernmental ties. As I see it, these relationships will never happen in Israel/Palestine. There will never be a cessation of hostilities, not to speak of the development of constructive interstate and interpeople ties. I think this for all the reasons I have outlined in my essay.

The best I would hope for is two separate states with borders clearly defined and policed and with a relatively low death toll on both sides. There will be some commerce and labor exchanges, but they will not be central to either economy and will largely be developed in spite of the existence of the two states. There will also be some people who will cross the cultural and political borders and genuinely interact with one another, but they will be, as they have been, very few in number and with no appeal to the masses, particularly the Palestinian masses who subscribe to the exclusivist teachings of intellectual and popular Islam.

Still, as the Bible itself records that forty years of reduced hostilities is an accomplishment, a goal to be striven for, I, for one, and I think many other Jews and Israelis, would be content with such a "peace," which is really a smoldering armistice, one that requires continued alertness and, unfortunately, the continued sacrifice of innocent lives on both sides. I think, too, that "peace" as I have outlined it might be a realistic short-term possibility at this time because of the peculiar historical juncture of the American insistence on democratizing the Middle East. This effort has a tendency to bring to the surface those who are ready for compromise, although it is not at all certain that they will survive long enough in Palestinian society to take the reins of power and make any significant changes in Palestinian society. Meanwhile, Israeli and Palestinian realists would do well to seize the moment and work diligently toward whatever peace is possible, while post-Shoah Western scholars would do well to disabuse themselves of the beliefs listed in my essay. Those beliefs do not further the cause of peace but actually inhibit it through an overly optimistic view of the possibilities that lie before us.

4. "Forgetting" the Holocaust: Ethical Dimensions of the Israeli-Palestinian Conflict

Leonard Grob

In 1988 the Israeli philosopher and historian Yehuda Elkana stunned fellow Israelis by writing an article entitled "In Praise of Forgetting." Elkana, himself a Holocaust survivor, urged Israelis to "uproot the domination of historical remembrance [of the Holocaust]" from their lives.[1] Elkana did not argue that the events of 1933-45 should — or could — literally be forgotten. What he had in mind was a radical critique of the role that some central forms of Holocaust remembrance had played in the lives of the Zionist leadership of decades past, as well as in the lives of his Israeli contemporaries.

In this chapter I examine some ethical dimensions of remembering the Holocaust insofar as such remembrance has played and continues to play a crucial role in determining Israeli political attitudes and policies in the ongoing conflict with Palestinians. There can be no doubt that although Zionism has millennia-old roots in the ethos of the Jewish people, the State of Israel was born, in some substantial sense, of the destruction of two-thirds of European Jewry. How, I ask, have alleged lessons of the Holocaust helped shape the dominant Zionist narrative?[2] Drawing primarily upon the works of three religious thinkers — Martin Buber, Emmanuel

1. *Ha-aretz*, March 18, 1988, cited in Baruch Kimmerling, "The Two Catastrophes," an adaptation of a speech given at a conference of the Israeli Anthropological Association, Nazareth, March 17-18, 1999, online at http://dir.salon.com/story/opinion/feature/2004/12/06/catastrophes/.

2. It is not my intention to contend that there is but one Zionist (or one Palestinian) narrative. There are many narratives constituting "Zionism," many Zionisms. I endeavor to speak to a master narrative retold by generations of mainstream Zionist leaders.

Levinas, and Irving Greenberg — I attempt to articulate some ways in which rethinking a Zionist narrative forged substantially in the shadows of the Holocaust might serve to memorialize more responsibly the six million who were murdered.

Abuse of Holocaust memory in the Middle East conflict does not fall within the province of Israel alone. Israelis and Palestinians each allude freely — and, I argue, largely irresponsibly — to the Holocaust in the process of shoring up a rhetoric of war. Palestinians frequently compare their situation in the territories with the treatment of European Jews by the Nazis. Likening, simplistically, the systematic genocide of European Jewry at the hand of the Nazis to (admittedly often heinous) abuses of power by Israeli leaders toward Palestinians fans the flames of hatred in the region. Memory of the Holocaust here has clearly been abused, militating against the development of dialogical approaches that might lead to a just peace.

Although both peoples employ Holocaust images in constructing their largely fixed, unyielding narratives — narratives that, in turn, drive public policy — I focus in this chapter, as I have noted above, on *Israeli* modes of remembering. Given an asymmetry of power between the warring parties, misuse of Holocaust memory by Israel is especially grievous. Such misremembering contributes substantially to Israel's failure to take the initiatives toward peacemaking that, morally speaking, are demanded of the more powerful party to a conflict in which each has legitimate claims to be in the right.

To speak of an asymmetry of power is not to say that we are in the presence of a clear-cut "David and Goliath" scenario: Palestinians are not merely helpless victims of Israeli power. Lacking firepower on a massive scale, extremist and even some mainstream Palestinian leaders have expertly utilized forms of power other than the machinery of conventional warfare to press their case both before the eyes of their own people and before the world community. Exploiting millennia-old, ingrained, and virtually worldwide antisemitic attitudes to demonize Jews; manipulating popular media to incite "the streets" (both at home and in neighboring countries) toward hatred of the alleged Jewish "outsider" in a Muslim world; utilizing Holocaust denial to invalidate the history of Jewish suffering that helped give rise to the need for a state where Jews could control their destiny; glorifying the *shaheed,* the martyr who has sacrificed his or her life to murder Israeli civilians — these are forms of power that some Palestinians employ in the service of their cause. The existential fear of Israelis that they may be driven from their land in the name of Greater Palestine — or worse, annihilated — is rooted, in some measure, in the reality of hatreds spawned by some Palestinians, as well as by leaders of some Muslim nations held captive to radical anti-Israel ideologies.

Although Palestinian firepower may be lacking on a large scale, increasingly sophisticated armaments have recently been employed against Israel by such extremist groups as Hamas, Islamic Jihad, and the al-Aqsa Martyrs' Brigades (a militant faction allied with the larger Fatah party). Especially worrisome to Israel in this regard is the current threat posed by Palestinian links to Hezbollah in Lebanon. The failure of Israel to destroy Hezbollah's capacity to fire rockets into northern Israel during the summer 2006 war gives further evidence of the military might of a well-funded band of several thousand guerrillas, waging war amid a local civilian population. These attacks, along with the sustained launching of Palestinian Qassam rockets from Gaza into southern Israel during 2005-6, demonstrate the considerable power of relatively small groups of guerrilla fighters imbued with an ideological commitment to harm Israel. Furthermore, perhaps most alarming is the link between Hezbollah and an Iran sworn to Israel's destruction and militarily capable of realizing that aim.

Yet, it cannot be denied that there remains an asymmetry of power in the region. To say, as has been argued by some supporters of Israel, that the image of Palestinian powerlessness is rooted in a distorted narrative of dispossession is to fail to acknowledge facts on the ground. Israel is not only the leading military power in the region but one of the leading such powers in the world. It is nonsensical to tell Palestinians that their image of powerlessness is contrived when they are confronted with Israeli jets, gunships, tanks, and high-powered artillery. If asymmetry in the conflict is still in doubt, one might add the unquestioned — and unquestioning — allegiance to Israel on the part of the United States, the world's sole superpower. Whether or not Palestinians have done all they can to lay the groundwork for a nation-state — an endeavor hard to conceive under current conditions — Israel can and does employ the full might of an organized state against a people suffering from the ravages of what is recognized internationally (and labeled by the former Israel prime minister) as occupation. Whether or not Palestinians have always negotiated peace in good faith, it is the Israeli leadership — often captive to the idea of Eretz Yisrael Shlema (Greater Israel) — that remains in control of access to the region via air, sea, and land. It is Israeli might that has allowed for the presence and ongoing proliferation (as of this writing) of 240,000 settlers in the territories. While both parties to the conflict must demythologize the narratives of suffering that would validate possession of the whole of a "land of two peoples" (there are no innocent parties in the region), Israel has a moral obligation to *initiate* the work of demystification.

And here, memory of the Holocaust comes to play an important role in preventing Israel from doing just this initiation. Holocaust imagery abounds in the present-day Israeli rhetoric, often used to shore up morally questionable political objectives. The Palestinian enemy has not alone been subject to ongoing "Nazification": Israeli supporters of a negotiated peace have been subjected with increasing frequency to such demonization as well. I do not need to return to archival material to cite instances of a misuse of Holocaust memory that demeans its victims. As of just one year preceding this writing, the following reports have appeared in mainstream newspapers:

1. Before the evacuation of Israeli settlers from Gaza, residents of the Gush Katif settlements announced their intent to wear Star of David badges to call attention to the evils of Prime Minister Ariel Sharon's disengagement plan.[3]
2. Nadia Matar, cochair of the grassroots movement Women in Green, referred to the Gaza disengagement administration as "a modern version of the *Judenrat*."[4]
3. Some settlers deemed Prime Minister Sharon's endeavor to evacuate Gaza settlements as designed to make the Land of Israel *judenrein*, free of Jews.[5]

Although each of the above accounts must be understood in the context of ongoing brutal hostilities in which the lives of military and civilian populations are at risk daily, and although many such reported expressions can be attributed to extremists within Israel, it is nonetheless true that Israelis of all political persuasions are haunted by Holocaust imagery. The highly charged term "Auschwitz borders" — alluding to borders deemed in-

3. Nir Hasson, "Badge Affair Symbolizes Rift between Pullout Factions," *Ha-aretz*, December 21, 2004.
4. Matthew Gutman, "Bassi: Most Wanted Man in the Country," *Jerusalem Post*, September 23, 2004. A *Judenrat* (pl. *Judenräte*) was a council of Jewish leaders established on Nazi orders in occupied territories.
5. Baruch Kimmerling, "Israel's Culture of Martyrdom," *Nation*, January 10, 2005.

defensible — was first employed by esteemed statesperson Abba Eban to refer to the Green Line (the 1948 borders of Israel). The alleged cowardice of those "who went like sheep to the slaughter" is compared, time and again, to the "new" Israeli Jew, who will stand firm in the face of the Palestinian Amalek, the inveterate enemy of the Jewish people who has returned anew to threaten its survival. And with great frequency do Israeli leaders of all political stripes appear to have gleaned one, *and only one,* lesson from the Holocaust: "Never again will innocent Jewish blood be shed with impunity."[6]

That allusions to the Holocaust abound in Israeli discourse is understandable. For a people traumatized by the systematic slaughter of one-third of its population just sixty years ago, how could the ghost of the Holocaust *not* haunt Jewish Israelis? *That* the Holocaust haunts the Israeli consciousness is thus not at issue in this chapter. My task here is to examine the moral implications of the use of Holocaust allusions that have so deeply permeated the Zionist narrative. In so doing, I will suggest ways of forgetting/remembering the Holocaust that might alter that narrative so as to honor the memory of the victims and, at one and the same time — from an avowedly utilitarian perspective — provide greater protection for the continued existence of a state with a Jewish majority.

And indeed, the State of Israel is in need of greater protection than can be provided by superior weaponry alone. Envisioning oneself as a community of victims — in Yiddish, *Shimson der Nebedicher* ("Wretched Samson," or "a superpower that can only see itself as victim")[7] — may, ironically, produce real victims. Israelis might well attend to the words of Holocaust scholar Zygmunt Bauman to the effect that Hitler may yet have a posthumous victory: The designers of the Final Solution "did not manage to turn the world against the Jews, but in their graves they can still dream of turning the Jews against the world, and thus . . . make the Jewish reconciliation with the world . . . all that more difficult, if not downright impossible."[8] Embracing a self-image of the eternal victim, Bauman implies, limits Israel's ability to forge the lasting peace with its neighbors that may provide for its genuine physical security.

Furthermore, in several post-Holocaust theologies, ahistorical im-

---

6. Words to this effect are attributed to former prime minister Menachem Begin.

7. The statement is attributed to former prime minister Levi Eshkol.

8. Zygmunt Bauman, "The Holocaust's Life as a Ghost," *Tikkun: A Bimonthly Jewish Critique of Politics, Culture, and Society,* July-August 1998, p. 37.

ages of absolute victimhood become paired with equally ahistorical images of absolute redemption:[9] Metanarratives arise, heralding in absolutist terms the movement from victimhood (during the Holocaust) to deliverance (with the founding of the State of Israel). Such metanarratives, I contend, must be reexamined for their role in helping create a Zionist mythos jeopardizing both the physical survival of Israel and the renewal of its tradition of justice toward the other.

For Irving Greenberg, for example, "Israel's faith in the God of History demands that an unprecedented event of destruction be matched by an unprecedented act of redemption, and this has happened."[10] For Emmanuel Levinas the founding of State of Israel is an event in Sacred History, a passage (in divine hands) from Auschwitz, the "Passion," to the State of Israel, the "Resurrection."[11] The metahistorical nature of the holy drama is reemphasized by Levinas's reference to the passage as a "Divine Comedy."[12]

What is the concrete danger, ethically speaking, in embracing these metanarratives, which have so deeply influenced post-Holocaust Zionism? As totalizing endeavors, such narratives are inevitably reductive in nature. They objectify the other, reducing him or her to the terms dictated by the overarching ideological framework within which the essential (often divinely ordained) nature of the nation is envisaged. The other is subsumed under categories devised for him or her in the course of a nation telling its story: Metanarratives become nothing other than autonarratives! The dominant Zionist narrative, influenced greatly by "holy dramas," runs the particular risk of exclusivism insofar as it fails to acknowledge the presence of the Palestinian other, who must share a land to which two peoples have legitimate claims. Normative Zionism has often been held hostage to an

9. I am indebted here to Mark Ellis's *Beyond Innocence and Redemption: Confronting the Holocaust and Israeli Power* (New York: Harper & Row, 1990), esp. pp. 1-15. In addition to the writings of Greenberg and Levinas cited below, selected writings of Elie Wiesel and Emil Fackenheim, noted by Ellis, address this theme. It should be noted that none of these theologians speaks of Israel's founding in terms of anything resembling restoration.

10. Irving Greenberg, "Cloud of Smoke, Pillar of Fire: Judaism, Christianity, and Modernity after the Holocaust," in *Auschwitz: Beginning of a New Era?* ed. Eva Fleischner (New York: Ktav, 1977), p. 32.

11. Emmanuel Levinas, "From the Rise of Nihilism to the Carnal Jew," in *Difficult Freedom: Essays on Judaism,* trans. Sean Hand (Baltimore, Md.: Johns Hopkins University Press, 1990), p. 221.

12. Emmanuel Levinas, "Demanding Judaism," in *Beyond the Verse: Talmudic Readings and Lectures,* trans. Gary D. Mole (Bloomington: Indiana University Press, 1994), p. 8.

all-encompassing mythos in which Palestinians are either largely absent or, when present, are most often assigned the role of Israel's current Amalek: In a drama largely forged by what I have termed misremembrance of the Holocaust, Palestinians are often regarded as little more than bit players.[13]

That both Greenberg and Levinas are aware of the risks incurred by adhering to the narrative-as-auto-narrative becomes immediately and abundantly clear in their further discussions of Zionism. Both philosophers speak directly to the need to incorporate sacred history *within* the profane, day-to-day life of the state. For Greenberg, the founding of Israel poses in its wake a dramatic litmus test of traditional Jewish ethics. "The assumption of power," Greenberg argues, "will now force . . . [Israel] to put up or shut up."[14] And for Levinas, the same dialectical tension between a prophetic vision and the realities on the ground is emphasized: The State of Israel is an "adventure," a "risk" insofar as the Israel of Holy History (subject to the ethical injunctions of the prophets) enters into Universal History (in which Realpolitik reigns supreme). For both thinkers, the mundane existence of the nation-state is to be sanctified by an ethic that takes into account the long tradition within Judaism in which just regard for the other — most especially the oppressed — hallows the ordinary everyday lives of both the individual and the collective. A call to justice protects against the dangers of triumphalism inherent in any metanarrative that would conclude on a note of redemption.

To avoid objectifying the other, I contend, metanarratives must be transformed into "internarratives," "intermyths." Such intermyths are continually formed and reformed in what Buber calls the Between — in this instance, the space between Israelis and Palestinians. More verb than noun, Zionism-as-intermyth is incessantly forged and reforged *in the presence of the face of the Palestinian,* who calls his or her Israeli other to account for the ethical import of his or her actions. Borrowing from Levinas's imagery system, the "said" — any static narrative — must subject itself to an ongoing critique *before the face of the other;* the "said" must perpetually transform itself into a "saying" that is respons-ible, that is, able-to-respond to (in this case) the Palestinian other.

Such a Zionism is called upon, for example (as of this writing), to re-

---

13. Ellis, *Beyond Innocence and Redemption,* esp. pp. 29-31.

14. Irving Greenberg, "The Third Great Cycle in Jewish History," in *Perspectives #1* (New York: National Jewish Resource Center, 1981), p. 15.

think the creation of each checkpoint, each sector of a fence/wall across the Green Line, each home demolition, each segment of Israeli-only by-pass roads, each uprooting of an olive tree. A Zionism perpetually reborn in what Buber calls "holy insecurity" must ask itself if these measures are just. Are they intended *solely* for defensive purposes? Do they provide gen-uine security for Israel? Might all these dehumanizing measures — tempo-rarily necessary as they may be — come to serve *in place of* facing the other in initiating the sacred work of forging a just peace?

Needless to say, the measures listed above for moral reassessment by Israel must be viewed in the context of the reality of murder of innocent civilians by extremist Palestinians. Never again to allow Jewish blood to be shed with impunity is *one* vital lesson of the Holocaust. There are times when the concrete face of the other is occluded, obscured from sight, by virtue of its hostility. As Buber argues, moral agents must endeavor to wring from each situation in which they find themselves the maximum amount of divinity that they can perceive it to permit. The moral "line of demarcation" between one action and another shifts from context to con-text. Genuine defensive action is indeed required at a given place and point of time. For Zionism-as-internarrative, each decision is undertaken in holy insecurity, in anguish, considering both the immediate danger to life and the call to establish a just peace with the Palestinians.

What is advanced here, then, is no pure Zionist ethic, no injunction to act according to an absolute standard of morality removed from its con-text in a lived world in which mortal enemies exist. Zionism-as-intermyth has ultimately no static content that would make it just one more narrative among the pantheon of nationalist ideologies, each realizing the aims of its totalizing narrative through a monopoly of power within its borders. Such a Zionism refuses to claim for itself the status of a static absolute: As a liv-ing absolute, this Zionism is enacted rather than posited, a tale "told-to-another," rather than one told-as-auto-narrative. A narrative told without the living presence of the other to whom one is responsible is a narrative that lacks ethical import.

To embrace this Zionism, what is needed, I have argued throughout, is "forgetfulness" of the Holocaust, forgetfulness of the elements that prompt Israelis to embrace perpetual victimhood and so often bring in their wake the ideology of Greater Israel. We must forget in order to better remember. To remember well the six million murdered at the hands of the Nazis is to engage in a doing (and redoing) that is a building of an interhuman, dialogical space in a land rightfully claimed by two peoples. To remember is thus, literally, to re-member, that is, re-collect, re-gather that which has been rent asunder. Such re-collection does not deny the irremediable nature of the genocide of Jews by their Nazi oppressors. But to re-member the victims we must no longer contribute to processes of dis-memberment. Israelis must stand as co-witnesses with the Palestinian people in the sharing of a contested land. The Holocaust was an attempt to destroy such co-witnessing, to destroy human solidarity, the possibility of creating interhuman space, the "between" of dialogue. To-forget-in-order-to-remember means to attempt to hear the silent screams of the victims calling upon the remnants and their descendents to no longer engage in those acts that might serve, as it were, to murder them a second time.[15]

Israelis might well begin this remembering-by-forgetting by owning up to the dispossession of Palestinians caused by the pressing need of Jews to establish a homeland in which they would be safe. To initiate the breaking out of a vicious cycle in which each party believes in the inviolability of its victim status — to accept the risk of acknowledging the pain one has caused without believing that this acknowledgment will result in even greater victimhood — this is a way to re-member, in a holy paradox, what has been (irremediably) dis-membered. Such an act not only humanizes the party acknowledged as wronged — "your pain is as important as mine" is now averred — but also humanizes the party doing the acknowledging: Freeing oneself of victim-identity allows for an empowerment not achievable as long as one is locked into the seemingly inevitable cycle in which victim-becomes-victimizer for the purpose of preventing further (real or often only perceived) suffering.[16]

A human tragedy has occurred: Jews, fleeing intolerable oppression, rushing for safety to the land for which their people had yearned for millennia, brought about the dispossession of large numbers of indigenous people. The tragedy will not end as long as each people holds fast to its own fixed narrative of suffering. Both peoples must demystify their narratives, but it remains incumbent upon Israelis to memorialize the dead of the Holocaust by taking the initiative in forgetting-in-order-to-remember.

15. Thoughts here reflect a conversation with Ernest Sherman, professor emeritus of philosophy, Pace University, New York, January 11, 2004.

16. I am indebted for these insights to an unpublished paper prepared by Jessica Benjamin for a lecture given at the conference "Impasse: Alternative Voices in the Middle East," held at Columbia University, New York, November 20, 2004.

Contributors' Questions for Leonard Grob

You repeatedly use the term "forging" peace, as though peace should and can be both initiated and achieved by only one party (the stronger). Given the Arab world as Palestinian allies, is Israel truly the stronger party? *Can* peace be achieved by only one partner? If you are the first to take the initiative, how do you get to the *inter-* of the internarrative? You say, "Israelis must stand as co-witnesses with the Palestinian people in the sharing of a contested land." You imply that they must do so unilaterally. How can this be accomplished? What if the other party is not prepared to give inter-narrative a chance?

You say that a new internarrative must be created, but since it is to be based on a "long tradition within Judaism" of attending to the needs of the stranger, does it not also require a metanarrative that is an autonarrative, namely the Jewish people's account of how they became chosen and sanctified by God's commandments? If so, then do the Jews need to return to an original metanarrative rather than create something new? How does one create a new myth? Might a new internarrative reconfigure Judaism in such a way as to endanger the notion of a Jewish state?

Response by Leonard Grob

Although it is clear that peace can never be "achieved by only one [party]," it is also evident that two parties to a conflict never approach one another with the same degree of openness to dialogue, moving at the same pace toward some mythological midpoint in the space that separates them. Neither individuals nor nations in conflict approach the peacemaking process in symmetrical fashion. As embodied, historical beings, we are always "in the midst of things," always caught up in the vagaries of history to which, paradoxically, we ourselves contribute and that inevitably result in relationships that are fundamentally asymmetrical in nature.

We thus cannot await a time when parties to conflict approach each other as willing — in equal measure at one and the same moment in time — to reconcile. There is no prerequisite to dialogue, no "readiness" formula that would ensure that dialogue will be successful: there is no way to dialogue; dialogue *is* the way. For peacemaking to take place, one of the two parties to conflict must refuse to operate according to quantifiable assessments of the degree of the other's preparedness-for-dialogue. In the midst of what cannot be other than an asymmetrical relationship, one party must take the "leap of faith" by means of which authentic dialogue is launched.[1]

How, more concretely, might we approach the question as to how authentic dialogue between Israelis and Palestinians might occur if one of

1. For several of the concepts articulated below, I am indebted to Prof. Ernest Sherman.

the two parties "is not prepared to give internarrative a chance"? I have argued throughout my chapter in this volume that it is incumbent on the *stronger* party to take that first step, which I now characterize as a leap of faith.[2] In this instance, Israel is the stronger of the two parties, measured both by its vast superiority in the possession of arms and by the advantage it maintains by virtue of its alliance with the United States. Although it is often noted that Israel, with its fewer than six million Jewish inhabitants, resides in the midst of forty million potentially hostile Arabs, it nonetheless remains the case that the Arab world has been, and continues to be, far from unanimous in active support of Palestinians, whose movement toward democracy poses threats to numerous autocratic Arab nations.

This is not to say there are foolproof guarantees that in taking such an initiative, Israel would maintain its current superiority. The Middle East is capable of vast changes in the allegiances forged among its nations. And the United States — motivated less by a moral concern to end the killing in the Middle East than by a determination to support its "sole democratic ally" in this oil-rich region — is certainly capable of withdrawing or limiting its assistance to Israel. There is indeed risk in initiating dialogue-as-peacemaking. If Israel initiates dialogue, Palestinians may or may not choose to become genuine partners in bringing about a peaceful resolution to the conflict. Yet there is also risk in *not* taking such an initiative. Force of arms and an alliance with the United States have thus far failed to guarantee Israel's long-term security. As of this writing, Israel — conceived as a refuge for Jews anywhere in the world — is the most dangerous place in the world for a Jew to live. Proceeding from a purely pragmatic calculus — negotiating solely from considerations of self-interest, narrowly conceived — has not won Israel the security for which it yearns.

While military might has failed to provide for Israel's security, I am not suggesting here that Israel abandon its strong defensive posture. Rather, in the spirit of the thought of Martin Buber, I am suggesting that such a strong Israel offer initiatives toward the cocreation — along with Palestinians — of what I have termed an internarrative. Insecurity occasioned by this initiative-taking is fundamentally different from that which

2. I have been asked by a fellow contributor to this volume why it is incumbent on the stronger nation to take such an initiative. The injunction to heed the call of the stranger, the widow, and the orphan (i.e., the weaker) is an injunction, I argue, that is sounded repeatedly throughout biblical and rabbinic texts.

inevitably accompanies any endeavor to forestall or end a conflict through force of arms alone. Named by Buber "*holy* insecurity," such uncertainty is nothing less than the "fear and trembling" that attends anyone who removes his or her "armor" designed — on the basis of analyses of strength and weakness alone — to ward off the enemy.

In holy insecurity, risk is present: Openness to dialogue may not be reciprocated. Yet if I am to move beyond calculations based on material considerations alone, if I am to engage in what Buber calls "prophetic politics," there is no alternative but to initiate the dialogue. For Buber, "One does not learn the measure and limit of what is attainable in a desired direction otherwise than going in this direction."[3] What I bring to the political decision-making process is an openness to what confronts me as something capable of manifesting a dimension of transcendence. I cannot *prepare* a world in which the divine manifests itself; what I can do, Buber argues, is to *prepare for* such a world. Initiating dialogue in the Middle East conflict is such a "preparation for." One cannot create peace unilaterally, but one can serve to initiate the sacred process through which peace becomes possible.

If creation of an internarrative, as I suggest, is the key to the resolution of the conflict in the Middle East, "how," I am asked, "does one create a new myth?" Furthermore, if such a myth is to be faithful to a "long tradition within Judaism," must not any new myth be rooted in "a metanarrative that is an autonarrative," namely, the biblical account of a people "sanctified by God's commandments"?

I would argue that the question "How does one create a new myth?" is itself highly suspect: Genuine myths are always in the process of being created. Authentic narratives evolve, develop, never succumbing to stasis, to "givenness." Narratives understood as mere dogma — permanently signed and sealed — are pseudonarratives, inviting belief that is nothing short of idolatrous. Indeed, the Holocaust has taught us well the dangers of belief in reified narratives. In engagement with tradition, genuine narratives are not created as new but are continually renewed, reforged in the fires of lived encounter.

As Buber argues, revelation is, at bottom, not a once-and-for-all occurrence. Rather, we live in the midst of perpetual, "streaming" revelation;

---

3. Martin Buber, "Prophecy, Apocalyptic, and the Historical Hour," in *Pointing the Way*, trans. Maurice S. Friedman (New York: Harper & Row, 1957), p. 206.

we engage in the ongoing "dialogue between heaven and earth," within which we become responsible (able-to-respond) to the divine manifesting itself in the world. For Buber, the recipient of revelation "receives not a specific 'content' but a Presence. . . . The assurance I receive of it does not wish to be sealed within me, but it wishes to be born by me into the world. . . . The eternal source of strength streams, the eternal contact persists, the eternal voice sounds forth. . . . All revelation is a summons and sending."[4]

The Judaic tradition to which I refer as a source for the creation of an internarrative has never taught that the revelation at Sinai was a static event, an "autonarrative" to which I am forever bound as a passive receptacle. Rather, the founding texts of Judaism remain perpetually open, subject to ongoing dialogue with those who would encounter them, interpreting their meaning in ever-new contexts. Jews are instructed to recall that not just the Pentateuch but the Talmud itself was revealed at Sinai. Torah, in its broadest sense, refers not just to the biblical canon but includes, as well, the responses of the rabbis.

This is not to say, however, that we are free to create narratives ex nihilo. We are neither totally *passive* creatures — receptacles for reified doctrinal truths — nor are we fully *active* creators of tradition, forging narratives as if there were no foundational teachings to which to turn for guidance. Active and passive at once, we continue the dialogue, continually harkening back to our tradition in the course of bearing witness to the particular context in which we find ourselves. Mining that tradition must ground the decision-making process in the Middle East conflict. It does not ground Zionism as some static teaching; rather, Zionism must be understood to be a living, growing body of thought. Ethical decisions that are faithful to Zionism, thus understood, must be forged anew at every turn. As Buber proclaims, the boundary lines "between service and service must be drawn anew . . . with that trembling of the soul which precedes every genuine decision."[5]

Zionism today must thus be perpetually reconceived before the face of the Palestinian partner. Every decision must be made — and remade —

---

4. Martin Buber, *I and Thou*, trans. Ronald Gregor Smith (New York: Collier Books, 1958), pp. 110-15.

5. Martin Buber, "The Validity and Limitations of the Political Principle," in *Pointing the Way*, p. 217.

within the bounds of that partnership. To be "sanctified by God's commandments" in this context, I argue, is to take the initiative in forging peace by ending the occupation of Palestinian land. The ancestral home of the Jewish people is also the home of an indigenous people — the Palestinians. For Buber, *the tradition of justice within Judaism* demands that the "redemption of the land" be fostered in conjunction with Palestinian co-witnesses to the work of the divine.

In supporting an ongoing transformation of autonarrative into internarrative in the course of my essay, I have never assumed that the process would be an easy one. Reconfigurations of deeply embedded mythic structures occur at a pace that is agonizingly slow. I come to realize only very gradually — and not without pain — that what I had believed to be *the* story is only *my* story. All such transformations, however, occur more rapidly when discursive arguments are complemented by existential encounters with the other: Each party to conflict must experience the space that Buber calls "the between"; each party must meet the other at moments when openings, small cracks occur in what were formerly understood to be closed systems of thought.

I will speak more personally at this point. Together with a Palestinian partner, I cofounded a not-for-profit organization called the Global Oral History Project (the Palestinian-Israeli Oral History Project). Our project was designed to provide the kinds of grassroots encounters that may allow for the creation of openings in what were previously fixed narrative structures. We endeavored to accomplish these goals by producing a series of books and films that were to reveal aspects of the ordinary lives of both peoples. In the endeavor to de-demonize the other, we asked Israelis and Palestinians to tell their stories to one another, to recount their histories. Through the sharing of narratives about elements of ordinary lives — sibling rivalries, first days of school, friendships, marriage, and so forth — simplistic understandings of the experiences of the other group were to be replaced by a more complex and morally nuanced grasp of these same experiences. Commonalities were noted, differences respectfully acknowledged. And what is perhaps most important, existential awareness was to complement didactic learnings. The primary audience for these books and films were Palestinian and Israeli school-age children. It was our hope that in reading and viewing these lived narratives, Palestinian and Israeli children would come to see, increasingly, that the enemy has a human face.

A final question remains to be addressed: I am asked whether an ongoing reconfiguration of the Zionist narrative such as the one I have pro-posed might eventuate in the abandonment of support for a Jewish state. It is my profound wish that at some time in the future all national borders will be called into question. However, given the history of a millennia-old antisemitism, culminating in the Holocaust, it must not be asked of the Jewish state to be "first in line" to relinquish its national sovereignty. For the foreseeable future, Jews must have a homeland within which they can, in substantial measure, control their own destiny. The forging of a just "two-state" resolution of the conflict can serve, however, both to preserve a Jewish majority within Israel and, at the same time, to model the process by means of which a seemingly intractable conflict can be justly resolved.

5. Dimensions of Responsibility:
A German Voice on the Palestinian-Israeli
Conflict in the Post-Shoah Era

Britta Frede-Wenger

I

January 27, 2005, the sixtieth anniversary of the liberation of Auschwitz, was a Thursday, the publication day for several German weekly newspapers and magazines. On that date the cover of *Stern*, one of Germany's most popular news magazines, featured a picture of Auschwitz-Birkenau. The caption read: "Sixty Years after the Liberation of Auschwitz: The Millennium Crime and the Question: Do we still have to feel guilty today?" This question made me wonder. It was and continues to be more telling than any of the answers presented by various politicians, scholars, and writers (German, Jewish, Romany, and Israeli).

It is no coincidence that my reflections on the Palestinian-Israeli conflict open with this question about Holocaust remembrance. In the context of this volume, my contribution is meant to provide a German perspective, but why is it assumed that there is "a German perspective" on this conflict? At the beginning of the twenty-first century, why not ask instead for a European as opposed to an American perspective? Or one might inquire, what qualifies as a "German" perspective where the Palestinian-Israeli conflict is concerned? For me, the answer lies less in the Holocaust events themselves than in the ongoing shadow they cast on both Germans and Jews. I believe that Dan Diner has such shadowing in mind when he speaks of a "negative symbiosis" between Jews and Germans after the Shoah: "After Auschwitz — how tragic — we can in fact speak of a 'German-Jewish' symbiosis, alas, a negative one: for both Germans and Jews, the results of this mass extermination have become the starting point for how they see themselves. This constitutes a kind of opposite mutuality [*gegensätzliche Gemeinsamkeit*], regardless of whether they like it or not. This negative symbiosis created by the Nazis will shape the relationship of both to themselves and, what is more, to each other."[1]

The history of the Holocaust binds Jews and Germans together. At the same time, it starkly sets them apart. For contemporary Germans and Jews, memory of the Holocaust marks the core of their identity — yet in fundamentally different ways. How Germans and Jews relate to that event influences not only the way we think about ourselves but also the way we think about and act toward each other. Diner goes even further: German and Jewish self-images are influenced by the negative symbiosis — that is, any search for German identity is confronted with the Jewish people, and vice versa. Therefore, the relationship between Germans and Jews, and especially the relationship between German society and the Jewish state, is not and cannot be "normal."

For these reasons, I claim that when Germans talk about the Palestinian-Israeli conflict, they often talk about themselves between the lines. The conflict is often seen and commented upon in terms of the Shoah. In other words, opinions on the situation in Israel and the Palestinian territories are influenced by the discourse on German identity after the Shoah. The complexities of these relationships mean, among other things, that I do not intend to present *the* representative German perspective on the Palestinian-Israeli conflict, if such a thing exists. I can present no more than *a* German *voice*, the voice of a white Catholic woman, born in 1971, who is not a political scientist, a historian, or a Middle East scholar.

To advance these reflections, I discuss the question posed on the cover of *Stern* in late January 2005, identify two possible reactions to the question of Holocaust guilt, and ask how they might influence perceptions of the Palestinian-Israeli conflict. In a second step, I look for a possible opposite of "guilt" in relation to the Holocaust and question whether "innocence" is a suitable term. I close with a suggestion for a distinctively German perspective on the Palestinian-Israeli conflict: to witness to both

1. Dan Diner, "Negative Symbiose: Deutsche und Juden nach Auschwitz," in *Ist der Nationalsozialismus Geschichte?* ed. Dan Diner (Frankfurt: Fischer, 1987), pp. 185-97, here p. 185. Here and throughout, the English translations are mine.

Israelis and Palestinians that people are responsible for their actions and especially for the suffering they have inflicted.

II

Let me go back to the beginning. Why did the question "Do we still have to feel guilty today?" disturb me? Because it suggests that there are people "out there" who hold the Holocaust against us Germans. But do they really? The *Stern* question also suggests that contemporary Germans do feel guilty. But do they really? Ten years ago, I first met Holocaust survivors and scholars. Only once or twice since then have any of them confronted me with hostility toward Germany. That hostility, however, was not addressed to me as a person or to my generation of Germans. Instead, I was welcomed, supported, and respected — and this readiness to enter into dialogue was not interrupted when I told people about my family background (which is a very mixed one and contains both devoted followers of Nazi ideology and a granduncle who was interned in a concentration camp). Very rarely have people given me reason to think that my German origin made them shy away from me — and when it did, it was they, not I, who felt guilty about that outcome. Speaking for myself, my dominant feeling has been insecurity. I have been and continue to be insecure as to how to meet and address the victims of the Holocaust. Also I have felt more anger than guilt. I am angry at the generation of my grandparents who have left me with a Holocaust legacy. I feel insecurity, anger, shame, and also helplessness — but not guilt.

The fact that in January 2005 a significant German news magazine asked, "Do we still have to feel guilty today?" implies first and foremost, however, that the question of guilt continues to be a serious one for the German public. That question is connected to a second one: *Should* we Germans feel guilty? Two possible answers are of immense importance. To identify and explore the first, note that the student movement in the late 1960s was a protest movement. In Germany, it included protest against the Nazi history of the parents. Accusing the perpetrators, it focused on their crimes. Gradually, however, this approach to Holocaust remembrance changed. What followed was the "discovery" of the Holocaust's victims, which included empathy with them. Surely the victims, their stories, their suffering, and their loss must be at the center of Holocaust remembrance. And yet, there are dangers: Empathy can turn into an overidentification with the victims and thereby lead to forgetting that today's Germans are the grandchildren or great-grandchildren of Nazi perpetrators. Overidentification can be escapism. Empathy, however, can also take another turn and lead to an overidentification with Holocaust guilt. This outcome can also be problematic. While a society may inherit the guilt of the past, young Germans today are not guilty in any personal or individual sense. What is the consequence in both these cases (overidentification with the victims or overidentification with the perpetrators)? I suggest that what follows is a paralysis. In both cases, a perceived "moral disqualification" of the perpetrator precludes a critical analysis of the Palestinian-Israeli situation.

There is a second way to relate to the question of Holocaust guilt. Although National Socialism has receded into the past, media coverage about it abounds in Germany. Commentators, however, observe a "fragmentation of memory." Coverage about Nazi politicians, army leaders, and wives, about German victims of allied bombings, about the expulsions of Germans from the East and their flight, and about the Holocaust of the Jews appear, more or less, side by side. This result does not necessarily have to be bad. On the contrary, I think it reflects a real need for a retrieval of the (family) history that the protesting German generation of 1968 condemned. Still, I doubt that this retrieval is critical enough. As Jan Ross of *Die Zeit* remarked: "In this fragmented plurality of remembrance, the question of how memory is transformed into politics (as well as fear of such a transformation) has lost a lot of its urgency."[2] Here it should be underscored that there are excellent examples of Holocaust education in Germany. They are confronted, however, by a growing readiness to speak of the "comparability" and even "similarity" of individual destinies, especially with regard to suffering. This tendency to find equivalences between the Holocaust and current problems can be observed even among people who are neither right-wing nor antisemitic. These ways of thinking are dangerous.

In January 2005 members of the Saxon state parliament from the extreme right-wing National Democratic Party (NPD) openly called the World War II firebombing of Dresden a "bomb-Holocaust" and refused the minute of silence in honor of the victims of the Holocaust because

---

2. Jan Ross, "Wie weit weg liegt Auschwitz? Gespräche mit Künstlern und Intellecktuellen über unsere Gedenkkultur," *Die Zeit*, no. 5, January 27, 2005.

they thought the victims of the Dresden bombing were not appropriately remembered. Such actions should provide warnings about a relatively new form of revisionism that is not an outright denial of the Holocaust but a subtle manipulation of memory based on selective attention to historical detail and context. According to this revisionist outlook, the Holocaust and the suffering of Germans during and after the war are more or less on the same level. Any feeling of guilt is denied; Germans suddenly appear as the true — or at least also as — victims. This mistaken equivalence is based on blindness about historical detail and context. Likewise, if adequate historical consciousness is missing with regard to the Palestinian-Israeli conflict, oversimplification is bound to occur, and the door for unhelpful polemics, including antisemitism, will remain dangerously open.

At this point, it must be stressed that the German political elite are clear and committed to facing the crimes of Nazi Germany and to accepting German responsibility for building a new, truly democratic, and nondiscriminating society. There is neo-Nazism in Germany, but overwhelmingly German society and its major political parties are determined to fight it. A few days after the events in the Dresden parliament, Horst Köhler, the president of the Federal Republic of Germany, traveled to Israel to celebrate the fiftieth anniversary of diplomatic relations between Germany and Israel.[3] Köhler's visit to Yad Vashem, the Israeli memorial to the Holocaust, showed even more than his words that German suffering and the suffering of the Holocaust victims cannot be measured against each other. Born in 1943, Köhler is the child of German farmers who had to flee, first, from Romania to Poland, then on to East Germany, and later to the West. Yet even with such family suffering, he broke into tears at Yad Vashem.

III

Thus far, I have developed two points: First, the relationship between Jews and Germans is special because the Holocaust binds them together in a "negative symbiosis." Second, the question of guilt continues to haunt the

3. Köhler spoke in the Knesset on February 2, 2005. His speech can be found at http://www.bundespraesident.de/Reden-und-Interviews-,11057.622155/Ansprache-von-Bundes praesident.htm?global.back=/-%2c11057%2c0/Reden-und-Interviews.htm%3flink%3dbpr _liste%26link.sDateV%3d02.02.2005%26link.sDateB%3d02.02.2005.

search for a positive German identity. I now move one step further and ask: What about the perception of Jews in this German search for identity?

The Jewish philosopher Emil Fackenheim called the Holocaust an abyss between Jews and Germans. If Germans are situated on the perpetrator side of this abyss — and therefore on the side of guilt — what terms do Germans use to describe the Jewish side, the side of the victims? "Innocent" seems to be an obvious choice, but I would argue that while "innocent" is correct, using this term might be dangerous, for two reasons. First, such rhetoric about innocence buys into the Nazi logic of a Jewish "crime." Second, this rhetoric also plays into the hands of the historical revisionism discussed above.

Fackenheim pointed out that National Socialism was based on a philosophical perversion. The idea that all human beings qua human beings have an inalienable right to live was foreign to Nazi ideology. In fact, this idea had been turned into its opposite. To prove this, Fackenheim refers to the *Häftlingspersonalkarte* (prisoner's identity card). Under the category "crime," one reads: "Hungarian Jew."[4] The fact that these identifications reflect a systematic camp categorization shows that the equation of Jewish existence with a crime and ultimately with a death sentence was not a minor matter. "At least as far back as 1938," Fackenheim states, "concentration camp prisoners had their respective categories emblazoned on their uniforms in the form of triangles: red for 'political,' green for 'professional criminal,' brown for 'unemployable,' pink for 'homosexual,' and yellow for 'Jew.' Once again, with the possible exception of the Gypsies (who were sometimes considered as inherently unemployable), everybody had to have done something in order to land in a concentration camp. Only Jews had simply to be."[5]

Fackenheim is not trying to compare individual sufferings here. Instead, he is identifying philosophically the nature of the Nazi attack. At least for Gypsies and Jews, the Nazi accusation did not relate to anything a person had done (or not done).[6] By asking a question, it becomes obvious

4. See "Midrashic Existence after the Holocaust: Reflections Occasioned by the Work of Elie Wiesel," in Emil Fackenheim, *The Jewish Return into History: Reflections in the Age of Auschwitz and a New Jerusalem* (New York: Schocken Books, 1978), pp. 252-72, here p. 255.

5. Ibid., p. 256.

6. Fackenheim pays practically no philosophical attention to the fate of the Gypsies. Especially when one looks at his reflection on the nature of the National Socialist attack, this omission must be considered a weakness in his writing.

that the meaning of "innocence" in relation to the Holocaust needs a second look: What made the victims of the Holocaust "innocent"? Were they "innocent" because they were "not guilty" of something they were accused of? The perversion of the idea of the right to live is the crime to which the innocence of the victims corresponds. In the Nazi logic, every Jew was to be murdered. The question whether they had done anything to deserve punishment did not even arise. Consequently, the victims of the Holocaust are innocent because life is innocent, not because all of them were "good people."

Earlier, I identified a recent form of historical revisionism characterized by a lack of attention to historical complexity. Against this background, it becomes even clearer why I argue that the term "innocence" is problematic. Where historical complexity and context are ignored, Jewish "innocence" can uncritically be assumed to be the opposite of German "guilt" for the murder of the Jews in the Holocaust. This duality, however, conjures up a metaphorical image of "the Jew" that does not correspond to reality. Where "guilt" and "innocence" are interpreted to be simply paired as opposites, a dangerous misunderstanding is bound to take place. It is fundamentally wrong to assume that anybody who has suffered must be "better" *because of* this history. Without critical reflection on "guilt" and "innocence," however, that problematic equation can be easily made. Such oversimplifications and equations might mean: If "the Germans" are guilty, "the Jews" are innocent. But what happens to this logic if "real" Jews or Israelis appear to be not so innocent? Then the equation shifts. If "the Jews" are not innocent, then "the Germans" cannot be all that guilty. Or (which is at least as unfortunate): Then the Jews are "just as bad."

On October 3, 2003, Martin Hohmann, who was then a member of the Christian Democratic Union (CDU), a conservative political party, and a member of the German Bundestag, gave a speech in which he called the Jewish people a "people of perpetrators."[7] This speech eventually led to his dismissal from the CDU. In my view, the context of Hohmann's remarks is at least as significant as their antisemitic content. October 3 is the German National Holiday (Tag der Deutschen Einheit). On that occasion, Hohmann's topic was "Justice for Germany." His reflections on German identity unavoidably led him to reflect on the Jewish people as well. Unfortunately, Hohmann's analysis suggested that "Justice for Germany" (= "ac-

---

7. The speech can be found at http://www.hagalil.com/archiv/2003/11/hohmann-3.htm.

quittal"?) was achieved when the Jewish people were identified as (another) "people of perpetrators." Again, I want to emphasize that the term "innocence" does apply to the victims of the Holocaust. Nevertheless, it is dangerous to pit "innocence" against "guilt" in the context of reflection about German identity. Doing so can put one on a slippery slope toward antisemitism and anti-Israelism.

IV

I started my reflections with the observation that Holocaust "guilt" still haunts Germans, even — and perhaps especially — young Germans. I conclude with remarks based on the insight that the question of guilt misses the point. Germany's postwar generations are not guilty for the Holocaust. What is frequently heard, however, is the notion of the "responsibility" that the younger German generation carries. Does such language do more than say the same thing in different terms? What are we responsible for?

Three points about the responsibility of the younger German generation — my generation — come to mind: First, we must ensure that those who are guilty for the Holocaust are held responsible for their crimes. Second, we must live up to the special responsibility for the safety and well-being of the Jewish people because Germans planned and carried out the Shoah. Third, we must keep alive the memory of what people are capable of doing to each other. As Fackenheim has written, "Auschwitz exacts a new concession from future philosophy: whether or not Man is infinitely perfectible, he is in any case infinitely depravable."[8] In a different but related context, Fackenheim adds that "the destruction of humanity remains possible, for in Auschwitz it was actual."[9]

Perhaps a German voice on the Palestinian-Israeli conflict can be raised with these three insights. All forms of political instrumentalization of the Holocaust, any analogy that is drawn between then and now, is for-

8. Emil Fackenheim, "The Holocaust: A Summing Up after Two Decades of Reflection," in *Contemporary Jewish Religious Responses to the Shoah*, ed. Steven Jacobs (Lanham, Md.: University Press of America, 1993), pp. 66-76, here p. 71.

9. See "Auschwitz as Challenge to Philosophy and Theology," in Emil Fackenheim, *To Mend the World: Foundations of Future Jewish Thought* (Bloomington: Indiana University Press, 1994), pp. xxxi-xlix, here p. xxxix.

bidden. Apart from the fact that such arguments are bound to be false, they do not lead anywhere that is helpful but render mutual understanding impossible. And yet we must admit that human beings are capable of inflicting immense suffering. Germans *know* how true that proposition can be, because Germans have inflicted suffering on a scale that is beyond measure, and they have been held accountable for it. I do not believe that, as young Germans, our choice is between paralysis and escapism. What we need — wherever possible — is solidarity with the victims. What we need is the critical ability to see oversimplifications for what they are. And what we need, first and foremost, is a political awareness that grows out of one absolute imperative (an absolute from the beginning, not just after the Shoah): There must be an end to suffering!

In the Oslo Accords, the leaders of both Israelis and Palestinians committed to keeping in mind not only one's own suffering but also the suffering of the other. Empathy with the victims should come first and foremost, but it must lead further. Empathy is only the first step in dealing with the question of responsibility: What caused this suffering? The situation needs to be faced in all honesty and in all its complexity. It must be followed by the question (and by sound responses to it): Who is to be held responsible for this suffering? It is my hope that the question of responsibility for suffering inflicted may reveal the ambivalence of actions and diminish suffering. There is suffering on both sides of the Palestinian-Israeli conflict — and both sides claim to defend themselves. Yet both sides are called to realize that even when acting toward a perceived good, they run the risk of inflicting suffering.

As a human being and as a German aware of my national history, I hope that both sides in the Palestinian-Israeli conflict will put the suffering into the center of their attention — the suffering on both sides. And I also hope that this placement will not lead to a perverse weighing of suffering against suffering but that both sides will see and accept their responsibility both for the suffering among their own people and for the suffering they have inflicted upon the other.

Contributors' Questions for Britta Frede-Wenger

You say that a German voice on the Palestinian-Israeli conflict can be raised with insights such as "human beings are capable of inflicting immense suffering" and "there is suffering on both sides of the Palestinian-Israeli conflict." While Israelis and Palestinians inflict suffering on each other, it can be argued that the vast majority of Israelis experience shame over the suffering they inflict, while tens of thousands of Palestinians literally celebrate in the streets. In that celebration, do you see any of what Fackenheim calls "the destruction of humanity"? What does this differing reaction to one's own acts of violence tell you about the Israeli-Palestinian conflict?

Do Germans, as you suggest, have less of a right to criticize the politics of the State of Israel because the Holocaust was perpetrated by Nazi Germany? Might collective guilt be playing a role in your analysis? Does what you argue not perpetuate a situation in which Jews become symbolic and so are seen and evaluated differently from all other peoples? Would it not be to the advantage of Jews, Israelis, and even Germans if Jews (or Israel) could be seen as just another people or nation with no call to special attention or evaluation?

Response by Britta Frede-Wenger

I begin with the second cluster of questions posed to me by the contributors to *Anguished Hope*. I want to emphasize that I do not argue that Germans have less of a right than anyone else to criticize the politics of the State of Israel. I have tried to show, however, that (and why) the relationship between Germans and Jews, and therefore also between Germany and Israel, is and will always be special. Neither am I arguing for hesitancy in speaking out against the politics of Israel. In this respect, I would rather have readers understand my argument as a reflection on the conditions for the possibility of a criticism that is both fair and fruitful. What must come first is self-awareness. No matter what we Germans do, the Holocaust is and remains part of our national history; no matter how much we wish it to be otherwise, if we want to call ourselves Germans, we need to be able to accept that this identity entails making clear where one stands regarding the crimes planned and committed by Germans in the Holocaust. For these reasons, I have tried to analyze how the question of guilt is dealt with by Germans who do not carry any personal guilt for the Holocaust. I think this phenomenon differs significantly from the question of collective guilt. Whether or not the Germans alive during the time of National Socialism share a collective guilt, the Holocaust casts a shadow over the German people alive today. This shadow is marked by the question: What becomes of guilt when all those who were actually guilty have passed away? It is unthinkable that all that happened becomes forgotten, forgiven, or somehow "dissolved."

My reflections point to the conditions of the possibility for responsible criticism of the politics of the State of Israel. To clarify this point, it must also be emphasized that discourse about German identity sets the context for the question of how to deal with Holocaust guilt. What does this have to do with the politics of the State of Israel? At first glance, perhaps nothing, but if one looks deeper, it is crucial to realize that answers to German questions about the Holocaust will also entail a narrative about the Jewish people. And if responses to Holocaust-related questions form the ground for German identity today, the accompanying narrative about the Jewish people will inform how we Germans look at the Jewish people. (Even neo-Nazis tell a story about the Jewish people when they explain what they think being German means — however distorted this story might be.) These relationships are part of what Dan Diner called the "negative symbiosis."

Should Germans and Jews/Israelis see each other as just another people or nation with no call to special attention or evaluation? It might be appealing to "forget" the Holocaust while focusing on the future, but it is impossible to do so; we cannot *not* reflect on national identity. Does that outcome perpetuate a situation in which Jews are a symbolic people and are evaluated differently from all other peoples? Not necessarily. Again, let me stress the importance of self-awareness. "When Germans talk about the Palestinian-Israeli conflict," I said, "they often talk about themselves between the lines." My claim pointed to the necessity of transcending a discourse in which the Jewish people have little more than symbolic value. While I hold that the relationship between Germans and Jews, including Israel, will always be special, an awareness of this special relationship might also be a (even, perhaps, the only) way of transcending the limitations of this discourse. It might then be possible to move beyond the identity discourse and to understand and value the Jewish people and the State of Israel in their nonsymbolic reality — in other words, to see Jews and the State of Israel as just another people. In a 2005 interview, Joschka Fischer, Germany's foreign minister at the time, remarked that many Germans do not realize what it really means that the legitimacy of the existence of the State of Israel is questioned by the majority of its neighbors.[1] I agree. He also emphasized that Europe has a vested interest in the economic development, cultural and academic excellence, and especially the safety of Israel, the only true democracy in the region. This interest does not grow out of a perceived historical responsibility only.

1. See "Anwalt Jerusalems," *Die Zeit*, no. 20, May 11, 2005.

A limited perspective on the State of Israel is not a good starting point for fruitful and constructive criticism. Such a starting point may not go further than apologetics and polemics. When criticisms of Israeli politics come up in the context of reflections on the German past, or when they are (and I can testify that this happens frequently) introduced by a sentence such as, "After sixty years, we should finally be allowed to say this again . . . ," we Germans should be extremely alert.

In the first set of questions, the other contributors point out differing reactions to acts of violence by Palestinians and Israelis, and they ask what these reactions tell us about the conflict. First, we must remember that the situation is immensely complex. Second, we must be extremely careful not to oversimplify a situation by uncritically applying philosophical arguments to historical realities. Fackenheim's idea of the "destruction of humanity" rests on the insight that the National Socialist ideology turned an axiomatic belief on its head, namely, the idea that a human being has an inalienable right to live.[2] Furthermore, during National Socialism the turning upside down of that axiomatic belief did not itself remain an idea but was part of the basic structure of society and its politics: Jews were killed because they "were," not because they had "done anything." Under National Socialism, the demonizing of "the Jew" culminated in genocide, whose perverted logic dictates killing the other merely because he or she has no right to live. Such demonizing surely plays an important part in the Palestinian-Israeli struggle. We support and applaud all initiatives that fight the demonizing of the Israelis by Palestinians and the demonizing of the Palestinians by Israelis, all initiatives that aim at dialogue and at getting to know the other as a human being like oneself.

We should not uncritically apply philosophical arguments to historical realities. I say this with care, for there is a great danger in taking Palestinian celebrations of terrorist attacks as signs of the "destruction of humanity." This accusation comes close to instrumentalizing the Holocaust. Neither side has a right to claim that the other is perpetrating a Holocaust. And yet, I want to hold on to what I wrote — not as a literal diagnosis of the situation but as a warning: Human beings are all too capable of committing genocide. And in a post-Holocaust world, if we do not take action against the first steps on the road to genocidal action, we come too late.

2. Obviously, this belief was not always respected before the Holocaust. One thinks, for example, of the fate of indigenous people and black slaves in the United States.

What do such considerations tell us about the Palestinian-Israeli conflict? They indicate that we must take seriously how both sides act toward each other, how they talk about each other, and what they teach their children about the other. Furthermore, we cannot stake our hope only on dialogue. What if it fails? What if propaganda and the daily experience of discrimination, oppression, or terrorism outrun the dialogue? In 1948, in the aftermath of the Shoah, the United Nations issued its Universal Declaration of Human Rights. Article 3 reads: "Everyone has the right to life, liberty and security of person." If anyone questions or violates this right with regard to any other person or group, the peoples of the world have the obligation to protest against those actions and to protect the victims. Dialogue is pivotal, but it not enough. In the Palestinian-Israeli conflict, both sides must be held responsible for the violence they inflict. There can be no double standard or finger-pointing here — not for the Palestinians, but neither for the Israelis.

II. RISKS

Part I identified challenges that need to be faced if there is to be a just and lasting reconciliation between Palestinians and Israelis. Challenges involve awareness of problems, consciousness of the circumstances (historic and contemporary) that bring dilemmas to the fore, and senses of possibility, which include opportunities for action, appraisals about them, and also alertness about what might happen if no action is taken. Challenges call for responses and await decisions.

When one considers how to meet challenges or moves to address them, risks require assessment, lest the responses become ill-conceived and unnecessarily perilous. Responses to the challenges posed by conflict in the Middle East, including its key Palestinian-Israeli dimensions, are risk-filled. Many of those risks became increasingly apparent as quandaries mounted in 2006 and thereafter. What would be the fate of democracy in the West Bank and Gaza with Hamas flexing its muscle, or in Lebanon with Hezbollah's rocket launches and Israel's military retaliation leaving Israel's northern neighbor in shambles? Was Israel's 2006 withdrawal from Gaza a failure that played into the hands of militant Islamic radicalism intent on Israel's ultimate destruction and quieted Israeli voices that called for negotiation? How would the aftereffects of the Israeli-Hezbollah violence later that summer play out, particularly with regard to the Palestinian-Israeli situation? Every response to the challenges embedded in such questions entailed risks that remain matters of life and death.

On July 20, 2006, the *Washington Post* quoted Dan Gillerman, then Israel's ambassador to the United Nations, as saying, "We will do whatever is necessary. We have no timeline." Gillerman referred to the steps that his government was prepared to take as violence between Israeli troops and Hezbollah militias raged in Lebanon and northern Israel. His remark, however, can also help to introduce the essays in the second part of *Anguished Hope*. What is necessary, after all, as one considers the risks that are integral to the Palestinian-Israeli conflict and every response to it? Furthermore, if no timeline can be set as far as a just and lasting settlement of that conflict is concerned, then what should be done — when, where, and in what order of priority? In the risk-assessing chapters that follow, scholars who speak from their base in Holocaust studies do not presume to answer such questions completely and finally. No reflection about the Palestinian-Israeli conflict could be responsible if it tried, let alone claimed, to do so. Instead, the contributors to Part II strive to shed light on some of the risks that most need to be considered and taken if renewed efforts toward peace and justice are to follow in the wake of violence. Above all, the risk that must be taken is that of long-term commitment to those efforts, even if, and especially when, their success seems far off, if it can be achieved at all.

Margaret Brearley underscores two tasks that are necessary for a just solution to the Palestinian-Israeli conflict. If risks are not taken to advance them, any timeline pointing in that direction will be indefinitely null and void. First, Brearley argues, an inversion of historical reality must be undone. That inversion, which equates Zionism with Nazism, is common to much Arab and Palestinian rhetoric. Challenging that inversion is risky because it entails undoing a strongly entrenched mind-set and the institutions that support and spread it. Second, while maintaining that Israel's primary obligation is to protect its citizens and that, in this regard, Israel should be judged as any other state in the world, Brearley also stresses that Jewish life and tradition, which are fundamental for Israel, include "exceptional duties of morality," including rigorous self-criticism, generous compassion, and a real-world holiness. Israel cannot be successful by acting alone, but the nation's traditions call for it to take risks for peacemaking and for "treating its neighbors and opponents with equity."

David Patterson emphasizes related aspects of risk-taking in an essay that aims to offer a Jewish view of the Jewish state in the aftermath of Auschwitz, which definitely includes the Palestinian-Israeli conflict. Because of his interest in a *Jewish* response to these matters, his essay draws upon the Jewish texts and the Jewish thinkers that the Nazis would have consigned to the flames. That focus leads Patterson to affirm that in the aftermath of the Nazis' attempt to erase from the earth not only Jewish presence but also Jewish testimony, the best way that Jews can respond to the Nazis is to maintain a distinctively Jewish presence in the world. Since it is not evident that another Holocaust is impossible, a Jewish state — a Jewish *haven* — is essential to maintaining a Jewish presence in the world. From a Jewish standpoint, a Jewish haven can be found only in the land of the Jewish covenant. At the same time, Jewish teaching attests to the sanctity of *every* human being. Thus, Jewish risks taken for an end to the Palestinian-Israeli conflict must affirm the dearness of Palestinian lives. The major difficulty here is that much of the conflict is driven by a hatred of the Jew as the incarnation of evil, that is, by a metaphysical hatred. Therefore, Jews also face the need and responsibility to determine how such hatred can be transformed into respect for the other. Patterson does not think that a definite timeline for justice and peace will be guaranteed if Muslims and Jews turn to the best wisdom of their sacred traditions, but absent that turning, the chances diminish for even anguished hope.

The title of Didier Pollefeyt's essay, "Between a Dangerous Memory and a Memory in Danger," amplifies the emphasis in Part II on risks. Specifically, he asks, how might a Christian Holocaust scholar contribute to a realistic and just peacemaking process in the Palestinian-Israeli conflict? Pollefeyt's response is to deconstruct the Manichaean outlook that not only drove the Nazi political system but also resurfaces in the Middle East. Manichaeism, Pollefeyt explains, is the radical ontological separation between good and evil. It entails attribution of goodness to oneself and evil to the other, an action in which one forgets and thereby even activates evil in oneself. Just as one cannot draw a self-evident comparison, let alone equivalence, between the Nazi genocide against the European Jews and the plight of the Palestinians in their conflict with Israel, Pollefeyt takes the risk of arguing that it is also not credible to draw a neat and complete moral line between Nazi decisions and those taken by the State of Israel in the Palestinian-Israeli conflict. A responsible use of Holocaust studies in addressing the Palestinian-Israeli conflict involves taking the risk of siding with all who suffer unjustly, wherever they are, and bringing criticism to bear not one-sidedly but wherever it is deserved and needed.

Brearley and Pollefeyt reflect on the Palestinian-Israel conflict from European perspectives. Patterson uses long-standing Jewish outlooks to inform his assessment. Myrna Goldenberg joins them by rooting her appraisal in study of the Holocaust, but she also brings American Jewish insights to bear on the struggle. Noting that the views of American Jews about the Palestinian-Israeli conflict have been diverse and often polarized and volatile, she finds that Israel "poses an agonizing struggle" for American Jewry. One thing is sure, she insists: American Jews cannot responsibly disengage from Israel and its conflict with the Palestinians and much of the wider Arab world. American Jews have a special responsibility to "work pragmatically towards a just, secure peace, a two-state solution that assures the dignity, integrity, and independence of both Israel and Palestine." That hope requires American Jews to press the government of the United States to keep taking risky steps that lead in those directions. Goldenberg is not overly sanguine that the existence of a Palestinian state, even one that is economically and politically viable, will necessarily relieve pressures and threats against Israel's future. "We cannot know until there is a Palestinian state," she concludes, adding that "we must take the risk, cautiously."

Taking the risk — that is not the only thing that must be done, and doing so assures very little, but without such steps the Palestinian-Israeli conflict is likely to go on and on, periodically flaring and escalating, deepening hatred and suspicion from one generation to another, moving from anguished hope to unrelieved despair. No good is likely to come from such trends. The risk of allowing that downward spiral to take place is one that nobody, not only Palestinians and Israelis, should take.

6. National Socialism, Israel, and Jewish/Arab Palestinian History: Myths and Realities

Margaret Brearley

As actual knowledge of the Holocaust recedes (nearly half of adults and 60 percent of those under the age of thirty-five in Britain have never heard of Auschwitz),[1] the mask of Nazi aggressor is now firmly attached to the face of Israel. Despite the fact that, according to recent surveys, 63 percent of Europeans know little or nothing about the Israeli-Palestinian conflict,[2] Israel is now regarded by 59 percent of Europeans as the world's biggest threat,[3] and over 50 percent of Germans believe that the Israel Defense Forces are equivalent to the Nazi army and that Israel is engaged in a "war of extermination" of Palestinians.[4]

The equation of Zionism with Nazism is a commonplace of Arab and Palestinian rhetoric. Official Syrian dailies claim that Israel pursues a "Holocaust policy" toward Lebanon[5] and has "surpassed even the Nazis in . . . murder, destruction and . . . disdain for humanity."[6] In Egypt, despite

1. BBC survey of four thousand adults, December 2004, online at http://www.bbc .co.uk/pressoffice/pressreleases/stories/2004/12_december/02/auschwitz.shtml.

2. ADL European Survey, May-June 2002, online at http://www.adl.org/PresRele/ ASint_13/4118_13.asp.

3. European Union Survey, October 2003, online at http://www.guardian.co.uk/ israel/Story/0,,1076084,00.html.

4. Poll by University of Bielefeld, December 2004, online at http://www.tomgross. media.com/mideastdispatches/archives/000044.html.

5. *Teshreen*, February 21, 2000, in an editorial by Mohammed Hir el-Wadi. See http:// www.mfa.gov.il/MFA/MFAArchive/2000_2009/2000/2/Growing%20Concern%20in%20 Israel%20at%20Rhetoric%20in%20Some%20Arab.

6. *Al-Thawra*, February 22, 2000, in an editorial by Muhammed Ali Bouzha. See Web site in n. 5 above.

widespread Holocaust denial ("the Zionists invented the matter of the crematoria in order to extort the world, especially Germany . . . the Holocaust is only a myth"[7]), Zionism is widely branded as "a new Nazism."[8] In 2002, the Saudi ambassador to London described Israel's "war of occupation" as "far more severe" than wartime German occupation of Europe.[9] In 1984 Mahmoud Abbas published his doctoral dissertation, entitled *The Secret Relationship between Nazism and Zionism*, while in 1982 a Moroccan writer argued that Zionism had actually created Nazism.[10]

In Europe, too, the equation is widely accepted. During the first intifada a German Lutheran pastor told me of his relief: "Now I no longer feel guilty as a German, for the Israelis behave just like Nazis — or worse, since they know what suffering is." Parallels have been drawn in cartoons and newspaper articles between Israeli "genocide" of Palestinians and the Holocaust genocide of Jews. The journalist Brian Sewell likened Palestinian suicide bombers to resistance fighters attacking German occupying forces in World War II. He indicated that Palestinian hatred of Israelis parallels British wartime hatred of Germans, but "the Palestinians under the Israelis have suffered far worse and far longer."[11] Until 2008, the Muslim Council of Britain boycotted Holocaust Memorial Day because of its omission of the "genocide" against the Palestinians.

The Soviet linkage of Zionism to Nazism in the 1970s, in typical condemnations of Israel's "Zionist gang . . . stained with the blood of crimes committed during the war by the Nazis,"[12] is now reflected among Western

7. See http://www.adl.org/egyptian_media/antisem_feb_may_2001.asp.

8. *Al-Ahali*, March 14, 2001. See http://www.adl.org/egyptian_media/media_2002/comparison.asp.

9. See http://www.telegraph.co.uk/news/worldnews/middleeast/saudiarabia/1400959/Israelis-%27are-worse-than-Nazis%27.html.

10. On these items, see David Pryce-Jones, *The Closed Circle: An Interpretation of the Arabs* (New York: Harper & Row, 1989), p. 215. On March 30, 2002, the *Independent* stated that the Sudanese foreign minister, Mustapha Ismail, "said [that] 'Israeli barbarism' had surpassed the acts of Adolf Hitler." See http://www.independent.co.uk/news/world/middle-east/arab-fury-at-foolish-illegal-aggression-655933.html.

11. *Evening Standard*, June 25, 2002. See http://www.thisislondon.co.uk/news/article-437320-details/After+50+years+of+suppression+we+too+would+become+bombers/article.do.

12. V. Bolshakov, *Anti-Sovietism — Profession of Zionists* (Moscow: Novosti Press Agency Publishing House, 1971), p. 14; *Soviet Antisemitic Propaganda: Evidence from Books, Press, and Radio* (London: Institute of Jewish Affairs, 1978), pp. 55-66.

intellectuals.[13] Tom Paulin, an influential Oxford academic, published a poem in which he described "another little Palestinian boy . . . gunned down by the Zionist SS."[14] In the Egyptian weekly *Al Ahram*, Paulin described Jewish settlers on the West Bank, for whom he "feels nothing but hatred," as "Nazis" who should be "shot dead," adding "I never believed that Israel had the right to exist at all."[15] In 2003 the *Church Times* marked Holocaust Memorial Day by carrying an article by Rev. Richard Spencer arguing that "in Ramallah, in reality, was the suffering and deprivation that I could only imagine in Auschwitz."[16] In Israel, he continued, the Holocaust is used "as a means by which anything is justified," a claim paralleling one made in Ramallah in March 2002 by Portuguese Nobel laureate José Saramago: "What is happening here is a crime that may be compared to Auschwitz."[17] John Pilger, noting Amnesty International's claim that Israel "murders and tortures 'systematically,'" wrote: "Goebbels would have approved."[18]

This inversion of historical realities serves many functions. It maximizes Israeli culpability and oppression of Palestinians while nullifying Palestinian culpability for terror. Its powerful imagery distracts attention away from far grosser humanitarian catastrophes such as recent or current genocides (Sudan, the Congo) and potential genocides in Zimbabwe and elsewhere. Moreover, the inversion is exculpatory; it deflects onto contemporary Jewish Israeli polity the guilt and shame of actual past involvement with Nazism, both of Western nations and of the Arab world. The myth of present Nazi Zionism conceals the truth of past Arab Nazism.

It is relevant here to examine briefly the Nazi connections of the grand mufti of Jerusalem, Haj Amin al-Husseini. Robert Wistrich has highlighted what he terms "Islamo-fascism," the "remarkable degree of ideological *rapprochement* between Islamic antisemitism and National Socialism."[19] Haj Amin and Fawzi al-Qawuqji, both Nazi sympathizers and rabid anti-

13. See Howard Jacobson's essay "The Incendiary Use of the Holocaust and Nazism against the Jews," in *A New Antisemitism?* ed. Paul Igansky and Barry Kosmin (London: Profile Books/JPR, 2003), pp. 102-12.

14. "Killed in Crossfire," *Sunday Observer*, "Poem of the Week," February 18, 2001.

15. *Al Ahram*, April 4-10, 2002.

16. *Church Times*, January 24, 2003.

17. See http://www.guardian.co.uk/world/2002/apr/16/israel2.

18. *New Statesman*, June 27, 2002.

19. Robert Wistrich, *Hitler's Apocalypse: Jews and the Nazi Legacy* (London: Weidenfeld & Nicolson, 1985), p. 169.

semites, instigated terror against Jewish villages and fellow Palestinians from 1936 until 1939. In 1938 alone, 69 British, 292 Jews, and at least 1,600 Arabs were killed, often with extreme brutality.[20] Haj Amin fled first to Baghdad, then to Berlin, where he remained from 1941 to 1945, "supervising Nazi propaganda broadcasts to the Middle East."[21] He met Hitler on November 28, 1941, and, together with Qawuqji, created an Arab legion that became an SS unit.[22] Haj Amin, an ally of Himmler, fully endorsed the genocide of Jews, declaring in March 1944: "Kill the Jews wherever you find them — this pleases God, history and religion."[23] He was close to Eichmann and probably visited Auschwitz in his company.[24] He recruited Bosnian Muslims in a Waffen SS company in 1943, which killed 90 percent of Bosnia's Jews and lobbied Hitler to prevent Jews from escaping Hungary.

While tens of thousands of Palestinian Jews were fighting with Britain against Germany, Baldur von Schirach toured the Middle East and Joseph Goebbels visited Egypt, which, like Saudi Arabia, Syria, Iraq, Algeria, Tunisia, and other Arab countries, developed significant alliances with Nazi Germany, a relationship "disastrous to the Palestinian Arabs,"[25] one that resulted in long-term negative consequences for Arab-Israeli relations: "Arab identification with Nazism, and Jewish suffering in the Holocaust, finalised open antagonism between the two communities after the war."[26] Moreover, Haj Amin's "legacy of uncompromising refusal to accept or recognize Zionism in any form" exerted enduring influence on later Palestinian policy.[27] Haj Amin's negationism was adopted both by his younger kinsman Yasser Arafat and by the Muslim Brotherhood, which in turn influenced Palestinian policy. Above all, the Zionism/Nazism nexus has been used to foster hatred of Israel and of Jews. Charles Krauthammer noted in the *Washington Post* that "Arafat has raised an entire generation

20. Pryce-Jones, *The Closed Circle*, p. 196.
21. Martin Gilbert, *Exile and Return: The Emergence of Jewish Statehood* (London: Weidenfeld & Nicolson, 1978), p. 269.
22. Hitler regretted that Germans had "the wrong religion" (Christianity's "meekness and flabbiness") rather than being "Islamized Germans" (Albert Speer, *Inside the Third Reich* [London: Phoenix Paperback, 1995], p. 150).
23. Pryce-Jones, *The Closed Circle*, p. 206.
24. Nicholas Bethell, *The Palestine Triangle: The Struggle between the British, the Jews, and the Arabs 1935-48* (London: Steimatzky/Andre Deutsch, 1979), p. 225.
25. Ibid., p. 33.
26. Pryce-Jones, *The Closed Circle*, p. 207; see also chap. 8, "The Impact of Nazism."
27. Peter Mansfield, *The Arabs*, 2d ed. (London: Penguin Books, 1985), p. 212 n. 14.

schooled in hatred of the 'Judaeo-Nazis,'" his indoctrination including "the rawest incitement to murder."[28]

The inversion of a historical Nazi/Arab alliance into anti-Israeli rhetoric has been achieved using techniques paralleling those deployed by National Socialism (which translated Hitler's vision of war as "cunning, deception, delusion, attack and surprise" into powerful, innovative propaganda).[29] In her 2004 study of Hezbollah, Judith Palmer Harik noted the power of visual imagery in Middle East politics: "A picture is worth a thousand words in this part of the world . . . the message gets across and the image lingers."[30] Already during the first intifada the Palestinians had proved "far more adept at exploiting the presence of the media to their advantage" than Israeli spokespersons.[31]

Early in the second intifada, the fabrication of a powerful iconic image, a helpless, twelve-year-old boy being shot by Israeli soldiers, was a brilliant propaganda technique. Its success lay in the ability of pictures, noted in Siegfried Kracauer's comments in 1947 on Nazi films, to "make a direct appeal to the subconscious and the nervous system." National Socialist film-making, influenced by earlier Soviet counterparts, employed "many devices . . . for the sole purpose of eliciting from audiences certain specific emotions," including the faking of events: "faked reality passed off as the genuine one."[32] So too the filming of Muhammad al-Dura's faked murder in November 2000 was a deception designed to create specific responses. It elicited emulation among Palestinian youth, outrage among Muslims worldwide (accustomed to lurid antisemitic propaganda against Jews as child-killers), and shock and sympathy for the Palestinian cause within Western audiences.

Simultaneously, the image tarnished Israeli soldiers as deliberate child-murderers. Muhammad al-Dura was filmed to be the intifada's foundational myth; his "death" was reenacted in many schools and sum-

28. *Washington Post*, March 26, 2002.

29. Hermann Rauschning, *Hitler Speaks: A Series of Political Conversations with Adolf Hitler on His Real Aims* (London: Thornton Butterworth, [1939]), p. 16.

30. Judith Palmer Harik, *Hezbollah: The Changing Face of Terrorism* (London: I. B. Tauris, 2004), p. 189.

31. Ze'ev Schiff and Ehud Ya'ari, *Intifada: The Palestinian Uprising — Israel's Third Front* (New York: Simon & Schuster, 1989), p. 159.

32. Siegfried Kracauer, *From Caligari to Hitler, a Psychological History of the German Film* (Princeton: Princeton University Press, 1947), p. 279.

mer camps. A romanticized TV account glorifies his "martyrdom"; "the soundtrack tells children that death in conflict with Israel will bring them to a child's Paradise."[33] The stratagem of filming a staged child murder was a strategy of warfare, an instance — like the purported Jenin massacre — of traditional Islamic warfare techniques of *taqiyya* (dissimulation) and *hila* (ruse).

The recent actual deaths of hundreds of Palestinian suicide bombers are also a form of strategic warfare with multiple purpose. Affirmed in April 2002 by Sheikh Tantawi of Cairo's al-Azhar University as the "highest form of jihad operations," they "strike terror into the hearts of the enemies of Allah," according to Ahmad al-Tayeb, Egypt's leading jurist.[34] Religiously sanctioned and designed to terrify Israeli Jews, suicide bombers also serve to distract attention from the PLO's terrorist past to a present where the only weapon appears to be an expendable body strapped with explosives. According to Adel Sadeq, "There is no middle ground. Co-existence is total nonsense. . . . The real means of dealing with Israel directly is those who blow themselves up. . . . There is no other way by the pure, noble Palestinian bodies. This is the only Arab weapon there is. . . . The Palestinian body is the only means in this battle."[35] The spilled blood of killer-martyrs sacralizes Palestine's soil and the uprising itself, as we hear from a refrain from the first intifada: "Every day the soil soaks up the blood of the pure."[36] This sacral role allotted to killer-martyrs' blood (strongly resembling the function of the sixteen Putsch Martyrs' blood in Munich in sanctifying the National Socialist revolution) reflects the glorification of death in militant Palestinian ideology and current propaganda to Palestinian youth.

But it also disguises the extent to which Palestinians are fighters by proxy, spearheading a war of attrition, demoralization, and propaganda, a long-term war designed to eradicate Israel as an autonomous Jewish state. The war is financed and supported by neighboring states. The vision of Iranian-backed Hezbollah "follows Ayatollah Khomeini's goal of exporting the Islamic Revolution throughout the region. Removing the Israelis from Jerusalem and the Holy Land and restoring the rights of the Muslim

---

33. Raphael Israeli, *Islamikaze: Manifestations of Islamic Martyrology* (London: Frank Cass, 2003), p. 209.

34. Alan M. Dershowitz, *Why Terrorism Works* (New Haven: Yale University Press, 2002), p. 80.

35. Israeli, *Islamikaze*, p. 285.

36. Schiff and Ya'ari, *Intifada*, p. 105.

community was a sacred imperative." Thus, "Hezbollah leaders made their sacred obligation to conduct jihad against 'the usurpers of Muslim lands' — the Israelis — their top priority."[37] Al Qaeda forged close strategic links to Hezbollah, trained Palestinians in terrorism, and sent funds to Hamas.[38] Hamas, the radical Islamic Palestinian group that pioneered suicide bombings against Israeli civilians — a tactic now adopted by Fatah and Al Aqsa Martyrs' Brigade — is funded mainly by Saudi Arabia and Jordan. (Saddam Hussein also diverted "oil for food" money to Palestinian suicide bombers.) Hamas is determined to end Jewish occupation of the whole of historical Palestine; Hamas leader Mahmoud al-Zahar declared: "From our ideological point of view, it is not allowed to recognize that Israel controls one square meter of historic Palestine."[39] Hamas, founded in 1988 from Muslim Brotherhood origins, published in that same year its "Covenant of the Islamic Resistance Movement — Palestine," in which it proclaimed "*jihad* as the 'personal obligation' of every Muslim, for Palestine was the 'soil of Islamic trust till the end of days' and the Jews . . . were an instrument of evil that turns the wheels of history."[40]

The second intifada, launched in September 2000 after Arafat's rejection of Camp David and Taba peace negotiations, was quintessentially a renewal of ongoing warfare in what Hassan Khaled, mufti of Lebanon, had declared in 1968 to be "a battle between two religions," Islam versus Zionism, since Zionism is "a very perilous cancer, aiming at domineering . . . the whole Islamic world." Khaled was speaking at a major conference of Middle Eastern Muslim theologians, held at al-Azhar University in Cairo in 1968 to discuss the Arab-Israeli conflict following the Six Day War. Eminent speakers demanded jihad of all Muslims against the Jews because Israel, "the possession of all Muslims," is "in the heart of the Arab and Muslim land." Therefore, "relinquishing the fight against the Jewish aggression is tantamount to unbelief and renunciation of Islam," especially since Jews are "the enemies of God," of "the Islamic Nation," and of humanity itself. Because they "love life" so keenly, they deserve humiliation and even torture.[41]

37. Harik, *Hezbollah*, pp. 16, 19.

38. Rohan Gunaratna, *Inside Al Qaeda: Global Network of Terror* (New York: Columbia University Press, 2002), p. 150.

39. *New York Times*, April 4, 2002.

40. Schiff and Ya'ari, *Intifada*, p. 237.

41. D. F. Green, ed., *Arab Theologians on Jews and Israel* (Geneva: Editions de l'Avenir, 1974), pp. 60, 48, 47, 11, 58, 10, 38.

Since the State of Israel and its 1967 victory represent both "the de-Arabization of Arab territory"[42] and de-Islamization of Muslim territory, Israel therefore confronts pan-Arab and pan-Islamic opposition to its very existence. This opposition is all the more intense because the dominant theology now championing pan-Arab and pan-Islamic unity is Saudi-based Wahhabism. Rejecting the cultural and religious heterogeneity prevalent in the Ottoman Empire, this austere theology — as formulated by Islamist thinkers, including Sayyid Qutb — affirms death as better than life and seeks to reflect *tawhid,* the unity of Allah, by creating cultural and religious uniformity on Wahhabi models. This position has radical consequences. One fundamental Wahhabi premise is that Western society, secular Muslim rulers, many non-Wahhabi Muslims, and all non-Muslim minorities are *jahiliyya,* in a state of pre-Islamic unbelief and paganism, and therefore not under the legal protection traditionally granted by Shari'a law to Christians, Jews, and heterodox Muslims. Saudi Wahhabi preachers have proclaimed Christians to be *mushrikun,* polytheists, and have therefore sanctioned their killing, including women and children.[43] Jews, labeled as heretics, traitors, and enemies of Islam, are now similarly vulnerable.

Such rigidly exclusionist teaching is potentially genocidal to non-Wahhabi Muslims, of whom hundreds of thousands have been killed in Algeria, as well as to non-Muslims. (When Young Turk leaders seeking pan-Turkic uniformity gained control of the Ottoman government, formally declaring jihad in 1914, this control led directly to the genocide of over a million Armenian Christians in 1915.) The Salafist-Wahhabi government in Sudan has committed actual genocide of some two million southern Sudanese Christians and animists since the early 1980s, and what Elie Wiesel has called "a genocide in slow motion" of black Sufi Muslims in Darfur today.

Like the Muslim Brotherhood before them, Hamas and Islamic Jihad are imbued with the Wahhabi vision and religiopolitical aims. Israel thus faces — as did Jews faced with National Socialism — both an exclusivist, potentially genocidal theology and political enemies that use terror to annihilate their opponents. Today, there are signs of hope in addition to the renewed Palestinian leadership: moderate Muslim voices express a new

42. Walid Khalidi, *Palestine Reborn* (New York: I. B. Tauris, 1992), p. 84.
43. Dore Gold, *Hatred's Kingdom: How Saudi Arabia Supports the New Global Terrorism* (Washington, D.C.: Regnery Publishing, 2003), p. 217.

malaise over the destructiveness of radical Islamism; Israel's withdrawal from Gaza in 2005 was termed by then prime minister Ariel Sharon "the new Zionism"; Sheikh Abdul Hadi Palazzi interprets positively the qur'anic "controversial verses" (Sura 5:20-21; Sura 17:104) regarding the Jewish homeland. Disturbingly, though, despite its own call for on ongoing cease-fire, Hamas, as of this writing, has had some involvement in Qassam rocket attacks on the south of Israel.

Israel's first duty is *pikuach nefesh*, saving its citizens' lives (the maligned, problematic fence — paralleling the British eighteen-feet-high barbed-wire Tegert fence erected in 1938 — has already saved hundreds of lives) and surviving as a state to become the post-Holocaust Jewish "house against death," as Catholic theologian Johann Baptist Metz termed it.

Yet Israel has inherently exceptional duties of morality. While Israel should be judged by others as a normal state, it should judge itself rigorously. For it is "the only land that responds physically to moral behavior," its crops and rainfall dependent, according to the daily Shema prayer, on ethical behavior and observing the commandments.[44] Emmanuel Levinas argued that duties of justice and holiness beyond the normal extend to Israel: "This country is extraordinary. It is like heaven. It is a country that vomits up its inhabitants when they are not just. There is no other country like it; the resolution to accept a country under such conditions confers a right to that country." For Israel to possess the land is to "sacralize the earth" by founding "a just community in this land."[45]

Rabbi Abraham Isaac Kook, writing before World War II, believed that Jewish love of Israel is a powerful life force that would move even seeming unbelievers toward practical holiness, "expressing the divine commandments concretely in image and idea, in song and deed. . . . The source of this power is in the Power of God."[46] Justice and practical holiness must emanate from Israel, above all from Jerusalem, as Abraham Joshua Heschel envisaged: "Let Jerusalem inspire praying: an end to rage, an end to violence. Let Jerusalem be a seat of mercy for all men. Wherever a sigh is uttered, it will evoke active compassion in Jerusalem."[47] (That a

44. Nachum Amsel, *The Jewish Encyclopedia of Moral and Ethical Issues* (Northvale, N.J.: Jason Aronson, 1996), p. 126.

45. Emmanuel Levinas, *Nine Talmudic Readings*, trans. Annette Aronowicz (Bloomington: Indiana University Press, 1990), pp. 69, 66.

46. Arthur Hertzberg, ed., *The Zionist Idea* (New York: Atheneum Books, 1973), p. 422.

47. Abraham Joshua Heschel, *Israel: An Echo of Eternity* (Woodstock, Vt.: Jewish

religious Jewish underground apparently sought and received rabbinic authorization for the murders of Palestinian mayors and innocent Palestinian civilians is the absolute antithesis of justice and holiness.)[48]

Rabbi Joseph Soloveitchik argued that holiness, "the descent of divinity into the midst of our concrete world," must result in real compassion and caring: "the actualization of the ideals of justice and righteousness is the pillar of fire which halakhic man follows when . . . he serves his community." Compassion must create solidarity with all suffering; the ideal of *tikkun olam,* mending the world, makes peace-seeking urgent. While inadequately mirroring Jewish values, Israel often reflects in practical reality those life-affirming qualities of Soloveitchik's ideal *halakhic* (Torah-abiding) man: esteem for the individual, for ideas, for innovative rationality. Israel must stand against "the forces of negation and nothingness." Israel should, and in certain ways already does, mirror Soloveitchik's ideal, building for the future, seeking self-renewal derived from self-critical repentance, and fostering "an active creative spirit" with passionate "yearning for creation."[49]

Ideals of holiness, "contracted . . . within a community," can thus imbue the far greater complexities of an endangered state so heterogeneous that its citizens come from over one hundred countries and many cultures, its forty Christian denominations and its large Muslim population highly diverse. Israel's multifaceted creativity and *chesed,* practical compassion, already extend far beyond its boundaries, especially during natural and man-made disasters.[50] Israel faces unprecedented challenges in terms of peacemaking, water sharing, confronting terror and superb propaganda, and treating its neighbors and opponents with equity, which demand an innovative, creative, and, ultimately, holy response, assured, in the words of Rabbi Nahman of Bratslav (1772-1810), that "despair does not exist at all . . . for you cannot take God from my heart."

Lights Publishing, 1997), p. 37. See also Arthur Miller, "Why Israel Must Choose Justice," in *Wrestling with Zion: Progressive Jewish-American Responses to the Israeli-Palestinian Conflict,* ed. Tony Kushner and Alisa Solomon (New York: Grove Press, 2003), pp. 166-69.

48. See Colin Shindler, *The Land beyond Promise: Israel, Likud, and the Zionist Dream* (London: I. B. Tauris, 2002), p. 190.

49. Joseph B. Soloveitchik, *Halakhic Man* (Philadelphia: Jewish Publication Society of America, 1983), pp. 108, 91, 107, 133-34.

50. Helen Davis, *Israel and the World* (London: Weidenfeld & Nicolson, 2005).

Contributors' Questions for Margaret Brearley

You say that "Israel's first duty is *pikuach nefesh,* saving its citizens' lives . . . and surviving as a state." You also say that Israel "has inherently exceptional duties of morality." In light of the destruction of two-thirds of European Jewry, does Israel's self-preservation now trump all other concerns? What happens when, as is often the case in this conflict, these two duties clash? How can you stand in support of the notion that Israel must realize the ideal of holiness when you fail to discuss the concept "occupation" in your chapter or to speak concretely about the suffering of Palestinians?

When you speak about Palestinians as "fighters by proxy, spearheading a . . . long-term war designed to eradicate Israel as an autonomous Jewish state . . . ," are you not in danger of engaging in an essentialist claim that would lump all Palestinians under the one heading? What do you mean by "*the* Palestinians?" What happens to individuals among the Palestinian people? Might not your characterization of the belief systems of pan-Arabism and pan-Islam oversimplify — and demonize — what may be diverse currents of thought among these individuals?

Response by Margaret Brearley

Regarding Israel's self-preservation: within rabbinic tradition, each human life is considered sacred, so sacred that it may not be sacrificed for the sake of a group. While one may risk one's life in the hope of saving another, it is forbidden to deliberately sacrifice one's life to save another; each person, however humble, thus has the overriding right of self-preservation,[1] unless it involves *chillul ha-Shem*, profaning God's name by murder, incest, or idolatry. (Some authorities, it should be noted, permit killing in self-defense.) By extension, a Jewish state has as prime duty its own self-preservation when faced with enemies aiming to destroy it — not for *raison d'état*, but solely in order to preserve the collective lives of its individual citizens. Even Jewish pacifists recognized the need to fight in self-defense (and ironically, Christian pacifists have supported Palestinian terror against Jews);[2] even the German Jewish philosopher Martin Buber stressed that although Jews "cannot *desire* to use force," they may have to use it: "If there is no other way of preventing the evil destroying the good, I trust I shall use force and give myself up into God's hands."[3]

Yet rabbinic tradition places self-preservation within strict moral and social boundaries. Since no individual is superior to any other, for all are created in the image of God, each is required to live with the utmost sensitivity

1. Samuel Belkin, *In His Image: The Jewish Philosophy of Man as Expressed in Rabbinic Tradition* (London: Belard-Shuman, 1960), pp. 97-99.

2. Evelyn Wilcock, *Pacifism and the Jews* (Stroud, Gloucestershire: Hawthorn Press, 1994), pp. 198, 206.

3. Martin Buber, as quoted in ibid., p. 110.

to the rights and dignity of others. One's primary obligation is to the rights of others, prioritized according to proximity: the first obligation is to one's poor relatives, then to one's neighbors, finally to strangers; a Jewish state, indeed any state, has roughly the same priorities. Yet Jewish ethics, based on *imitatio Dei,* imply supererogation; they demand friendship and kind acts toward enemies, a constant search for peace between Jew and non-Jew, and the duty specifically to help even religious enemies and those who hate Jews.[4]

The Jewish state thus embodies implicit demands for holiness, both toward its own citizens and toward those of other states, including its enemies. Despite their failures and the demands of survival and Realpolitik, Israeli leaders have acted from certain core moral values: preparedness to relinquish land for the hope of peace (Sinai, the buffer zone in South Lebanon, more recently Gaza); a historical readiness to negotiate and accede to proposals for partition, however limited; permission for soldiers to disobey orders on grounds of conscience;[5] the refusal to use public rhetoric of hatred or annihilation of enemies parallel to that employed by many past Palestinian leaders; *havlagah,* self-restraint, in the limiting of civilian casualties and in the ruthless suppression of Jewish terrorism — best exemplified in the near-suicidal decision to enter booby-trapped Jenin in April 2002 with infantry, of whom fifty-four died, in order to minimize Palestinian civilian casualties.[6]

I do not mean to avoid reference to the "occupied territories" or to skirt around Palestinian oppression by Israel. To discuss in detailed terms "the suffering of Palestinians" seemed unnecessary, since no postwar uprooted population in the world has had its homelessness and sad plight so well documented or disseminated, particularly the many hundreds of deaths caused by the Israeli army during the first and second intifada. The suffering of Palestinians, however, is not all caused by Israel. No Arab state apart from Jordan (with about 1.8 million Palestinian refugees) has granted citizenship or equal rights to Palestinians; Jordan itself massacred 5,000-10,000 Palestinians in September 1970. Intimidation, torture, and murder used by Fatah and other factions against dissidents have resulted in hundreds of Palestinian civilian deaths.

---

4. Belkin, *In His Image,* pp. 125, 227-47.

5. Wilcock, *Pacifism and the Jews,* p. 201.

6. Benny Morris, *Righteous Victims: A History of the Zionist-Arab Conflict, 1881-2001* (New York: Vintage Books, 2001), pp. 94-95, 136.

I omitted, too, the suffering of the 900,000 Jews dispossessed and exiled from Arab lands from 1948 (750,000 went to Israel), and the suffering between 1968 and May 1992 caused by international Palestinian terror, leaving at least 217 Israelis and Jews, as well as 501 non-Jews, dead and 1,095 wounded. From April 1994 to February 2005, Islamic Jihad, Hamas, Fatah Al Aqsa Martyrs' Brigade, the Palestinian Front for the Liberation of Palestine, and Tanzim (a militant faction of Fatah) killed at least 649 and wounded at least 4,349 civilians in Israel. Arguably, the Lebanese civil war of 1974-76, involving 40,000 deaths, was largely caused by Palestinian violence and the Druze/Palestinian alliance against the Maronites.

Since revisionist historian Benny Morris, among others, consistently writes "the Palestinians," the term clearly has legitimacy. Yet in my essay "the Palestinians" is found only in quotations by Brian Sewell and by Ze'ev Schiff and Ehud Ya'ari (and "the Palestinian body," by Adel Sadeq). I deliberately refrained from writing "the Palestinians" precisely so as not to oversimplify the complex phenomenon of Palestinian identity. Like Israeli identity — consciously fashioned from both Palestine-born Jews and refugees and immigrants from over 100 countries bound by a common faith and history of persecution — Palestinian identity is a construct. Palestinians include descendants of indigenous Arabs and of Muslims, including Circassians, Turks, and Kurds brought "in an effort at 'Islamization'" by the Ottoman authorities, from the empire's northern and Balkan peripheries in the late nineteenth century.[7] They further include descendants of many immigrants from Syria, Lebanon, Egypt, and further afield in the 1920s, 1930s, and 1940s, drawn by high wages.[8] Palestinian identity is a passionately held vision of self, allegiance, and nationhood. Individuals have great diversity of religious, social, and political affiliations, in which family, village, clan, and geographic location are of critical importance, and as Abigail Jacobson has shown in her recent article contrasting Musa Kazim Husseini and his older brother Hussein al Husseini,[9] individuals can hold distinctly nuanced views.

Yet ultimately, in most nondemocratic societies, the affiliations and beliefs of the few individuals with power determine the lives of the entire

7. Ibid., p. 13.

8. Joan Peters, *From Time Immemorial: The Origins of the Arab-Jewish Conflict over Palestine* (New York: Harper & Row, 1984), chaps. 12 and 13.

9. Abigail Jacobson, "Alternative Voices in Late Ottoman Palestine," *Jerusalem Quarterly File and Institute of Jerusalem Studies*, no. 21, Spring 2004.

people. It was perhaps a tragedy for Palestinians and for Jews that the Husseini clan gained hegemony and influence over more moderate Nashashibis and other *effendi* (highly educated) families. Haj Amin Husseini, given sole religious and secular authority and vast unsupervised funds by the British in the early 1920s, held an ideological hatred of Jews and fomented mass violence against them from 1920, culminating in the Great Revolt of 1936-39, deadly terror against his Palestinian opponents, and affirmation of Nazi genocide of Jews: "Germany battles world Jewry, Islam's principal enemy. . . . my enemy's enemy is my friend," Haj Amin declared in a speech to the Nazi SS Handschar Division in January 1944.[10] His radicalized thought stemmed from the pan-Islamist writings of Jamil al Din Afghani and Afghani's brilliant disciple Muhammad Rashid Rida, Haj Amin's Cairo tutor before World War I. Afghani, a militant, innovative creator of pan-Islamic nationalism, called Muslims to arms against imperialist incursions, while Rida, president of the Syrian National Congress from 1920, created a blueprint for an Islamic state.

But I suggest that a key additional factor in the grand mufti's experience may well have been the Armenian genocide. While training in the Ottoman Military Academy in Constantinople from late 1914 to mid-1915, Haj Amin must have been aware of the deportations and mass murders of Christian Armenians both in Constantinople and within the army itself. Remaining as a junior officer in the Ottoman army until November 1916, he must have known of the well-attested expropriation and murders of over one million Armenians by late 1915. In 1919 he spent several months in Damascus, where hundreds of thousands of deported Armenians had died of starvation, ill-treatment, and exposure in the previous three years.

Was Husseini's intense Jew-hatred and opposition to Jewish immigration and settlement thus fueled both by Salafist pan-Islamism and by firsthand knowledge that forcible dispossession and mass murder of despised dhimmis (non-Muslims living in countries with Muslim majorities) are achievable, and without international opprobrium? And by immediate knowledge that large-scale terror actually gains substantive political concessions, as his appeasement by the British authorities from 1920 until his prewar flight later proved? The successful genocide perhaps crucially inspired Haj Amin, who, with kinsmen Musa Kazim and Abdel

---

10. Cited in Richard Bonney, *Jihad: From Qur'an to bin Laden* (London: Palgrave Macmillan, 2004), pp. 275-76.

Qader (who like other *effendis* — though not Haj Amin himself — accumulated great wealth from secret land sales to Jews), instigated and maintained extremist policies of anti-Jewish violence, terror, and uncompromising rejectionism. These policies dominated Palestinian politics from 1920 until the recent death of their younger relative, Yasser Arafat, and involved violent suppression of more moderate individuals and factions.

The Egyptian revolutionary Muhammad 'Abd al-Salam Faraj made the following pronouncement: "Fighting the near enemy is more important than fighting the distant enemy. In *jihad* the blood of the Muslims must flow until victory is achieved. . . . The first battlefield of the *jihad* is the extirpation of these infidel leaderships and their replacement by a perfect Islamic order."[11] Professional Arab armies proved incapable of destroying Israel and its "infidel leadership" in 1956, 1967, and 1973, so Syria, Egypt, Iraq, Iran, and Saudi Arabia have funded and used Palestinians, closest to the "near enemy," to spearhead the attack on Zionism. (Samir al-Khalil described "the 'Palestinianization' of the struggle against Zionism," with scant regard for the well-being of Palestinians not directly involved in the struggle. Indeed, prolonging innocent Palestinian suffering maintained what Aijaz Ahmad termed Orientalist "narratives of oppression": "colonialism [i.e., Israel] is now held responsible not only for its own cruelties but, conveniently enough, for ours too.")[12]

Jihad against Israel is "a legal precept binding upon every Muslim,"[13] likely to remain permanently in force, however much land Israel cedes and however much Israel renounces in pursuit of peace. For Hezbollah, for example, "the liberation of all Palestine and Jerusalem in particular was . . . an Islamic, rather than a purely Palestinian duty." This position is valid, in part, because according to Islamist thinkers such as Sayyid Abu'l-A'la Mawdudi (1903-79), "the objective of Islamic jihad is to put an end to the dominance of the un-Islamic systems of government and replace them with Islamic rule." Islamist jihad thus threatens both Israel and, potentially

---

11. Muhammad 'Abd al-Salam Faraj, *Al-Jihad: Al-Farida al-Gha'iba* (n.p., [ca. 1982?]), cited in Bernard Lewis, *What Went Wrong? The Clash between Islam and Modernity in the Middle East* (London: Weidenfeld & Nicolson, 2002), p. 107.

12. Samir al-Khalil, *Republic of Fear: The Inside Story of Saddam's Iraq* (London: Hutchinson Radius, 1990; orig. pub. Berkeley: University of California Press, 1989), p. 250; Aijaz Ahmad, *In Theory: Classes, Nations, Literatures* (New York: Verso, 1994), pp. 196-97.

13. 'Abd al-Salam Faraj, *Al Jihad,* cited in Emmanuel Sivan, *Radical Islam* (New Haven: Yale University Press, 1985), p. 20.

at least, other non-Islamic governments, since, according to Sayyid Qutb, "Islam demanded (and continues to demand) the elimination of all governments that are contradictory to its ideology. The universal nature of Islam means that it seeks to govern the whole world, not just a portion of it." Moreover, Qutb argues that the Qur'an (9:123) "advocates fighting those who live next to the land of Islam 'without reference to any aggression they may have perpetrated. Indeed, their basic aggression is the one they perpetrate against God. . . . It is this type of aggression that must be fought through *jihad* by all Muslims.'"[14] Israel is thus challenged by jihad on multiple grounds, being un-Islamic, non-Arab, "next to the land of Islam" and, paradoxically, within Islam's heartland. The outlook therefore seems bleak, especially if Bat Ye'or's vision of a powerful Euro-Arab anti-Israeli alliance were to be justified.[15]

Some authors, perhaps surprisingly, suggest that there are grounds for optimism. Olivier Roy writes of "post-Islamism," arguing that radical Islamism is transmuting into neofundamentalism and that, despite Qutb's ubiquity on neofundamentalist Web sites, there is "Wahhabi condemnation of Sayyid Qutb."[16] Bonney claims that, although Wahhabism has denied "the inherent diversity within the Islamic tradition . . . there may be signs of a change of attitude among younger scholars."[17] Hope just might lie in the very teachings that inspired Haj Amin's hatred. Al-Afghani, Rida, Abdu, al Banna, and other radical Islamists, while stressing that the Qur'an is "final, unique and most authentic," also urged the importance of *ijtihad*, creative independent interpretation,[18] though Roy cautions that "the Salafis and Wahhabis support *ijtihad* . . . as a way of bypassing the tradition of the different religious schools, and not as a way of adapting to new situations."[19] The current *ijtihad* of the Italian Sheikh Palazzi, surprisingly, envisages Zionism and Israel as benign and Arab-Jewish brotherhood as realizable.

14. Bonney, *Jihad*, pp. 297, 203, 218, 220.

15. Bat Ye'or, *Eurabia: The Euro-Arab Axis* (Madison, N.J.: Fairleigh Dickinson University Press, 2004).

16. Olivier Roy, *Globalised Islam: The Search for a New Ummah* (London: Hurst, 2004; first published as *L'islam mondialisé* [Paris: Editions du Seuil, 2002]), p. 250.

17. Bonney, *Jihad*, p. 169.

18. Dilip Hiro, *Islamic Fundamentalism* (London: Paladin Grafton Books, 1988), p. 270.

19. Roy, *Globalised Islam*, pp. 243-44.

7. Toward a Post-Holocaust Jewish Understanding of the Jewish State and the Israeli-Palestinian Conflict

David Patterson

Tohu is a green line around the globe from which darkness emanates, as it is written: "He made darkness His secret place surrounding Him" (Psalms 18:11).

Bereshit Rabbah 1:21

After 1,900 years of exile, persecution, and slaughter in other lands, Jews have reestablished the Jewish state in the realization that, as long as they are guests in someone else's house, their lives are in peril. There is no more radical proof of this truth than the Shoah. Thus, there can be no Jewish thinking about the Jewish state apart from the context of the Shoah. Jews do not live alone in the land, however; they never have, and they never expected to. But they live in the land with a people called "the Palestinians," who not only lay claim to the land but would remove the Jews from the land, "from the river to the sea." And yet, the same Torah that defines the Jew as a Jew also commands the Jew to live at peace with non-Jews in their midst, particularly in the Land of the Promise (see, for example, Exodus 23:9; Deuteronomy 10:19; 20:10).

Because, according to the halakhic tradition of rabbinic law, the Torah determines the relation to the land, the Jewish relation to the land is not merely political, where power can justify anything. If the Israeli-Palestinian conflict amounts to something more than a power struggle, it is because the Jewish state, in the words of Emmanuel Levinas, "stems from the religion which modern political life supplants."[1] The Third Reich attempted to supplant that religion through the extermination of the Jews as a policy of state. It is in these exterminationist contexts that the post-Shoah Jewish state must be understood — not as some kind of compensation for the Shoah but as the embodiment of what was targeted for annihilation during the Shoah: the tradition of Torah and Talmud that, in the words of Nazi ideologue Alfred Rosenberg, had poisoned Aryan blood.[2]

André Neher understood the metaphysical scope of these contexts when he wrote, "Is not the State of Israel, in its very existence, a meta-state? And surely the war launched against Israel on Yom Kippur, October 6, 1973, was not only horizontal. . . . Zion, which is only a fragment of Jerusalem and the Land of Israel, is a word one can neither play around with, nor play tricks with, nor beat around the bush with. It is the key word of the 'meta' of Jewish history. Through Zion, Zionism becomes bi-dimensional. The vertical is interlocked with the horizontal."[3] One dimension is interlocked with the other because both the Shoah and the advent of the Jewish state are part of *sacred* history, not just for the Jews, but also for any tradition that regards the Torah as Holy Writ. Because that biblical tradition was slated for annihilation in the Holocaust, the issue of the Land of Israel has implications not merely for political expediency but, more profoundly, for sacred history in the post-Holocaust era.

As Levinas has rightly said, "The Shoah re-establishes the link — which up until then had been incomprehensibly hidden — between present-day Israel and the Israel of the Bible."[4] If the advent of the State of Israel has no metaphysical meaning — if the Land of Israel is not the Holy Land — then the religious traditions that rest upon the biblical testimony rest upon an illusion. If that is the case, then the absolute nature of the prohibition against murder is an illusion. And if that is the case, then we lose all grounds for any objection to the killing that continues in the Israeli-Palestinian conflict. The issue of the land, therefore, far transcends issues of power, territory, or even survival — it is an issue of human sanc-

---

1. Emmanuel Levinas, *Difficult Freedom: Essays on Judaism,* trans. Sean Hand (Baltimore, Md.: Johns Hopkins University Press, 1990), p. 217.

2. See Alfred Rosenberg, *Race and Race History and Other Essays,* ed. Robert Pais (New York: Harper & Row, 1974), pp. 131-32, 181.

3. André Neher, *They Made Their Souls Anew,* trans. David Maisel (Albany: State University of New York Press, 1990), p. 58.

4. Levinas, *Difficult Freedom,* p. 12.

tity as determined by the testimony of Torah and by the commandments of G-d. The Jewish return to the land as the *Holy* Land is central to a return of holiness to the human being in the post-Holocaust era.

The Significance of the Jewish Return to the Holy Land

The holiness of the Holy Land derives neither from its history nor from its shrines but from the divine commandments concerning the land, from the *mitzvot,* which are not just "commandments" but also "connections" between G-d and the land. Indeed, the Maharal of Prague maintains that "G-d's Name is identified with the Land of Israel,"[5] because G-d is known through his commandments. The One who commands us concerning the land, as in when we can plant and when we can harvest, also commands us concerning love for our neighbor. Because the holiness of the land is central to the notion of human sanctity, without that holiness, power is the only reality and weakness is the only sin. From a traditional, halakhic Jewish standpoint, then, the holiness of the land does not mean I can justify any action to maintain possession of the land; rather, it means that I must justify *every* action before G-d and humanity, according to the commandments of Torah.

In the aftermath of the Nazis' attempt to erase from the earth not only Jewish humanity but also Jewish testimony on the sanctity of humanity, the one way that Jews can respond to the Nazis is to maintain a distinctively Jewish presence in the world. Since it is not evident that another Holocaust is impossible, a Jewish state — a Jewish *haven* — is essential to maintaining both the Jewish presence and the Jewish testimony. And since the holiness of Zion is central to that testimony, a Jewish presence in Zion is central to a Jewish presence in the world. To argue against Zionism is to argue that another Holocaust is either impossible or desirable. A Jew cannot accept either proposition and remain a Jew, not merely in the name of survival but, above all, for the sake of the commandment to love G-d and neighbor, which is just what defines a Jew.

From a traditional, halakhic Jewish standpoint, then, a Jewish haven can be found only in the land of the Jewish covenant, only in the Holy

---

5. Yehuda Loeve, *Maharal of Prague: Pirke Avos,* trans. R. Tuvia Basser (Brooklyn, N.Y.: Mesorah, 1997), p. 322.

Land. Like the presence of the Jews in the world, the presence of the Land of Israel signifies a teaching and a commandment concerning our absolute responsibility to and for our fellow human beings. After the Nazis' attempt to eradicate that divine commandment from the world, the Jews must abide in the Holy Land because the Jews and the land *together* signify the truth of the covenant that commands love and forbids murder. The covenant and its commandments are what make Israel the Erets Hakodesh, the "Holy Land." If the land is no longer viable as something holy, then the covenant is no longer viable. Without the covenant, neither the commandment to love nor the commandment to refrain from murder is viable.

Perhaps for this reason Levinas insists that the State of Israel, "in accordance with its pure essence, is possible only if penetrated by the divine word," which always speaks in the imperative.[6] From the Land of Israel a voice emanates into the world precisely because the Jews once again dwell in the land. It is a voice that declares what the Nazis set out to silence; it is a Jewish presence that the Nazis set out to annihilate; and it comes from a land that, with the help of the Haj Amin al-Husseini, the Nazis hoped to dominate through their Arab Muslim allies.[7] Because the State of Israel is thus "penetrated by the divine word," it has an inescapable, metaphysical significance. Therefore, as Levinas states, "the State of Israel will be religious because of the intelligence of its great books which it is not free to forget. It will be religious through the very action that establishes it as a State. It will be religious or it will not be at all."[8] Israel's great books are the vessels of the testimony that enters the world through the Jewish people, a testimony through which all the nations of the world are blessed (see, for example, Genesis 12:3). "Zion is absolute in the world," says the Maggid of Mezeritch; "it is the life of all countries."[9] The action that establishes Israel

---

6. Emmanuel Levinas, "Zionisms," trans. Roland Lack, in *The Levinas Reader*, ed. Sean Hand (Oxford: Basil Blackwell, 1989), p. 271.

7. The Palestinians were pleased to be deemed honorary Nazis after their leader, Haj Amin al-Husseini, paid homage to Hitler. In 1938 Haj Amin began his recruitment of between 6,000 and 20,000 Muslims to serve in the SS. While many Christians have been embarrassed by the conduct of Pope Pius XII during the Holocaust, Muslims have been silent on Haj Amin's complicity in the murder of the Jews.

8. Levinas, *Difficult Freedom*, p. 219.

9. Quoted in Louis I. Newman, ed., *The Hasidic Anthology* (New York: Schocken Books, 1963), p. 301.

as a Jewish state is the action that preserves this universal blessing, as well as a universal responsibility to and for the other person.

Because the post-Shoah world — including much of the Arab Muslim world — continues to harbor the exterminationist designs upon the Jews that defined the Shoah, in such a world the holiness of the land can endure only through a Jewish rule over the land. And just as the land is the center of post-Shoah Jewish life, so is Jerusalem the center of the land. Any other capital of the Jewish state would reduce it to just another political entity engaged in the power struggles of the world.

The Place of Jerusalem in Jewish Consciousness

In the Israeli-Palestinian conflict the conflicting claims to Jerusalem parallel conflicting views of humanity. Just as the Jewish state signifies the sanctity of every human being, so does the Holy City demand an openness to every human being. That openness has been attained only since Jerusalem became reunified as the capital of the Jewish state in 1967; since that time, everyone has been free to pray in the Holy City.[10] From the standpoint of Jewish thought, that openness is a defining feature of the holiness of the Holy City. By contrast, one need only look to Mecca to see what the notion of "holy city" means in the Muslim world: it is closed to all except Muslims. Whereas Mecca signifies the truth of Islam, Jerusalem signifies the holiness of humanity — that is what makes it G-d's dwelling place. That is what makes Jerusalem the Holy City. Religiously speaking, Jews do not claim Jerusalem as their own; rather, in our prayers, it is *irkha,* "your city" — that is, G-d's city.

Understood as G-d's dwelling place, Jerusalem signifies G-d's presence in the world. Far more than a political capital belonging to the Jews, Jerusalem signifies the divine authority and the divine commandment to affirm the sanctity of our neighbor and thereby sanctify the Name signified by Jerusalem, as it is written: "There are seventy names of G-d, Israel, Torah, and Jerusalem" *(Yalkut Shimoni, Naso).* On a mystical level, each of these terms is a synonym for the other. On a human level, each summons us to a human community that, as Martin Buber has argued, requires two

10. While the Holy City is open to all who come in good faith, it is closed to those who come to murder people.

things: each member of the community must live in a relation to a transcendent center, and each must live in a relation to the other that is expressive of the higher relation.[11] The Holy City is that center.

The holy texts articulate this significance of the Holy City by saying, "This world is likened to a person's eyeball: the white of the eye [corresponds to] the ocean which surrounds the whole world; the iris to the [inhabited] world; the pupil of the eye to Jerusalem; the face in the pupil to the Temple" (*Derekh Erets Rabbah* 9:13). That is, Jerusalem is the lens through which G-d looks upon the world and puts to each human being the question he put to the first human being, Where are you? Similarly, the Midrash teaches, "When a person prays in Jerusalem, it is as though he prays before the Throne of Glory, for the gate of heaven is in Jerusalem" (*Midrash Tehillim* 4:91:7). Not a Jew, the text reads, but a *person* — any person, any child of Adam. Indeed, through Jerusalem each of us is tied to Adam and, through Adam, to each other. "In the place whence Adam's dust was taken," it is written, "there the altar was built."[12] As the Holy City's Holy of Holies, the altar signifies the link between G-d and humanity; as the place from which Adam's dust was taken, it signifies the bond between human and human.

Furthermore, since exile is a metaphysical and not a geographic condition, one can be in exile even within the walls of Jerusalem. To be sure, in the book of Lamentations, which we Jews chant on the anniversary of the destruction of the two temples, the city itself is said to have become a *nidah,* or a "wanderer" (see Lamentations 1:8); Jerusalem itself follows us into exile. And Jerusalem itself returns to the land with the return of the Jews to Jerusalem, to the extent that the Jews allow the Holy One entry into Jerusalem by living according to the commandments of Torah. In the Talmud, Rabbi Yochanan teaches, "The Holy One, blessed be He, said: 'I will not enter the heavenly Jerusalem until I can enter the earthly Jerusalem'" (*Taanit* 5a). When can G-d enter an earthly Jerusalem? When every human being can enter the earthly Jerusalem.

11. Martin Buber, *I and Thou,* trans. Walter Kaufmann (New York: Charles Scribner's Sons, 1970), p. 94.

12. *Tanna debe Eliyahu: The Lore of the School of Elijah,* trans. William G. Braude and Israel J. Kapstein (Philadelphia: Jewish Publication Society, 1981), p. 411.

Implications for a Jewish Understanding
of the Israeli-Palestinian Conflict

In the light of the foregoing, what are the implications for a Jewish understanding of the Israeli-Palestinian conflict? To answer this question, we begin with the basis of traditional, halakhic Jewish understanding — with the Torah, where we are warned, "The sword shall bereave you of children without, as shall the terror from within" (Deuteronomy 32:25). In a commentary on this passage, the Talmud urges us to move to the inside, even if there, too, terror threatens to bereave us of our children (see *Bava Kama* 60b). Levinas elaborates: here we "see the entire problem of present-day Israel appear, with all the difficulties of the return. One must withdraw into one's home. . . . And even if 'at home' — in the refuge or in the interiority — there is 'terror,' it is better to have a country, a house, or an 'inwardness' with terror than to be outside."[13] Once again, the point in having a house is not mere survival; rather, it means having a community — an *edah*, in Hebrew, which also means a "testimony." It means bearing witness to the holiness of the human being from within the center that commands that testimony. It means a Jewish presence in Jerusalem and in the Land of Israel.

Levinas articulates what this internal terror means for a Jewish understanding of the Israeli-Palestinian conflict by saying, "Do we not smell here . . . the odor of the camps? Violence is no longer a political phenomenon of war and peace, beyond all morality. It is the abyss of Auschwitz or the world at war. . . . One must go back inside, even if there is terror inside. Is the fact of Israel unique? Does it not have its full meaning because it applies to all humanity? All men are on the verge of being in the situation of the State of Israel. The State of Israel is a category."[14] The Americans suffered 9/11, the Spaniards and the British the attacks on their trains, and the Iraqis the assaults on their new government not because they gave aid to Israel but because they strive to represent the openness to humanity, regardless of creeds, that Israel represents. Any nation that would attest to the sanctity of every human life is subject to the terrorist attacks of those who insist that only the life of the "believer" has value, as has become the case in Wahhabi Islam.

13. Emmanuel Levinas, *Nine Talmudic Readings*, trans. Annette Aronowicz (Bloomington: Indiana University Press, 1990), p. 190.
14. Ibid., pp. 190-91.

And yet, because Jewish teaching attests to the sanctity of *every* human being, negotiations for an end to the conflict must affirm the dearness of Palestinian lives. The major difficulty here, however, is that much of the conflict is driven not merely by ethnic or political differences but by a hatred of the Jews as the incarnation of evil, that is, by a metaphysical hatred, found among some Muslims. The very opposite of the holiness that the Jews attach to the land, it is a hatred that justifies any measure taken to murder Jews, including the training of one's own children to kill themselves in the process of murdering Jews. Whereas in the Jewish tradition, as in other traditions, martyrdom means dying in a refusal to commit murder or to defile G-d, in the Islamic teaching it has come to mean dying precisely in order to commit murder and thereby to glorify Allah. One may say, "Well, that is how they define martyrdom." But as we have learned from the Nazi assault on language, a word does not mean whatever we will it to mean. Some Muslim Arabs may regard the killing of oneself in order to kill Jews as martyrdom, but just as the Nazis were wrong in their definition of Jews as subhuman, so are those Muslims wrong in their definition of martyrdom as dying in the effort to murder Jews and others.

As for the metaphysical, exterminationist hatred of the Jews expressed among some Muslims, consider the following:

- The spurious *Protocols of the Elders of Zion* is axiomatic truth in much of the Muslim world. Excerpts are included in article 32 of the Hamas covenant, as well as in the *Al-Shuhada* manual of the Palestinian Border Guards.
- Holocaust denial is the norm in much of the Muslim world. Those who deny it include Professor Hassan al-Agha of Gaza's Islamic University and the Palestinian official Mahmoud Abbas. The theme of a Muslim scholars' conference held in Amman, Jordan, on May 13, 2001, was that the Holocaust never happened.
- Not only is belief in the invidious blood libel part of Muslim popular culture but, thanks to intellectuals such as Dr. Muhammed bin Saad al-Shwa'er, in some quarters it is part of the Muslim culture of "higher learning" as well.
- Leaders such as Bashar Assad and Bassam abu Sharif (former adviser to Yasser Arafat) have proclaimed to the Christians that the Jews are behind the crucifixion of Jesus, even though Islam denies that the crucifixion took place.

- And, of course, there are the repeated urgings of Muslim imams to "kill Jews everywhere."

The horrific irony is that, although many Holocaust scholars make much of paying attention to the "warning signs of genocide," too many of them ignore these warning signs of contemporary genocidal designs upon the Jews. The challenge facing the Jews is to determine how to transform such hatred into tolerance.

Recommendations for Peace

The Jews of Israel cannot transform Muslim hatred into tolerance unless Jewish existence is secure. Therefore, the world must not turn its back on the Jews, as it did in the time of the Shoah; Israel's security must be assured. This imperative is especially incumbent upon Holocaust scholars. Furthermore, we must continue to support measures such as Israeli-Palestinian family contacts, joint development of educational curricula for peace, and joint economic and academic endeavors. The idea here is that people who can recognize each other's humanity and thus see the need for each other are much less likely to kill each other. The world should also honor the tremendous courage on the part of Palestinians who truly seek peace. These seekers of peace, and not those so bent on murder that they would die in order to kill, are the true martyrs among the Palestinian people. They include Suleiman Faraj, Samer Goma Ofeh, Rajah Mahmoud Ali, Ikhlas Yassin, Abdullah abu Alhawa, and Tahseen abu Arkub, to name just a few of the hundreds who have been subjected to lynching and public execution, their bodies left on display or dismembered and dragged through the streets.

Finally, my recommendation for peace between the Muslims and the Jews is the following: let us turn to the wisdom of our sacred traditions. In the Qur'an it is written, "Allah does not alter the condition of a people until they first alter what is in their hearts" (13:11). And the Mishnah teaches, "Peace alone can be a vessel of blessing for Israel" (*Uktsin* 3:12). In the time of the Shoah the teachings of the holy texts came under a radical assault, as the *tohu*, or chaos, of a primeval darkness threatened to engulf the world. Perhaps in our own time those teachings can transcend the green line of chaos that cuts through the land and surrounds the globe.

Contributors' Questions for David Patterson

Are land and covenant, as you suggest, completely inseparable? How can such a linkage avoid ethnocentrism and religious nationalism, narrowly conceived? In what sense is Israel more imbued with the divine word than any other land in the world? Is it not the case that *any* land can become sacralized through one's ethical response to the other? Does not your assertion that a given plot of land is sacred move us toward idolatry, toward a "veneration of rocks"? Is any land inherently holier than any other? Does not Levinas speak of Israel as "risk," implying that holiness is not an attribute of place but rather a command to be responsible?

"If the advent of the State of Israel has no metaphysical meaning," you claim, "then the religious traditions that rest upon the biblical testimony rest upon an illusion." What about someone who is born Jewish, who feels strongly committed to living as a Jew, but who does not necessarily believe that a metaphysical meaning accrues to the State of Israel? Is that person outside the Jewish fold? Is Judaism limited by place? Does your essay allow for a pluralistic understanding of Judaism? Perhaps most important, does such an individual, as you imply, have no basis for rejecting murder absolutely?

Response by David Patterson

Let me begin by identifying a few premises underlying my essay and this response to the issues raised about it. Written in the aftermath of the slaughter of nearly half of world Jewry, the essay should be understood in the light of a diametric opposition between two worldviews: a Nazi worldview, which takes the value of a human being to rest on natural accident and personal will, and the worldview of traditional, halakhic Judaism, which takes the value of a human being to lie in his or her creation in the image of the Holy One. Contrary to the Nazi viewpoint, I adopt the premise that, for a Jew in a post-Holocaust world, the traditional, halakhic Judaism slated for annihilation by the Nazis provides the one means of reestablishing the sanctity of the human being. This restoration of what the Nazis set out to destroy is not merely a matter of survival for its own sake; what is at stake is a testimony to the very meaning of our humanity.

My adoption of traditional, halakhic Judaism as a premise for my thinking brings me to a question raised in the first set of issues: "Is it not the case that *any* land can become sacralized through one's ethical response to the other?" The short answer is no. Ethics never sacralized anything. From a Christian standpoint, Golgotha became a "sacralized" piece of ground when the Son of G-d was crucified there. Was that an "ethical response to the other"? Stated differently, the Holy Land is holy not because ethical responses to the other have taken place there; no, it is holy because it signifies the One who commands ethical responses to the other *everywhere*.

Sacralization is determined by two things: covenant and commandment. Land and covenant are not inseparable, but *holy* land and a covenant with the Holy One are inseparable, as the Torah indicates (e.g., Genesis 15:18). In this sense Israel is "more imbued with the divine word than any other land in the world"; the covenant of Torah concerns Israel more than any other land in the world, at least as that land has been understood among Jews, Christians, and Muslims. Millions of people throughout the world understand the term "Holy Land" to refer to Israel, and not to Manchuria, regardless of whether the land is in fact holy. Similarly, one may reject the idea that Torah and covenant are from G-d and thus proceed from a premise other than the one I have adopted. But in a post-Holocaust era, to ask the Jews to reject Torah is precisely to ask them to go along with the Nazis — at least with regard to the status of Torah.

As for the commandments that sacralize the land, yes, they include ethical commandments regarding our treatment of others, but the sacred is never reducible to ethics. Rather, it is what makes ethics possible. Thus the commandments that sanctify the land concern not only our treatment of others but also our treatment of the land itself (e.g., Exodus 23:10-11), as well as certain rites and rituals to be performed in the land (e.g., Leviticus 23). Because the Covenant of Torah is a covenant of commandments — of *mitzvot* — it is a covenant of *connections* with the Holy One, as the root of *mitzvah, tzavta* (attachment, bond), suggests. These connections, and not ethical systems or even ethical actions, are what make the Holy Land holy. And they are what make *this* land and *this* covenant inseparable. The Land of Israel is not "*inherently* holier than any other"; it is holier because, of all the lands of the earth, it is a central focus of divine commandment.

The matter of inherent holiness brings me to another excellent question raised by my respondents: "Does not your assertion that a given plot of land is sacred move us toward idolatry, toward a 'veneration of rocks'"? No religious tradition is more sensitive to this issue than Judaism. For this reason the rabbis constantly warn the Jews who pray at the Kotel (Western Wall), "Be sure you pray *at* the Wall, not *to* the Wall." The Torah that commands us with regard to the land also cautions us against idolatry; as each commandment is tied to the other, so both are tied to the commandments to love the neighbor and to refrain from murder. From a traditional, halakhic standpoint, one cannot take a cafeteria approach to the commandments, selecting the ones that make sense and rejecting the ones that do not, as if our own reasoning were higher than divine commandment. Therefore, in traditional Judaism, the Jews cannot embrace the holiness of the person and reject the holiness of the land, any more than a Christian can affirm the crucifixion but reject the resurrection.

One way in which Judaism seeks to avoid a veneration of rocks can be seen in the liturgical references to Jerusalem, as well as in the openness of Jerusalem. Judaism views Jerusalem not as an object of worship but as a vehicle of divine commandment and divine presence. The Holy City is more an opening than an entity; contrary to the Muslims, who allow only Muslims into Mecca, the Jews open the Holy City to all who wish to worship there in peace. This stance is precisely the opposite of idolatry.

With regard to other issues raised, let me turn first to the one deemed "most important": does one who rejects "the biblical testimony" have "no basis for rejecting murder absolutely"? This question applies to anyone — Christian, Muslim, or Jew — who views the prohibition against murder as something that comes from G-d, and not from international opinion, human decency, or rational deduction, all of which played into the hands of the Nazis. The key word here is "absolute," which means regardless of universal reason, personal inclination, cultural convention, and other ideals that Auschwitz has shown to be utterly bankrupt. If G-d does not command me, from beyond the ontological totality, not to murder my neighbor, then why — and in the name of what — should I refrain, if it is profitable, expedient, and I can get away with it? So far I have heard no real answer to this question, no viable alternative to the *divine* prohibition against murder, which makes it an *absolute* prohibition *absolutely* incumbent upon me, regardless of cultural context or personal inclination. Invoking the divine prohibition, moreover, has nothing to do with sophomoric systems of reward and punishment in an "afterlife"; rather, it has to do with a metaphysical connection that imposes upon me an absolute responsibility, regardless of contexts and contingencies.

Do we really need a holy land to determine such a connection? Yes, we do. Those of us who are made of earth and who dwell in space and time need just such a symbol, just such a sanctified earth, to remind us of the commandment to sanctify life. The sanctity of the land does not remove the limits of justification — precisely the opposite: because the sanctity is rooted in the commandment, it imposes limits on what can be justified in the Israelis' treatment of the Palestinians, as well as the Palestinians' treatment of the Israelis. Indeed, this notion of limit is crucial, as the limitations placed upon the land — with respect both to its borders and to its treatment — parallel the limitations placed upon our actions toward our fellow human beings. The absence of limitations characterized the discourse of the Nazis, for whom there were no divinely commanded absolutes. The Nazis did not commit the unimaginable — they committed everything imaginable, for the imagination was their only limit.

As for a person "who feels strongly committed to living as a Jew, but who does not necessarily believe that a metaphysical meaning accrues to the State of Israel," according to the traditional, halakhic premise I adopt, such a person is most certainly *not* "outside the Jewish fold." But it is a fold of responsibility, not of privilege. Anyone who is born Jewish enters the world with all the responsibilities of any Jew, regardless of whether he or she accepts those responsibilities. Similarly, Judaism cannot be anything anyone wants it to be, according to the opinion of just any Jew, from Karl Marx to Menachem Schneerson. Judaism can no more do without the Covenant of Torah — and therefore of the land — than Christianity can do without the doctrine of the Trinity or the incarnation.

This is not to preclude pluralism or questions or challenges. Indeed, Judaism encourages questions and challenges, even challenges to the One who sanctifies the land as a holy land. The Talmud, for instance, presents *all* the arguments, and not just the prevailing arguments, on any given issue. Precisely because Judaism is pluralistic, the Land of Israel is itself pluralistic, allowing room for religious freedom, including freedom for non-Jews, and a haven to *every* Jew. There can be no stronger affirmation of pluralism, nor can such pluralism be found anywhere else in the Middle East. Of all the religions of Abraham, Judaism is the most pluralistic, insisting, as it does, that one need not be an adherent of Judaism to have a place with the Holy One or to have a place in the Holy Land. This difference is definitive between the Jewish state and the Arab Muslim countries. It is also at the heart of the Israeli-Palestinian conflict. Whereas many Jews have no problem with a Muslim presence in the Jewish state, many Palestinians have a serious problem with a Jewish presence in the future Palestinian state.

Finally, from the perspective of Judaism, *anyone* can become a Jew; Judaism thus avoids the pitfalls of nationalism and ethnocentrism. The Jew "who feels strongly committed to living as a Jew" simply because of culture or birth must think of "being Jewish" either in ethnocentric or in nationalistic terms. If he or she embraces a distinctively Jewish state, it must be in ethnic or nationalistic terms; if he or she embraces a universal humanity opposed to ethnicity or nationalism, that one must reject the distinctively Jewish state in the name of human egalitarianism. Indeed, apart from ethnocentric and nationalistic self-interest, for such a Jew there is no particular reason why the Jews should not simply be absorbed into the fabric of a benign humanity. Nor is there any reason to make peace with one's enemy if killing the enemy is more expedient.

8. Between a Dangerous Memory and a Memory in Danger: The Israeli-Palestinian Struggle from a Christian Post-Holocaust Perspective

Didier Pollefeyt

In contemporary Jewish thought, the legitimacy of the State of Israel is mainly defended out of the need for Jewish political self-determination, particularly following upon the tragic situation of utter powerlessness during the Holocaust in Europe. According to the influential Jewish theologian Emil Fackenheim, Jews have the holy obligation "not to give Hitler a posthumous victory."[1] They may not carry out what Hitler failed to do: destroy Judaism and its ethical message. After Auschwitz, Jewish survival has itself become sacred, a moral — even religious — obligation.

The logic behind this approach is certainly understandable and legitimate: no people can ignore concern for their safety. One can refer here to the post–World War II critique of Jewish victims of the Holocaust for having allowed themselves to be led as "sheep to the slaughter" in Auschwitz.[2] One cannot criticize the Jewish people for being too passive in confrontation with anti-Jewish violence and, at the same time, reject their efforts to establish a safe social and political space. To continue choosing or undergoing powerlessness as a community would be completely immoral for the Jewish people, both in light of their catastrophic history in Europe and in light of the current and unremitting death threats made by some Arab peoples to the State of Israel.

1. Emil L. Fackenheim, *To Mend the World: Foundations of Future Jewish Thought* (New York: Schocken Books, 1982), p. 10.
2. Hannah Arendt, *The Jew as Pariah: Jewish Identity and Politics in the Modern Age* (New York: Grove Press, 1978), pp. 246-48.

While the legitimacy of the State of Israel and the entrance of the Jews upon the political scene are certainly not being questioned, one can nonetheless discuss an underlying ethical and theological frame of thought that is often employed in legitimating this political coming into being. In Fackenheim's thinking, Jewish survival simply becomes a witness for the Good against the forces of Evil in the world. In this Manichaean scheme of thought, the distinction between authenticity (loyalty) and inauthenticity (betrayal) is often theologically and ethically redefined in terms of an either-or: unconditional support for Israel or the posing of a threat to Israel's very right to exist. A critique of the politics of the State of Israel becomes almost completely absent or impossible to conceive.

At this point, it immediately becomes clear how complex the relationship can be between Holocaust studies and the Israeli-Palestinian debate, especially for a Christian scholar. As a Christian Holocaust scholar, one can devote oneself to the correction and eradication of anti-Jewish elements in Christian theology and praxis, and one can engage in Jewish-Christian dialogue as a moral and theological response to the Holocaust. This response will imply the recognition of the *historical* and *theological* legitimacy of the claims of the Jewish people on the *Land* of Israel. In this way, one can build up trust and even restore relations between Judaism and Christianity on the individual and the institutional levels — relations that have been disrupted for many centuries mainly because of religious and theological arrogance of a powerful Christian majority.

But when it comes to a *political* discussion on the *State* of Israel, some Jewish partners in dialogue expect Christian engagement in post-Holocaust interreligious dialogue to translate automatically into unconditional support for the politics of the State of Israel. Even more, some Jewish partners in dialogue assume that because of the Holocaust — and especially because of the collective guilt of Christendom for the Holocaust, in which all Christians participate — Christians should unconditionally support the State of Israel and all its political positions.[3] This a priori political support for the State of Israel then becomes a kind of litmus test for the trustworthiness of Christians after Auschwitz. A Christian Holocaust scholar who dares to nuance this scheme will run the risk of being depicted

---

3. See my contribution "Forgiveness after the Holocaust," in *After-Words: Post-Holocaust Struggles with Forgiveness, Reconciliation, Justice*, ed. David Patterson and John K. Roth (Seattle: University of Washington Press, 2004), pp. 55-69, esp. pp. 65-66.

as unreliable, as someone who has not overcome antisemitism sufficiently and who cannot be trusted with regard to the safety of future Jewish generations. This suspicion can easily lead to the accusation that one is opening the gate for a new Holocaust against the Jewish people. Not only Christian scholars run risks when they engage in discussion about the future of the State of Israel. Anyone who enters this discussion — as a scholar, as a Jewish, Christian, or Muslim believer, as a politician, or as a civilian — will have to take a stand about that matter. Doing so, however, means that the individual then risks being judged and even condemned as loyal or disloyal to this or that ideological or nationalistic perspective.

The point of departure for my position is to reject Manichaean patterns of post-Holocaust thought that choose automatically to characterize any criticism of Jewish political self-determination as evil. Instrumentalizing the Holocaust for political ends, this Manichaean impulse alleges that criticism of Jewish political self-determination constitutes a betrayal of the victims of the Holocaust. The crucial flaw of this outlook is that such instrumentalization of the Holocaust can ultimately lead to indifference about the liberation of others — in particular, the Palestinian other. My thesis is that Manichaean uses of the Holocaust are disloyal to the legacy of the Holocaust and the solidarity that this legacy demands for *all* victims in the world, non-Jews as well as Jews. Furthermore, my analysis is driven by the idea that being a victim of past evil does not automatically immunize oneself from the risk of becoming a perpetrator in the future. Paradoxical though it may seem from a Manichaean perspective on the Holocaust, my stance is grounded in a moral and theological concern to protect both the memory of the Holocaust and Jewish survival. The ongoing ideological reconstruction of the Holocaust as an argument in blind support of contemporary Israeli politics is becoming a new source of criticism and rejection of the Holocaust. Such reconstructions are also serving as a source of renewed antisemitism, not only in the minds of some extremely dangerous Arab terrorists, but — perhaps even worse — in the minds of many "ordinary" people throughout the world. My stance intends to combat both of those unfortunate and dangerous tendencies.

My position entails preserving a delicate balance between honoring the memory of the Holocaust and entering into political history. While I wholeheartedly recognize that the future of the Jewish people can be guaranteed only by having a state, I also argue that Jewish selfhood should ulti-

mately be bound up with the liberation struggle of others.[4] Becoming politically powerful is suspect when, in the course of acquiring that power,
others are victimized. If the Jewish people do not allow themselves to be
challenged by the memory of their own powerlessness, then the danger of
hardening oneself to the suffering of others unfolds. If such hardening
takes place in Jewish life, it becomes increasingly difficult for Jews to act
ethically in ways that reflect the deepest awareness of their history of suffering, their biblical tradition of respect for the stranger, and the moral lessons offered by the Holocaust.

Despite having persecuted Jewish people both religiously and socially through its anti-Judaism, perhaps Christianity — particularly
through the contributions of Christian liberation theology — could help
to set Judaism back on the path of its own traditions of an exodus from
slavery and a prophetic "no!" against injustice and idolatry. In this way
Christianity would challenge Judaism to recapture vital aspects of its own
history. Admittedly, these suggestions are risky. They can be seen as a sign
of Christian arrogance and thus neutralized. True interreligious dialogue,
however, presupposes a kind of elementary symmetrical relationship between partners in dialogue. In dialogue of this kind, Christians can learn
from Jews, and Jews can learn from Christians — even if, for historical and
moral reasons, Christians are to be the first to listen and learn, and Jews are
to be the first to speak and to teach. In such symmetrical dialogue, however, Christians can also, at certain points, serve to mirror to their Jewish
partners the idea that the Jewish people can be true to their own biblical
values only by showing solidarity with the liberation struggle of others.
The Jewish people must be prepared to cooperate toward ending the ongoing spiral of violence in the Middle East. Self-determination can never be
an end in itself, neither is it ever unambiguous. It is merely an intermediate
stopping place along the way to liberation, or, to use Nelson Mandela's
phrase, on "the long walk to freedom."[5] Without the guidance provided by
ethics and by a passionate feeling of solidarity with all who suffer, power

4. See three works by Mark Ellis: *Toward a Jewish Theology of Liberation: The Uprising
and the Future* (Maryknoll, N.Y.: Orbis Books, 1989), *Ending Auschwitz: The Future of Jewish
and Christian Life* (Louisville, Ky.: Westminster John Knox Press, 1994), and *Toward a Jewish
Theology of Liberation: The Challenge of the Twenty-First Century* (Waco, Tex.: Baylor University Press, 2004).

5. See Nelson Mandela, *Long Walk to Freedom: The Autobiography of Nelson Mandela*
(Boston: Little Brown, 1994).

on its own — even power exercised for the sake of survival — creates new evils and signifies a tragic end to the hope for the full liberation of all.

Yigal Amir, a young Orthodox Jewish citizen of Israel, assassinated the Israeli prime minister Yitzhak Rabin on November 4, 1995. Rabin had dared to go against an established and even sacralized distinction between the "good Jew" and the "bad Palestinian" and had instead reconnected strongly with the biblical tradition of respect for the stranger as bearer, par excellence, of the image of God. As an astute politician and experienced soldier, Rabin also realized that a military defeat can best be avoided by making peace while one is strong. With the 1993 handshake between Rabin and Yasser Arafat on the lawn of the White House in Washington, D.C., the end of a downward spiral of violence — in the course of which Jewish Israelis had served both as victimizers and victims — seemed to be at hand. For the first time in the history of the Middle East, a hopeful perspective was opened for a lasting peace between Israelis and Palestinians. Rabin's words expressed the hope: "We who have fought against you, the Palestinians — we say to you today in a loud and clear voice: Enough of blood and tears. Enough. . . . We, like you, are people who want to build a home, to plant a tree, to love, live side by side with you — in dignity, in empathy, as human beings, as free men."[6]

By murdering Rabin, Amir had attempted to reinstate the certainty and validity of the Manichaean pattern of "Jews *against* Palestinians," but paradoxically, Amir's action pointed in the opposite direction. It led numerous Jewish Israelis to the shocking realization that evil could color *their* narrative, too. For the whole world to see, Amir's act falsified the ethical and theological framework he sought to defend. His crime was essentially inspired by a fear of the universal character of Jewish ethics — more precisely, by the fact that the Jewish covenant can be fully realized only when one accepts the concept that Jews and Palestinians share a single destiny and that the question is only one of how best to share this destiny in the most human way possible.

Rabin's murder was a hateful protest against Israel's attempt to set an end to the spiral of Palestinian-Israeli violence. While one can point to the Orthodox religious background of Amir, one should also note that his ba-

---

6. Yitzhak Rabin, "Remarks by Prime Minister Yitzhak Rabin on the Occasion of the Signing of the Israeli-Palestinian Declaration of Principles, Washington, September 13, 1993." The full text is available online at http://www.mfa.gov.il/mfa/archive/peace+process/1993/.

sic convictions were shared — whether explicitly or in milder forms — by Jews from extremely disparate religious and political backgrounds. We should not socially and politically isolate or marginalize Amir as "an extremist exception," as some Jewish commentators tried to do. Such efforts reflected how the wider political community in Israel sometimes attempted to shift blame from itself and avoided confronting the degeneration of fundamental ethical norms into the ethnocentric politics of self-interest.

But to this line of criticism a sharp warning must be added. Earlier in this chapter, I emphasized prophetic criticism of current Israeli politics, as well as a post-Auschwitz exhortation to radicalize and universalize a Jewish ethic that welcomes the stranger. Jewish victimhood carries with it no moral prerogatives. The murder of Rabin by a fellow Jew and citizen was shocking proof that evil does not merely lurk in the other but also is in oneself. Christians might be tempted to exploit Rabin's murder by one-sided finger-pointing at the Jewish people with respect to Israeli conduct in the Israeli-Palestinian conflict.[7] When the Christian world today finds itself so easily incensed on behalf of the lot of Palestinians in the region, it should first confront its own moral anger. Christians who think that the Middle East problem is merely a Jewish problem forget, in fact, to confront themselves with their own history of centuries of Christian anti-Judaism, a history that has made Jewish life so problematic. In other words, if Christians — especially those living in Europe — are indignant only about the historical wrongs of Israelis and not also about their own history of anti-Jewish wrongs, then they are not much different from those Jews who see only the historical wrong that was done to them and fail to see the wrong that Israelis themselves inflict. Christians have no right to level ethical questions at Israeli Jews without at the same time *and with equal urgency* becoming engaged in looking for a solution to the centuries-old and legitimate question of Jewish (in)security. The one-sided European indignation at Israeli injustice to the Palestinians should thus be a reminder and challenge for Christians to face up to their own historical responsibility for the drama in the Middle East. When Christian peace movements lose sight of this responsibility, their interventions in the political debate regarding the Middle East are arrogant, and thus they lose credibility.

7. Darrell J. Fasching, *The Ethical Challenge of Auschwitz and Hiroshima: Apocalypse or Utopia?* (Albany: State University of New York Press, 1993), pp. 157-60.

A key part of the difficulty and paradox of the Israeli-Palestinian conflict is that both communities are at the same time a minority and majority.[8] Palestinians are an alien minority within Israel, but simultaneously Israeli Jews remain an alien minority within an inimical Arab world that is part-Christian, part-Muslim. The Middle East is no simple story of the strong and evil Israel over against the good and weak Arabs, as many people in Europe think. The Middle East is an unfathomable world of cogwheels within cogwheels, of secret drawers that hide a complex network of secret alliances and inter-Arab plots — plots that have often victimized the Palestinian people themselves! When the Jew welcomes the Palestinian-as-stranger without the reverse happening, the scene is inevitably set for what amounts to suicide for Israel and perhaps for the Jewish people as a whole. Christian Holocaust scholars have naturally not resigned themselves to this tragic situation. Rather, they have tried to help find a way toward a future in which human beings can choose to live in a shared world where there is mutual recognition among peoples.

There is no way out of the ongoing conflict if one adopts one-sided positions. Some Christian voices currently argue that if Israelis were to resolve the Palestinian question, they would win recognition and respect in the Middle East. Such statements not only fail to appreciate the enormity of anti-Jewish sentiment in the Middle East but also claim that the root causes of Middle Eastern tensions are solely a "Jewish problem." Such "logic" makes the Jewish people the exclusive cause of all anti-Jewish resentment. At the same time, such claims free the surrounding Arab world from the responsibility of fully engaging themselves in the challenging issues surrounding a peaceful resolution of the conflict in the Middle East. Such one-sided analyses unnecessarily add fuel to already inflamed situations. Just as Israelis needed to bring self-critical moral reasoning to bear on the murderous act of the fundamentalist Jew Yigal Amir, so Muslims must speak out self-critically as well. Muslims all over the world, both individually and collectively, must condemn the blind terrorist violence by Islamic fundamentalist groups and must show solidarity with innocent victims, Jews as well as non-Jews. In many cases, the silence of the Muslim world makes it guilty by omission. Here, Christians have specific responsibilities to develop Christian-Muslim relations alongside Jewish-Christian

8. G. H. Cohen Stuart, *Een bevrijdend woord uit Jeruzalem? In gesprek met Joodse en Palestijnse bevrijdingstheologie* (The Hague: Boekencentrum, 1991).

dialogue; they must promote, as well, a trialogue among Jews, Christians, and Muslims.

The murderous suicide bombings by Muslim extremist groups such as Hamas also indicate how extremely fragile an ethical option has become for Israelis. These attacks legitimate military responses — not as ends in themselves, but as a political means that is sometimes (yet always in due proportion) necessary. Nevertheless, a choice needs to be made between two fundamentally different scenarios. In the first scenario, Jews as well as Palestinians run the risk of immersing themselves in comfort-giving-but-violent schemes in which "the bad Palestinian" or "the bad Jew" retaliates in kind for past hurts. The repetition of such acts undermines possibilities for an ongoing peace process. The danger now becomes real that suicide bombers will have assured themselves, in some tragic way, of a posthumous victory. In the second scenario, Jews and Palestinians will be able to condemn evil together, mourn as one, and allow their hurts to heal. Real security is guaranteed more fully through having good relations with one's neighbors, rather than by two parties maintaining an all-consuming spiral of violence.

What can be the specific contribution of a (Christian) Holocaust scholar to this peacemaking process? Holocaust scholars should start with an adequate historical-critical analysis of the Holocaust. The Holocaust happened in a very specific historical context. It was a historical event with unique contextual characteristics. This historical analysis forms a critique of easy comparison between the Holocaust and the political conduct of the State of Israel. Israeli actions aimed at securing Israel's existence are in no way to be equated with the Nazis' genocidal deeds. Holocaust scholars can show how drawing such analogies is completely wrong, both historically and morally.

Holocaust scholars, however, should rethink some basic assumptions regarding the forces that produced the Holocaust. Study of the Holocaust leads one to examine universal human and social phenomena. As I have argued elsewhere, Manichaeism informed the basic structure of the Nazi political system.[9] Manichaeism is the radical ontological separation be-

9. Didier Pollefeyt, "The Kafkaesque World of the Holocaust: Paradigmatic Shifts in the Interpretation of the Holocaust," in *Ethics after the Holocaust: Perspectives, Critiques, and Responses,* ed. John K. Roth (St. Paul, Minn.: Paragon House, 1999), pp. 210-42; Didier Pollefeyt, ed., *Incredible Forgiveness: Christian Ethics between Fanaticism and Reconciliation* (Leuven: Peeters, 2004).

tween good and evil, as well as the attribution of good to oneself and evil to the other, a movement in which one forgets (and thereby activates!) the evil in oneself. Even if the Holocaust is not reproduced historically in the Israeli-Palestinian conflict, a fundamentally Manichaean structure has reproduced itself there, creating new forms of violence in new contexts, with regard to the actions both of Israelis and of Palestinians. Manichaeism is both the consequence of and an "answer" to an individual or social situation of a violation of trust, giving "destructive entitlement" to its victims in an endless circle of self-fulfilling prophecies.[10] Only through a process of deconstructing Manichaeism can a real horizon of peace be created for the Israeli-Palestinian conflict. Holocaust scholars should not ally themselves unthinkingly with the politics of the State of Israel as such; rather, they should side with the victims of all conflicts — including those in Israel and Palestine. Through this embrace of all victims, Holocaust scholars should help groups in conflict empathize with one another — that is, help them to see how the other arrived at his or her position, including any resort to violence. This perspective in no way excuses violence but can help each party to understand and ultimately de-diabolize the other as each reassesses its own position.

In her book *Eichmann in Jerusalem,* Hannah Arendt broke with the Holocaust paradigm of Manichaeism.[11] She also analyzed the origins of totalitarianism.[12] It may now be time to reconsider her proposed political solution for the Israeli-Palestinian problem, a proposal emerging — not accidentally — from her analyses of binationalism.[13] With regard to the Israeli-Palestinian conflict, binationalism is a proposed solution based on the idea that Israel should be transformed into a secular-constitutional state with both Jews and Arabs as its national citizens. It can be summarized in the saying "One Land for Two Peoples."[14] Binationalism is to be

---

10. Ivan Boszormenyi-Nagy and Barbara R. Krasner, *Between Give and Take: A Clinical Guide to Contextual Therapy* (New York: Brunner Mazel Publishers, 1986), p. 415.

11. See Hannah Arendt, *Eichmann in Jerusalem: A Report on the Banality of Evil* (New York: Viking Press, 1963).

12. See Hannah Arendt, *The Origins of Totalitarianism,* 5th ed. (New York: Harcourt, Brace & Jovanovich, 1973).

13. Amnon Raz-Krakotzkin, "Bi-nationalism and Jewish Identity: Hannah Arendt and the Question of Palestine," in *Hannah Arendt in Jerusalem,* ed. Steven E. Aschheim (Berkeley: University of California Press, 2001), pp. 165-80.

14. Among the most famous proponents of binationalism in the United States and Is-

distinguished from the more familiar "two-state solution," according to which two states, one Israeli and the other Palestinian, coexist side by side. It is also to be distinguished from the current situation in which one established State of Israel coexists next to scattered Palestinian areas in what are known as the Occupied Territories.

Binationalism embodies a value system that aims at coexistence between peoples and communities that live on the same territory — in this case, the territory of historical Palestine — on the basis of equality and respect for the distinctive characteristics of each group. This system is the opposite of a philosophy of separation that informs the current conflict between Israelis and Palestinians in essential ways. The philosophy of separation is Manichaean: the less contact with the other, the better; "they with them, we with us."[15] Endorsing binationalism implies a radical change in the political approach to the Israeli-Palestinian conflict for both Israeli and Palestinian authorities. This approach departs from Manichaean ethics and politics. Instead of two conflicting parties, each appealing to international law as arbiter, Israelis and Palestinians accept each other's moral and juridical rights as members of a single polity. Two historically persecuted minorities now become full citizens of a new state, whether that state is to be called "Israel" (as is assumed here), or whether another name is to be chosen for the binational entity. Instead of engaging in discussions regarding a division of territories, both Israelis and Palestinians living within a binational state come to share ownership, rights, and privileges in such areas as law, education, the economy, and so on. A binational solution demands a shift from two competing blocs (at war with one another or subject to terrorist acts by one another) toward individual citizens and groups all living within one polity, all asking for justice meted out by one court of judges committed to protecting all inhabitants of the land on the basis of universal, democratic, and constitutionally guaranteed civil rights.

This defense of binationalism is in line with my critique of Nazism's Manichaean thought and violence during the Holocaust. Binationalism entails an end to an "ethics of war" between conflicting parties fighting for "the good" and against "the evil" in acts that result in more and more

---

rael are the Palestinian American writer Edward Said and Azmi Bishara, a Palestinian-Israeli member of the Israeli Knesset.

15. Michel Warschawski, *Israël-Palestine: Le défi binational* (Paris: Seuil, 2001), p. 33.

deaths on both sides. It replaces Israeli military power and Palestinian martyrdom by an "ethic of the legal claimant," who, according to Lama Abu-Odeh, is "rights-obsessed, constitution-fixated, friend of the lawyer, unwelcome but tireless visitor to the courtroom."[16] It brings the same weights and measures to both Israelis and Palestinians: ethics and justice. According to Odeh, "The argument for binationalism is that it would force both parties to engage in each other's discourses: force the Israelis to rise up to their claim of being an island of liberal democracy in the middle of an authoritarian desert, and force the Palestinians to give up the fantasy of military triumph in a war waged across the borders."[17]

Enormous problems exist for such a social and political model, several of which account for the fact that presently there is not much political support for this proposed solution to the conflict. A binational proposal, for example, demands a (constant) redistribution of the economic wealth, something that the region lacks at present. Binationalism is not, however, a merely romanticized model for peacemaking. It would face many problems, but at least it has the ability to diminish or prevent (but not necessarily to eliminate completely) violence among the citizens of the area in question. With its critique of the violence inherent in Manichaeism, binationalism can be an answer to the post-Holocaust imperative not to hand Hitler posthumous victories.

The goal of this book is not primarily to discuss concrete political solutions to the Israeli-Palestinian conflict but, rather, to scrutinize the role of Holocaust studies as it confronts this problematic situation. Research in Holocaust studies on the role of memory has shown how remembrance of the past is never a pure reproduction of the historical facts but always a reconstruction of those facts, one that reveals not only history itself but also the assumptions of those who reconstruct it. Such a reconstruction is also influenced by events that have taken place during the time that elapses between the original historical event and the contemporary moment. These factors mean that new post-Holocaust political agendas can enter the scene according to the ways that remembrance of the Holocaust has been reconstructed. The more historical distance grows between the context in which

16. Lama Abu-Odeh, "The Case for Binationalism," in *Boston Review: A Political and Literary Forum,* December 2001/January 2002, online at http://bostonreview.net/BR26.6/abu-odeh.html.

17. "Lama Abu-Odeh Replies," in *Boston Review: A Political and Literary Forum,* December 2001/January 2002, online at http://bostonreview.net/BR26.6/abu-odeh2.html.

the Holocaust occurred and our contemporary context, the less it is evident how we are to draw an immediate line between the Holocaust and concrete, contemporary political or moral issues. Just as one cannot draw a self-evident *comparison* between the Nazi genocide and the current treatment of Palestinians by Israelis in the twenty-first century, so one cannot draw an absolute *moral distinction* between the Nazi genocide and concrete decisions made in the politics of the State of Israel today. What should be noted in these cases is the risk of a "fundamentalist" reading of the meaning of the Holocaust (either in the form of an outright negation of Jewish national aspirations or in the extreme forms of Zionism that would seemingly be legitimated by the Holocaust). Holocaust studies should criticize such interpretations of the Holocaust, both those offered by the enemies of the legitimate struggle of the Jewish people to survive politically today and the forms of Israeli politics that would constitute an insult to and an instrumentalization of the legacy of the Holocaust's victims.

Such a critique of the ideological (mis)use of the Holocaust is also an important antidote to the "Holocaust fatigue" that is growing — at least in Europe — as a consequence of such (mis)use of the Holocaust.[18] "Holocaust fatigue" refers to a phenomenon of people responding with irritation, resistance, cynicism, or indifference when the Holocaust is brought up in politics, social life, the media, educational settings, or daily conversations. Arguably, this fatigue is a softer anti-Jewish phenomenon than is found in hard and explicit Holocaust denial; nevertheless, such fatigue is as dangerous, if not more dangerous, with regard to the future of the Jewish people. Among other things, "Holocaust fatigue" is the result of a certain canonization of the history in the Holocaust, which fixes the meaning of the Holocaust to serve certain clear or (seemingly) hidden moral, ideological, or political agendas. Unless these mistakes are corrected and the memory of the Holocaust is not allowed any longer to be "a dangerous memory" for the politics of the State of Israel, Israel itself can become a danger for the memory of the Holocaust ("a memory in danger").

18. See Tzvetan Todorov, *Les abus de la mémoire* (Paris: Arléa, 1998).

Contributors' Questions for Didier Pollefeyt

You urge the creation of a binational state. How would a binational state, presumably including Hamas and Islamic Jihad, be peaceable? Are many Muslim and Jewish religious leaders prepared to live in one state? In attempting to avoid Manichaeism, you abandon hope for a resolution that would result in the creation of two states. But might you be demonizing two-state solutions? Might not "two" embody the spirit of "one," insofar as the states in question would work toward a confederation that both allows for ethnic majorities to exist in each and also clears a path toward reconciliation in the moral sphere? *Must* "two" connote (a binary) opposition?

You suggest that both Israelis and Palestinians are Manichaean in their representations of each other. But is there a moral equivalence here? Are not Palestinians more radically Manichaean in their blatantly antisemitic rhetoric, including Holocaust denial? Does this practice not send warning signals of genocide that Jews must take seriously? Is it not of critical importance for there to be a state, for the first time in 1,900 years, in which Jews constitute a majority? Given the demographics of the region in question, can Jews feel safe in a binational state in which they would inevitably become a minority?

Response by Didier Pollefeyt

As the violence in Palestinian-Israeli conflict continues without an apparent end, an increasing number of people in the world are thinking that a separationist two-state idea is unable to produce a realistic and effective solution. The two-state idea to divide the contested territory into two nation-states on ethnic grounds seems not to be realizable because it fails to take into account either the complexity of the conflict or the degree of intertwining that exists and will continue to exist between the conflicting parties in the region. The goal of my essay is not to demonize the two-state solution as such but, rather, to look for alternatives that perhaps can bring peace closer in the area. At the same time, my approach is a critique vis-à-vis the policy of the isolation of the Palestinian territories by the Israeli government as an (admittedly) excessive variant of a two-state solution. It is not understandable how a two-state solution can be defended at the same time that a fence/wall is being built to separate the two peoples. One Israeli journalist proclaims: "You can erect all the walls in the world here but you won't be able to overcome the fact that there is only one aquifer here and the same air and that all the streams run into the same sea. You won't be able to overcome the fact that this country will not tolerate a border in its midst."[1]

The former deputy major of Jerusalem, Meron Benvenisti, further compares the Israeli situation with the situation in South Africa, where an attempt to create a "homeland for the blacks" failed to solve the problems

1. Ari Shavit, *Ha'aretz*, August 8, 2003.

between blacks and whites. When it became clear that this scenario of "decolonization" was made to expel or transfer blacks, the proposal collapsed from within and was condemned by the international community. As the possibility for a two-state solution fades in the Middle East, there is an opportunity to advance new ideas as to how to escape the bloody impasse by creating an alternative conceptual universe. Originally the enfant terrible among the solutions for the Middle East, the democratic binational solution is moving more toward the center of contemporary discussions; it is being discussed by people from different ideological and political backgrounds — not only from the Palestinian side, but from the Israeli side as well. According to Benvenisti, "[We Israelis] should start to think differently, talk differently. Not to seize on this ridiculous belief in a Palestinian state or in the fence. Because in the end we are going to be a Jewish minority here. And the problems that your children and my grandchildren are going to have to cope with are the same ones that de Klerk faced in South Africa. The paradigm, therefore, is the binational one. That's the direction. That's the conceptual universe we have to get used to."[2]

A binational solution is a combination — possible in many variants — of unity with diversity, of "one" and "two." For this reason, most modern binationalist proposals involve a form of federalism or the recognition that the state can comprise a number of self-governing regions (or "states"), united by a central ("federal") government. This federal perspective is not a European solution for an Arab problem but a solution that has been adopted in many parts of the world, such as in the United States, Australia, Brazil, Canada, Germany, and India. For historical Palestine, it could mean a division of the land into Jewish and Arab cantons.

Binationalism is an alternative to a two-state solution, which connotes, in my view, an unfortunate binary opposition that binationalism does not entail. The two-state *non*solution is a self-fulfilling prophecy. It is a solution for the Manichaean mind trapped in binary thinking. It is at one and the same time the ideal and the impossible solution. It is the ideal solution because it divides the conflicting parties, but at the same time it is the impossible solution because neither party trusts the other enough to realize it. Many people in the Muslim world do not begrudge Israel a safe and independent future, but the two-state solution is not acceptable to most Muslims. Furthermore, an independent Palestinian state would pose

2. Meron Benvenisti, *Ha'aretz*, August 8, 2003.

a greater security threat to Israelis than a binational solution because such a state would house millions of Palestinians who have endless claims that Israel cannot meet. In this sense, the two-state solution fails to provide long-term security for Israel. A two-state solution is presented by many as the only way out of the conflict, yet the violence continues day after day, and a two-state solution is not likely to change that state of affairs.

In the summer of 2005 Ariel Sharon, the Israeli prime minister at the time, decided unilaterally to evacuate twenty-one settlements in Gaza and the West Bank. Without any consultation with the Palestinian president Mahmoud Abbas, Sharon demanded that the Palestinians disarm Hamas and Islamic Jihad. The evacuation from Gaza was eventually completed "successfully," and the Palestinians celebrated. But this division of territories did not bring peace to the region. The Gaza Strip is one of the most densely populated areas in the world. The 2006 population stands at close to one and a half million, giving the region a population density of 3,750 people per square kilometer (9,712 people per square mile).[3] As of this writing, Israel continues to control the borders and the airspace of Gaza. Gaza is, in this sense, an immense open-air prison. Unemployment in this region is over 40 percent. Almost 66 percent of the inhabitants have to live on less than two dollars a day. In this context, it can be predicted that organizations such as Hamas and Islamic Jihad will continue to receive the support of many Palestinians. By withdrawing from Gaza, Sharon put the ball in the Palestinians' court, but in this context, Palestinian authorities will not be able to stop suicide attacks. Even more recently, Israel's war with Hezbollah means that Jewish settlements in the West Bank are not likely to be withdrawn. The "ideal" two-state solution continues to be the impossible solution.

The binational approach tries to bring another kind of resolution to the conflict by directly critiquing the process of mutual diabolization — the engine driving the conflict — and the two-state solution that is bedeviled by that process. It is characteristic of this process of mutual diabolization that both parties to the conflict situate evil solely in the other. Meanwhile, goodness is situated in oneself. Each selects from the identity of the other all those aspects that sustain and strengthen the construction of an evil "other"; at the same time, each party avoids self-criticism. In this way, both parties can act violently in the name of the Good.

3. Online at http://en.wikipedia.org/wiki/List_of_countries_by_population_density.

The question posed to me, "Are not Palestinians more radically Manichaean?" is a typical Manichaean question presented from the Jewish side. If Palestinians had contributed to this volume, some could have asked exactly the same question, but from the opposite perspective within a Manichaean worldview. The bottom line of these kinds of questions is: "You are more evil then I am," or "I have more reasons to mistrust and to violate you than you have to mistrust and to violate me." Israelis will always find reasons why the Palestinians are more Manichaean than they are, but at the same time Palestinians will always find more reasons why Israelis are more Manichaean than they. Of course, these reasons have some objective grounding; the other *is* to a certain degree Manichaean. The problem is not in the facts but in the selection and the one-sided reconstruction of these facts. In the course of time, so much evil and violence have happened, legitimized by these constructions on both sides, that it has become impossible to say who is more or less evil than the other. At this point, the discussion mainly shifts to the question as to who has started the violence and injustice, and who is "in the right."

Conflict resolution theories propose that these kinds of questions will never bring about peace but are themselves part of the problem. With regard to conflicts such as the one studied in this book, these theories argue for "multidirected partiality." Such a stance is not one that strives for unattainable objectivity but one that exerts effort toward a critical understanding of the perspectives of *all* the parties to a conflict. Instead of arguing who is most *evil*, my approach starts by attending to the legitimate *goods* that each party to the conflict wishes to protect: a safe future for its own people. In this approach, the question is not who is most evil but how one can do justice to a realization of the goods that each party wants to protect. This outlook criticizes evil on all sides. It recognizes and defends the need for a safe place for both the Jewish people and the Palestinian people. Because of the demographic situation, it argues for a binational state with equal rights for both Israeli Jews and Palestinians. If, as I have argued, it seems impossible to divide the land, then one state would give all the land to all the people. In fact, this solution is not extreme. It realistically accepts the undeniable fact that Israel and the Occupied Territories already form one single state sharing the same transportation network, the same telephone system, and the same international frontiers.

With the practical implementation of a binational state, many questions will arise. One central question is whether Jews can feel safe in a binational state in which they will inevitably become a minority. I understand the Israeli fear that large numbers of Palestinians would enter the binational state, making Israelis a protected but less than all-powerful minority. Social politics make clear, however, that richer citizens have enormous and uneven power in liberal-democratic states. Even if Israelis constitute a quantitative minority, in light of their much better economic situation, they would still exercise overwhelming power in the new state. Moreover, in a binational context, the actual central line of division between Israelis and Palestinians would be progressively replaced by many other lines of division; as in every other society, dividing lines would pivot around social class, worldview, gender, race, or local differences. From a socioeconomic perspective, the binational solution is more of a problem for Palestinians than for Israelis. Palestinians have reasons to fear that in one state in which they would be excluded from substantial economic and educational opportunities and goods, the international conflict will merely be transformed into internal economic and social strife between two peoples, strife that would now be more hidden from the international community. The binational solution must therefore be accompanied by a political program to foster social and political justice.

I understand that many Muslim and Jewish religious leaders are not prepared to live together in one state. Many Israelis and Palestinians have been educated to deny, distrust, and even hate each other to such an extent that recognizing the humanity of the other is a very big step to take within one generation. Yet in a democratic binational state, there would be no place for Hamas and Islamic Jihad — groups that feed on hate. Such extremist movements constitute a problem for *every* proposed solution to the conflict in the Middle East. The binational solution takes away the fertile soil of Manichaeism on which such movements flourish. Violence is the result of the absence of viable political alternatives to an unacceptable status quo. An important element of the binational solution is the call to the Palestinians to change drastically their politics of armed and violent struggle. When Israelis and Palestinians are treated on an equal basis under the law, fewer Palestinians will be motivated to blow themselves up; movements such as Hamas will become less popular when both sides realize that the fight is over and when they start to know each other in constructive ways.

A common home for Israelis and Palestinians cannot be built in one day. The process will be as long as it is transformative. It will probably take more time than the lengthy effort that has already been given — without positive results — to a proposed two-state solution. The binational solution cannot be imposed on people, but educational, juridical, economic, social, and political conditions can be created to favor it. Binationalism is an open, contextual, and always growing process. It will have to start with small steps and local initiatives by grassroots peace movements — but also with political movements on a national scale. I am convinced that political processes will lead in that direction. Here are some concrete examples of my thesis: the presence of a room for Muslim prayer in the Knesset (Israeli Parliament) and the idea to translate the Knesset Web site into Arabic.[4] And if the binational solution cannot be realized as a practical, on-the-ground possibility, it can at least expose the problems that a two-state solution faces and remain as a sign of promise for a better future in the Middle East.

Is binationalism loyal to the memory of the victims of the Holocaust? The Holocaust proved that Jews need a safe place. But it does not follow from the Holocaust that Jews deserve unconditionally to have a state established at the expense of another people. If every people in the world were to ask unconditionally for a national state, this world — with more then 5,000 peoples and only 200 nations — would end up embroiled in global nationalistic war.[5] The idea that for every people there needs to be a nation is more characteristic of nineteenth-century nationalism than of the internationalism of the twentieth-first century. The Holocaust was the outcome of the dangers of exclusive nationalism ("Ein Volk, ein Reich, ein Führer" [One people, one empire, one leader]). The effort to come to a more inclusive nationalism can be considered and experienced as a way to do justice to the memory of the victims of the Holocaust.

4. Online at http://www.knesset.gov.il/main/arb/home.asp.
5. Luc Reychler, "Het 5000-200 probleem: Enkele nota's over etnische en nationalistische conflicten," *Cahiers van het Centrum voor Vredesonderzoek* (Leuven) 30 (1991).

9. The Middle East Conflict, the Responsibility of History and Memory, and the American Jew

Myrna Goldenberg

We will have peace with the Arabs when they love their children more than they hate us.

Golda Meir

But for the Holocaust, the State of Israel would not have come into being in 1948. As Dennis Ross reminds us, "at the very time that the need for a haven for Jews was becoming more acute," the likely and logical safe harbor for Jews was less and less realizable. Ross succinctly summarizes Israel's pragmatic obsession with security and sovereignty: "The Holocaust, an unimaginable evil for the rest of the world, was an unspeakable reminder for the Jews of Palestine that the worst can happen; that weakness begets tragedy; that others can never be relied upon; and that they must have a state of their own."[1] Indeed, the Holocaust was unimagined by Jews and non-Jews. The establishment of the State of Israel was a late response to the tragedy and evil of Nazism, the indifference of the world, and the collusion of the British with the Arabs. Israel was — and still is — in the minds of many, many Jews, the permanent refuge that Jews did not have in the 1930s. And were it not for American support for the state, Israel would not have come into existence as it did in 1948. In the wake of the Holocaust, American Jewry rallied, both as political constituents and as private citizens, and helped to reshape the Middle East to include a nation-state for Jews.

1. Dennis Ross, *The Missing Peace: The Inside Story of the Fight for Middle East Peace* (New York: Farrar, Straus & Giroux, 2004), p. 18.

Besides being a safe haven for Jews everywhere, the State of Israel promised normalcy. Moreover, a Jewish state was the fruition of both the biblical covenant and secular sociopolitical ideals: Jews would never again be stateless or as vulnerable as they were in Europe from 1933 to 1945. In those early years, American Jewish support for Israel was strong and widespread though not unanimous. Indeed, with the exception of the non-Zionist American Council for Judaism, Jewish organizations were "galvanized . . . not only scared but determined."[2]

Whether it was welcomed as a religious, political, or ethical response to the Holocaust, Israel was, for the majority of American Jews, a dream come true — authentic, long-awaited, and just. The very fact of the State of Israel was a source of pride as well as security. As a Talmud Torah student in Brooklyn, I carried my little Jewish National Fund blue box (a *pushke*) from apartment to apartment and from building to building, collecting coins to buy every inch of Eretz Yisroel from the Arabs. I filled more than a few such *pushkes* and was proud of my contributions to Zionism. For decades, I carried the myth of a Zionist-*purchased* homeland. My vision of this ideal Jewish state was reinforced, even concretized, through popular literature, film, and music. Like many Jews and non-Jews, I was impressed with Leon Uris's *Exodus,* particularly the film with its unalloyed heroism and uncomplicated justice and magnificent musical score. That story and other fictionalized early versions of the Holocaust, such as John Hersey's *The Wall* and Fred Zinnemann's *The Search,* proved to me that my childlike trust and optimism were not misplaced. Contemporary Israeli writers continue to echo the early dream: Amos Oz, for example, put that vision into the mouth of the father in *Panther in the Basement,* who in 1947 holds fast to an ideal Israel: "[Israel] must evidently set a model of justice to the world, even toward the Arabs if they choose to stay and live here among us. Yes, despite everything the Arabs are doing to us, because of the people who are inciting them and egging them on, we will treat them with exemplary generosity, but definitely not out of weakness. When the free Hebrew State is finally established, no villain in the world will ever again dare to murder or humiliate Jews."[3]

2. Leonard Dinnerstein, *Antisemitism in America* (New York: Oxford University Press, 1994), p. 149.

3. Amos Oz, *Panther in the Basement,* trans. Nicholas de Lange (New York: Harcourt Brace, 1995), p. 19.

Generally, for most American Jews, the establishment of the State of Israel was a remarkable concrete response of the triumph over Nazism and the "Final Solution," of good over evil, of hope over despair, and of self-respect over shame. Indeed, a strong, just Israel helped restore American Jewish self-respect in the face of the shame of their impotence to influence the government to intervene against Hitler's Final Solution. And although the United States recognized Israel immediately, it actually offered no help to this fledgling state in its war of independence against all odds.[4] American Jews were called on as *private citizens* to support the new nation — and they did.

In recent decades, however, American Jewish responses to Israel and the Middle East conflict have become highly polarized and volatile, ranging from the shouts of "Never again!" to the cries of "Peace now!" and voices for and against disengagement from Gaza and the West Bank. For American Jews, the changing political and military situations of the Middle East are causes for hope or despair, sometimes alternatively. Sometimes framed as historical recitations of facts versus myths, the versions of the history of the region vary, and statements about the Israeli-Palestinian conflict are usually polemical. Not limited to reasoned and articulate arguments or acerbic cartoons in the press, opinions about Israelis and Palestinians are often expressed vigorously and uncivilly on college and university campuses, on Internet blog sites and Web sites, in supposedly unbiased television documentaries, even on the popular television series *West Wing*, and lately as strong-selling books.[5] The least disputed element of the arguments is the relationship of the establishment of the State of Israel to the Holocaust. Thus, consciously or otherwise, the entire subject of the Middle East conflict returns to the Holocaust, albeit somewhat circuitously and, astonishingly, ironically. (Ironically, in that extremes on both sides have invoked

---

4. According to Ross, the United States "allowed private assistance to flow to Israel, but would not provide direct military assistance for more than twenty years after Israel's founding" (*The Missing Peace*, p. 20).

5. To name a few: Phyllis Chesler, *The New Anti-Semitism: The Current Crisis and What We Must Do about It* (San Francisco: Jossey-Bass, 2003); Alan Dershowitz, *The Case for Israel* (Hoboken, N.J.: John Wiley & Sons, 2003); Abraham H. Foxman, *Never Again? The Threat of the New Anti-Semitism* (San Francisco: HarperSanFrancisco, 2004); Tony Kushner and Alisa Solomon, eds., *Wrestling with Zion: Progressive Jewish-American Responses to the Israeli-Palestinian Conflict* (New York: Grove Press, 2003); Ron Rosenbaum, ed., *Those Who Forget the Past: The Question of Anti-Semitism* (New York: Random House, 2004); and Ross, *The Missing Peace*.

Holocaust imagery and language to condemn the actions of the Israeli government in its treatment of Palestinians, on the one hand, and, on the other, to condemn Israeli policies that aimed at withdrawal from Gaza and from at least significant portions of the West Bank.) And although the Holocaust has been invoked less frequently than it had been during the first intifada, it has been conspicuous in antisemitic rants, especially from the Muslim world.[6] At some level, the Holocaust is thus the subtext of the responses of American Jews to the Israeli-Palestinian crisis.

I argue that a reasonable solution to the Israeli-Palestinian conflict is informed by the Holocaust, not only by its history, but also by respect for the moral imperatives that are embedded in that catastrophe. There needs to be a "both-and" solution: both Palestinian respect for Israeli security and Israeli respect for Palestinian desire for political integrity are essential to the permanent resolution of this conflict. A solution will take active and honest leadership — Israeli, Palestinian, and American. It will also take honest and substantial cooperation and support from the Arab "neighborhood" (300 million strong), as well as unequivocal European support in the negotiation process and outcome. A just solution will require control of the extremist Muslim factions that feed Arab/Palestinian anti-Zionism both in the Middle East and in Europe.

Though Jews have been more comfortable and politically assimilated in the United States than they were in any other nation in modern times, the American Jewish community was itself not entirely secure in the first half of the twentieth century. In the wake of the pogroms that brought millions of refugees to America at the turn of the century, Jews in America were subject to vocal and activist antisemitism that included the lynching of Leo Frank in 1915 and found expression in the activism of Henry Ford, Father Coughlin, Charles A. Lindbergh, Gerald L. K. Smith, and a sizable group of U.S. senators and congressmen. Many corporations and universities did not welcome Jews. Antisemitism was at "high tide" during the years of World War II,[7] and there was little happening in the United States

---

6. Consider, for example, the ominous words by Malaysian prime minister Mahathir bin Mohamad to 1.3 billion Muslims at the Organization of the Islamic Conference summit, October 2003: "The Europeans killed six million Jews out of 12 million, but today Jews rule the world by proxy. They get others to fight and die for them" (quoted in Kalman Sultanik, "The New Antisemitism," *Together,* August 2004, p. 7).

7. Leonard Dinnerstein, "Antisemitism at High Tide: World War II (1939-1945)," in *Antisemitism in America,* pp. 128-49.

to mitigate the concerns of American Jews about antisemitism, certainly not from the noninterventionist, obstructionist U.S. State Department. Clearly, American Jews were unprepared, except in isolated but conspicuous instances, to form a grassroots movement on behalf of Europe's Jews. Rabbi Stephen Wise and Peter Bergson (Hillel Kook) orchestrated very successful theatrical events and rallies but did not influence the government to alter its policy, open its borders, or bomb Auschwitz. Furthermore, the *New York Times'* anemic coverage of the Holocaust reflected the prevailing caution about raising the issue of antisemitism.[8] American Jewry responded feebly, and the government's response (i.e., no response) to the Holocaust left American Jewry in a confused, precarious state: America was safe for Jews, but within limits and not entirely; furthermore, American Jews could not take that safety for granted. The Holocaust proved that antisemitism was neither history nor abstraction.

Recent memory, coupled with the influx of Holocaust survivors and their impact on the American Jewish community, shaped a strong pro-Israel stance that has, over the decades, silenced or muted Jewish public criticism of Israel. Politically, since 1948, the U.S. government's support of Israel has been unwavering, not only because it is the only democracy in the Middle East, as well as the only nation in that region with whom we share Western values, but also because American Jews have been highly articulate and activist. Criticism of Israel, at virtually any level, whether stated by Jews or non-Jews, was barely tolerated. Public criticism of Israel is often construed as anti-Zionism, which in practical terms is, at its core, antisemitism.[9] In the United States, in effect, criticism and condemnation of Israel have been conflated, preventing serious discussion of the moral issues surrounding the conflict, including, for example, increased Israeli settlement in the West Bank or Israel's abuse of the human rights of Palestinians. Instead, the volatility of the conflict has created shrill positions that inevitably have a silencing or deadening effect.

For many American Jews today, Israel poses an agonizing struggle. While American Jews, especially Orthodox and ultra-Orthodox Jews, still

---

8. See Deborah E. Lipstadt, *Beyond Belief: The American Press and the Coming of the Holocaust* (New York: Simon & Schuster, 1993); Laurel Leff, *Buried by the Times: The Holocaust and America's Most Important Newspaper* (New York: Cambridge University Press, 2005).

9. "Catholic Church Equates Anti-Zionism with Anti-Semitism," *Israel Line*, July 9, 2004, quoted in *Golda Magazine*.

emigrate to Israel in substantial numbers, support for Israel has become far less unqualified, mostly as a result of the military's — and, by extension, the government's — treatment of the disaffected and highly politicized Palestinians. The aftermath of the 1967 war and the consequent reclamation of the West Bank and Gaza as Israeli territory exacerbated antagonism among Israeli political parties. In addition, the increase of settlements and their growing militancy, Israeli political power struggles, inconsistent Israeli leadership, the paucity of credible Palestinian leadership, the duplicity of Palestinian messages, Israeli repression on the one hand and Palestinian violence on the other, the fervor and growing influence of the religious Right on Israeli policy and strategies, and the passage of sixty years have led to the polarization, volatility, and erosion of American Jews' unquestioned devotion to Israel.[10] For a time, disengagement from Gaza and the West Bank seemed to offer hope, but whether that hope can be sustained in the aftermath of Hamas's electoral victory and Israel's 2006 war with Hezbollah remains to be seen.

Before 1948, few voices in America and elsewhere acknowledged the legitimate presence of Arabs in Palestine,[11] especially not the blue-collar Zionists I knew. The history of the Israeli-Palestinian conflict tells us otherwise, but it also reminds us of the relentless sequence of wars that Israel had to fight simply to survive. Indeed, from 1948 to 1967, the Palestinians did not propose the creation of a Palestinian state. Nevertheless, since 1967 Israel has compounded its unjustifiably harsh, even brutal, treatment of Arabs and dismissed Palestinian territorial claims by building permanent settlements. Nevertheless, the Palestinians' claims to victimhood should hardly engender only sympathy and support. Yasser Arafat's corrupt leadership and the continued indifference of other Arab nations to Palestinian pain, except as that pain is convenient as a political tool against Israel, have exploited and virtually anesthetized a people who have the education, the communication skills, and the potential leadership to shape themselves into a respected, reasonable political entity. That they have not done so and have resorted to terror and dishonest sensationalism in the press is ev-

10. Israel, too, has acknowledged the erosion of American support: "The United States is virtually our only friend, so we must remember that it, too, supports a withdrawal almost to the borders of 1967" (Leonard Fein, quoting Ehud Olmert in *Forward,* August 20, 2004, p. 8).

11. Kushner and Solomon, "Zionism and Its Discontents — Historical Documents," in *Wrestling with Zion,* pp. 13-36.

idence of a will to maintain the struggle, possibly in the hopes of winning the war against Israel through attrition.[12] Indeed, Arafat's ironic crafting of the Palestinians into a victim group at the mercy of an aggressive bully — a reversal of the David and Goliath struggle — proved a useful though sadistic tactic for the Palestinians, gaining them attention and support in the short run. Ironically, using Nazi propaganda tactics, Palestinians and other Arabs have waged a smear campaign to vilify Jews as the new Nazis, complete with cartoons of a swastika-adorned Sharon.

The rise of a "new" type of antisemitism that blends the "old" European antisemitism with Muslim or Islamist virulent and violent anti-Zionism seems to have inspired the American Left and American universities to take up the Palestinian cause. Traditional political alliances are being overturned. For example, American campuses hosted quasi-secret Palestinian Solidarity Movement's Divestment from Israel conferences that fed on students' ignorance of history and natural affinity for the underdog.[13] And American Jews were urged to respond to the *Christian Science Monitor* poll on divestment from companies doing business with Israel to ensure that a move in 2004 by the Presbyterian Church, U.S.A., to divest did not go unchallenged.[14] In addition, long-standing American Jewish leftist groups, such as Friends of the Courage to Refuse, B'rit Tzedek, A Jewish Voice for Peace, The Tikkun Community, and Jews against the Occupation (JATO), cite examples of Israeli military behavior that echo Nazi humiliation and degradation of the Jews in the early 1930s and condemn — not entirely without justification — such incidents in the name of failing to learn from the Holocaust.

At the same time, the Arab press barks vicious statements about Israelis, picked up in the European press, juxtaposing these smears with

---

12. Stephanie Juffa, "The Mythical Martyr," *Wall Street Journal Europe,* November 26-28, 2004, exposing as a hoax the story of Israeli soldiers supposedly shooting Muhammad al-Dura in a crossfire on September 30, 2000. See also Peter Haas's discussion of this incident in chap. 1 above. The Mitchell Report cites this incident as one of the events that "sparked the Intifada." See also the following analysis of the "bulldozing incident": Joshua Hammer, "The Death of Rachel Corrie," *Mother Jones,* September/October 2003, pp. 69-75, 98-102.

13. Wayne Firestone, "Deconstructing Divestment and Duke," *Jewish Week,* December 17, 2004, p. 19. See also Laurie Zoloth, "Fear and Loathing at San Francisco State," in Rosenbaum, *Those Who Forget the Past,* pp. 258-62.

14. Jane Lampman, "From Churches, a Challenge to Israeli Policies," *Christian Science Monitor,* December 6, 2004, http://www.csmonitor.com. See also chap. 2 in this volume.

statements denying the Holocaust, all of which is reinforced by Arab curricula that are blatantly antisemitic.[15] Charges that Israelis are the new Nazis must be dismissed as ludicrous if not obscene: Israeli policy has never been extermination, and there is no parallel between the ethos, goals, and methods of Israel and those of Nazi Germany. There are, however, ironic echoes of Hitlerism in the Palestinian cry to "drive the Israelis into the sea." Except for the ignorant and the blindly ideological, the comparison between Israel and Nazi Germany is absurd. Of course, the abuse of Palestinian noncombatants is immoral and indefensible, Jewishly and ethically, but the tendency to diminish the unmitigated cruelty of Palestinian suicide bombings or to rationalize them as responses to untenable frustration or to ignore educational processes that train youngsters to become martyrs flies in the face of reason, morality, and justice, and it impedes the peace process.[16]

For sixty years, a substantial number of American Jews and their organizations unquestioningly identified with and supported Israel. For many, though, the last twenty years and the increasing violence have eroded unequivocal support. Moreover, as the memory of the Holocaust fades and the resistance to resolution continues, support for Israel seems less urgent, even though it is axiomatic that Israel owes its existence to the Holocaust and that Israel's security is by no means assured. Demands by some American Jews to Congress to withdraw support for Israel renew, for other Jews, their awareness of the nature and relevance of pre-Shoah Zionism in a post-Holocaust, post–9/11 world. Discussion groups, as well as solidarity and reconciliation movements, have been growing in intensity and are polarizing the American Jewish community further. On the one hand, the longer the conflict continues, the more likely it is to fragment American Jewry, and, I would argue, the further removed American Jewish responses will become from the memory of the Holocaust. On the other hand, for over a decade the Palestinians have rejected resolution of the conflict, and other Arab voices have not publicly helped the process. American Jewish Holocaust scholars are unable to ignore the history that

15. Harold Evans, "The View from Ground Zero," Index Lecture, June 2, 2002, reprinted in Rosenbaum, *Those Who Forget the Past,* pp. 36-56. This is an excellent source about the propaganda that characterizes current Muslim antisemitism.

16. In a roundtable discussion on March 9, 2003, transcribed in Kushner and Solomon, *Wrestling with Zion,* Irena Klepfisz raised the issue of suicide bombings as a deterrence to bringing Jews to the peace table (see p. 365).

resulted from indifference or neutrality. Without America, Israel does stand alone, while the Palestinians are funded and supported by their Arab "cousins."

Still, some Americans, even some American Jews, continue to see the Palestinians as the underdog and, almost on principle, support them. Other Americans, particularly those familiar with Jewish history, know otherwise. As Dennis Ross argues, there can be no Middle East peace unless Israel's Muslim partners (whether Syrian, Palestinian, Egyptian, Jordanian, Iraqi, or Iranian) want peace.[17] Israel the nation is infinitely stronger than the Jews of Europe were, but it cannot withstand endless, relentless assaults. Moreover, to ask Israel to ignore Palestinian attacks, let alone those that came from Hezbollah in the summer of 2006, in order to further the peace process is to reposition Israelis as vulnerable "helpless victims."[18] American Jews must not tolerate such inequity. Neither can we witness continued concessions of land and security measures without equivalent concessions on the other side, beginning with the cessation of violence. And yet, American Jews cannot tolerate Israeli oppression of the Palestinians. The moral question is thorny. Neither Israeli nor American Jews can control Arab/Palestinian behavior, but American Jews have a moral obligation to pressure its government to influence the peace process by continuing to exert pressure on Arab nations to condemn, in words and action, Palestinian violence against civilians. The post-Holocaust generation carries the moral burden of the six million, a burden that requires us American Jews to urge our government to take action that would stop the violence. Our government can acknowledge and reward Arab leaders who exert pressure on Palestinian groups. Finally, we can aggressively take steps to reduce the geopolitical advantage that oil-rich Arab countries now enjoy. It is no less important for the United States to continue to condemn unequivocally and publicly the Islamic antisemitism that fuels hatred and violence across the Muslim world and the Palestinian tactic of demonizing the Israelis.[19] America must also use its considerable power to influence its partners to do the same. At the same time, American Jews must do their

17. Ross, *The Missing Peace*, p. 763.

18. Jonathan Rosen, "The Uncomfortable Question of Anti-Semitism," in Rosenbaum, *Those Who Forget the Past*, p. 10.

19. Robert S. Wistrich, "The Old-New Anti-Semitism," in Rosenbaum, *Those Who Forget the Past*, pp. 71-90.

part to convince Israel to advance policies that will produce a just and lasting peace.[20]

Clearly, understanding the role of oil in formulating American diplomacy is critical to understanding American responsibility in and for these conflicts. We must also recognize that the current Iraqi war and the long U.S. history with oil-producing Arab countries complicate the resolution of the conflict because Arab leaders contend, more firmly and loudly than ever, that settling the Israeli-Palestinian conflict is a prerequisite to settling the Iraqi conflict, an argument without merit, as well as a diversionary tactic that further politicizes both conflicts. This argument has become a mantra in that it conveniently reinforces old or classical antisemitism that contributed to the isolation of Europe's Jews in the 1930s. In late 2001, when Daniel Bernard, then the French ambassador to Great Britain, called Israel "that shitty little country," he was refueling the genteel antisemitism of the past, a comfortable, timeless "blame the victim" mentality, and the expedient geopolitics of the present.[21] With the presidency of George W. Bush, direct White House intervention in the peace process diminished, at least publicly, but basically Bush supported Ariel Sharon and his policies. In fact, for a growing proportion of American Jews, the Israeli-Palestinian conflict became a bullet issue in the 2004 election, much like abortion rights and the environment to other constituencies.

20. A hopeful sign of the value of such policies is the withdrawal of a small secular Jewish settlement in Gaza. See Greg Myre, "Tiny Collective of Jews Agrees to Leave Gaza under Plan," *New York Times,* December 27, 2004.

21. The Daniel Bernard incident produced a firestorm of controversy, including an immense number of reactions that can be found on the Internet. Among others, the following sources are helpful: Barbara Amiel, "Islamists Overplay Their Hand but London Salons Don't See It," http://www.telegraph.co.uk/opinion/main.jhtml?xml=/opinion/2001/12/17/do1701.xml; "'Anti-Semitic' French Envoy under Fire," December 20, 2001, http://news.bbc.co.uk/2/hi/europe/1721172.stm; Douglas Davis, "French Amb. to UK Blasts Israel as 'Threat to World Peace' — Report," Combined News Services, 12-21-1, http://www.rense.com/general18/rep.htm; Jamie Glazov, "Anti-Semitism: France's National Shame," January 10, 2002, http://www.frontpagemag.com/Articles/ReadArticle.asp?ID=228; Tom Gross, "'A shitty little country': Prejudice and Abuse in Paris and London," January 10, 2002, http://www.tomgrossmedia.com/ShittyLittleCountry.html. The Bernard canard is also referenced in Steven H. Zipperstein, "Past Revisited: Reflections on the Study of the Holocaust and Contemporary Antisemitism," J. B. and Maurice C. Shapiro Annual Lecture, U.S. Holocaust Memorial Museum, Washington, D.C., January 16, 2003, which is available online at http://www.ushmm.org/research/center/publications/occasional/2003-06/paper.pdf.

The 2004 election, in fact, reflected a small increase in Jewish support for Bush because of his stated support for the Sharon government.

And yet, the continuing stalemated peace process and the alarming rise of antisemitism, especially in Europe but also in the United States, must give pause to expressions of anti-Israeli/anti-Jewish/anti-Zionism. We have learned the consequences of taking antisemitism lightly. We are experiencing a tidal wave of Jew hatred, "unprecedented, and anyone who makes the most cursory examination cannot fail to be stunned."[22] Current Muslim antisemitism draws on discarded Christian lies, Nazi stereotypes, and the vast Arab network that has rejected Israel's right to exist since 1948. This antisemitism is pervasive, and it has encouraged and even strengthened non-Muslim antisemitism in Europe and America. Have we come full circle? Do we need Israel now as we did in 1930s? It is alarmist to think this way, but it is also natural in the face of our history: "one cannot dismiss anti-Semitism just because it offends one's sense of rationality."[23]

And yet again, an honest analysis of this conflict resurrects the guilt that stems from American passivity during the Holocaust and impels American Jews to react vigorously and realistically. Offering ideal rather than realistic solutions prolongs the conflict and leads to continued cynicism and violence. American Jews have an obligation — a moral, religiously rooted obligation that is supported by the history of events that transpired in Europe between 1933 and 1945 — to work pragmatically toward a just, secure peace, a two-state solution that assures the dignity, integrity, and independence of both Israel and Palestine.

22. Evans, "The Voice from Ground Zero," pp. 44-45. See also Anne Bayefsky, "One Small Step: Is the U.N. Finally Ready to Get Serious about Anti-Semitism?" June 21, 2004, http://www.opinionjournal.com/extra/?id=110005245.

23. Ruth Wisse, "On Ignoring Anti-Semitism," in Rosenbaum, *Those Who Forget the Past*, pp. 189-207.

Contributors' Questions for Myrna Goldenberg

Given the "tidal wave of Jew hatred" you refer to, do American Jews have a moral obligation not to add to that hatred with public statements severely critical of Israel? Is it even morally sound for American Jews, who do not have to live with the conflict, to offer criticism at all? Or — though you use such terms as "polarization" and "fragmentation" among American Jewry in a seemingly pejorative sense — might it be the case that creative dialogue between oppositional groups in the United States may better serve the cause of a just reconciliation of the conflict than would one (partisan) voice?

You cite the fact that before 1948, few voices in America acknowledged the legitimate presence of Arabs. This silence, of course, goes back decades earlier to British and French colonial governments after World War I. The denial of many Palestinian claims continues in much of Israeli society to this day. Are there legitimate Palestinian claims that need to be heard and addressed in some way today? To what extent might a failure to acknowledge the legitimate presence of Arabs in pre-1948 Palestine — to acknowledge that an indigenous people was largely dispossessed — contribute to the growth of Arab anti-Zionism in our time?

Response by Myrna Goldenberg

Before and during the Holocaust, American Jews often whispered, "*Sha sh'till.* Don't draw attention to us." Indeed, keeping a low profile is a familiar strategy of Jews. In the long run, it did not and does not make a difference, either in the United States or in Europe. Antisemitism is a presence with or without Jews. In the short run, however, a low profile can be a reasonable safety measure. For example, in France, Belgium, England, and Italy today, Jews protect themselves from potential physical abuse by not wearing a *kipah* or a *Mogen David* in public. Such tactics are simply common sense, regrettable though that may be.

American Jews today, however, enjoy the freedom to discuss and debate the status of Israel. And they do so with vigor — in both political parties — on talk shows and in American and American Jewish publications. Is Israel endangered by such talk? Assuming that such talk is well-informed (how much of it is well informed is a good question!), I would like to argue that Israel is not endangered by such discussion, but I cannot be sure. Surely, when *Tikkun*'s Michael Lerner urges Jews to ask Congress to withdraw funding from Israel, his words are not benign. They are precisely the words that American anti-Zionists want to hear to support their attacks on Israel. Pat Buchanan and his ilk are vindicated by such pleas. Lerner went to the extreme; his rashness served no purpose but self-aggrandizement. In fact, such public utterances and rants do not lead to reasoned debate; they do not engage the opposition in reasoned discourse.

Inflammatory speeches feed the already committed antisemites and reinforce but do not create negative attitude toward Israel. Serious, informed debates about Israel's relationship to the Palestinians, however, particularly within the Jewish community, encourage thoughtful and, one would hope, creative responses. American Jews do have a moral responsibility to support Israel, and responsible, empathic criticism is part of that responsibility. The New Jewish Agenda, for example, was founded for this reason — to provide an alternative type of support for Israel.

But moral responsibility is not limited to American Jews. Particularly on two matters, Israelis also need to accept responsibility. First, they need to respond promptly and ethically to false and exaggerated accusations by Palestinians and other Arabs about historical, religious, and political claims to the region. Israeli silence suggests disdain or even contempt for all non-Israelis. Moreover, in the wake of the Holocaust, silence can never be an option in the face of suffering. Second, Israel also needs to accept responsibility and, where necessary, culpability for intensifying the conflict through mistreatment and humiliation of the Palestinians. To some extent — and probably unreasonably so — Israel's security is a function of perception about its degree of morality. As Daniel Doron puts the point: "The erosion in Israel's moral stature has weakened not only its international standing, but also its most valuable ally, the American Jewish community. Jews no longer feel the pride and self-confidence that they felt after Israel's upset victory in the Six Day War, or after . . . Entebbe. . . . One must not underestimate the potential danger that erosion in Israel's moral position poses. . . . This danger must be met by mounting a massive educational effort to arm U.S. Jews, especially its leadership, with a better understanding of the nature and history of the Middle East conflict."[1]

In all likelihood, each side will refuse to yield its master narrative, but ultimately the truth of both sides may reach common ground in the face of documentary evidence. Knowledge of the facts is everyone's responsibility, including American non-Jews when they join the discussion. They have every right to voice their opinion and, indeed, often their role as outsider or "other" helps illuminate the issue. Yet I am somewhat uncomfortable with their involvement simply because they were not and are never likely to be faced with imposed statelessness. My parents' dilemma about whether to protest or not protest during the Holocaust stemmed from their own insecurity as immigrants and their fear of being both conspicu-

1. Daniel Doron, "There's Danger of U.S. Jews Remaining Ignorant," *Washington Jewish Week*, June 16, 2005, p. 15.

ous and unwanted. The memory of immigrant Jews from Poland and Russia included pogroms, and that experience diminished their sense of security, even in the United States. The Ethel and Julius Rosenberg trial, for example, fed their fears. Irrational? Perhaps, but undeniable all the same.

In the end, the tone and context of informed "oppositional dialogue" are the keys to positive and fruitful debate. Jews in America must be involved, if only because by virtue of their material support for Israel they are already involved. On a higher level, their reasoned involvement may lead to creative solutions and a deeper commitment to protect and preserve the State of Israel.

Denial of legitimate Palestinian claims aggravates and emboldens Israeli actions. Such denial is foolish and untenable, even when articulated by Golda Meir when she ingenuously stated that there is "no Palestinian people." Legitimate claims need to be acknowledged, beginning with the 1947 U.N. partition plan, which called for two states and which was accepted by Israel but rejected by the Arabs, and continuing until the present, with fair adjudication of community boundaries. But this is not the heart of the matter. First, Palestinians have repeatedly denied Israel's right to exist. Second, and probably more important, compensation for land, which would constitute public acknowledgment of the presence of Arabs, would not satisfy Palestinian demands for territory. In this regard, a two-state solution calls the Palestinian bluff, if it indeed is a bluff. Would a Palestinian state, assisted by American material support and Israeli political and social support, constitute an end to Arab demands? We cannot know until there is a Palestinian state. We must take the risk, cautiously.

At the same time and in the same vein, the relatively peaceful disengagement from Gaza and part of the West Bank seemed promising, but it is fraught with problems. Palestinian gloating and irresponsible claims that violence achieved the goal of driving Jews from the land is, at best, discouraging and, at worst, frightening. Israel took a first step. It is time for Palestinian leaders and the Arab world to encourage and support the next steps, that is, the development of a viable Palestinian state that respects the rights of its citizens, as well as the right of other peoples to live freely. In this complicated and extraordinarily sensitive topic, we tend to avoid the contribution of Jordan and other Arab states to the conflict. It is hardly reasonable or fair to place blame on Israel for all the woes of the Palestinian people, for the fact is that the wealthy Arab world has exacerbated the Palestinian problem through its Machiavellian exploitation. Particularly with Saudi Arabia and Kuwait, the United States can and should exert its considerable influence.[2] Yet, realistically, it is useless to wait for other Arabs and the colonialist nations who helped create the present impossible situation to accept their share of responsibility. In fact, for the United States to wait, to not act, is to invite more violence and to leave Israeli children and grandchildren with a persistent, unsolvable conflict. That is surely an immoral legacy.

2. Saudi influence in the United States is serious and effective, with its "infiltration" into our higher education system through funding scores of pro-Palestinian, pro-Islamist, pro-Arab Middle East Centers. See Lee Kaplan, "The Saudi Fifth Column on Our Nation's Campuses," April 5, 2004, http://www.frontpagemag.com/Articles/Read.aspx?GUID ={7634EF94-18DC-471C-A93F-6D0C0E15F610}.

III. POSSIBILITIES

Speaking in Cairo, Egypt, in July 2006, while the twenty-first-century's worst Middle Eastern violence to date continued to escalate, Amr Moussa, secretary-general of the Arab League, proclaimed that "the Middle East peace process has failed." As chants in Arab streets called for Israel's destruction, Moussa was not the only Muslim leader to pronounce the peace process dead. Hezbollah leader Sayyed Hassan Nasrallah concurred. On the Israeli side, as well as for many international journalists who covered the debacle unfolding in Lebanon, little confidence, let alone enthusiasm, remained for any hope that the clock could be turned back — not even to the status quo on the day before June 25, 2006, when Palestinian gunmen seized an Israeli soldier and the Israel Defense Forces retaliated by moving into Gaza, the Palestinian territory from which Israel had previously withdrawn. As one step led to another, fatefully some might say, new possibilities — many of them fraught with menacing challenges and risks — were at hand.

Nevertheless, no one knows exactly what will happen next. This consequence is one of promise and peril in human experience, which is never completely determined because yet-to-be human decisions play crucial parts. The past and even events as they happen cannot be retrieved and undone. Some trends, once they have gone too far, are irreversible, but history does not move completely in a fated lockstep. We cannot responsibly escape this realization because we know experientially that senses of possibility are inseparable from human existence. True, humanity's senses of possibility may at times be unrealistic; they can be too idealistic to have credible chances for fulfillment. They may also be too pessimistic, which makes them self-fulfilling prophecies that give despair more power than it deserves. Even in times that are bleak and dark, possibilities remain. They can suggest that there is no good exit or even that circumstances will get worse and never get better. They can also suggest, especially if thinking as imaginative as it is critical is brought to bear on admittedly dire human predicaments, that there are still ways forward toward healing, justice, and peace. To deny or ignore those possibilities is to give up too much and too soon.

Beginning with Henry F. Knight's aptly titled essay, "Beyond Conquest," the chapters in Part III of *Anguished Hope* emphasize and echo themes related to the importance of possibilities. Coming as they do from scholars whose thought is grounded in study of the Holocaust, none of these chapters suggests a quick fix. Each has a long-term perspective, one that underscores the need for persistent and lasting effort to make good things happen. Knight begins appropriately in a mood of modesty that incorporates a sense of awe about the possibilities that the Palestinian-Israeli conflict includes. Rightly, such awe ought to affect anyone who reflects on the Palestinian-Israeli conflict from Holocaust-related perspectives. Furthermore, as a post-Holocaust Christian, Knight realizes how dominant and destructive the pressure toward conquest can be. Christianity tried to "conquer" Judaism. That attempt contributed substantially to the Holocaust. Impulses to conquest, whether they emanate from Arab or from Israeli quarters, virtually always invite conflict and even disaster because they are driven by narratives of scarcity, by commitments that ensure that the victory of one group must mean the loss of the other. While acknowledging the power of such perspectives, Knight's sense of possibility differs from them fundamentally. Tentatively, cautiously, and soberly, he looks for ways beyond conflict, locating them in creative imagination that resists the fate of being "trapped in an endlessly escalating spiral of violence in which we all lose."

As a Holocaust scholar who is both Christian and African American, Hubert Locke also knows a great deal about the logics of scarcity and conquest. He is also fully aware of the stakes in struggles of survival against power, human rights abuses, and violence that threaten the very existence of one's people and the traditions they hold dear. Where the Palestinian-Israeli conflict is concerned, Locke's sense of possibility suggests that the right ways forward are unlikely to be taken unless unfinished business pertaining to antisemitism and racism is dealt with. In making that judgment,

Locke has in mind specifically, but not only, an ongoing dialogue between Christians and Jews. On the Christian side, there are at least two problems that involve what may be, at least, a latent antisemitism. Among the Christian Right, especially but not only in the United States, there appears to be unwavering, even uncritical, support for Israel. This support, however, rests theologically on a problematic narrative about Israel's possession of the land. According to this narrative, Israel's return to land, which was allegedly given to them by God, turns out to be the prelude for the second coming and triumph of Jesus Christ, an ironic outcome in which Jews are supported by Christians before Christians abolish them. In other Christian quarters, however, Israel is subject to harsh and often unfair criticism, which may also harbor versions of ancient Christian hostility toward Jews. In one way or another, the result may be a tragic bifurcation between Jews and less politically conservative Christians, whereas the two groups actually share much of importance.

Turning to his appraisal of Jewish outlooks, Locke takes the risk of suggesting that the Palestinian-Israeli conflict may involve Jews who have become "participants in the problem of race, as well as its victims." That danger, he adds, can be found on the Palestinian side of the volatile equation as well. At the very least, neither group is totally innocent or immune when it comes to using dehumanizing epithets and canards against the other. What would help to make "harmonious relations" possible in the Middle East, Locke concludes, is the possibility that Jews, Christians, and Muslims may be able to find ways to work "assiduously to overcome centuries of racial hostility between and among them." The Holocaust should serve as a warning of the cost of failure.

When suicide bombers detonate and rockets fall randomly on civilians, when air strikes engulf their targets in flames and there is little hope that the grief and hatred caused by killing can be assuaged, what possibilities remain for education? There are, of course, numerous possibilities of that kind, and by no means are all of them good. Both children and adults can be educated by experience, by political ideology and propaganda, and by schools and universities to buy into the logics of scarcity, conquest, antisemitism, racism, and other poisonous outlooks that breed hatred and hostility. Amy H. Shapiro, however, defends the possibility that there can still be hope for education that involves the critical thinking about self-identity that is much needed if there is to be peace between Israelis and Palestinians. "The Israeli-Palestinian conflict," she argues, "is no doubt a conflict between socially constructed realities." If so, education focused on critical thinking about self-identity could defuse the struggle and even help to heal its wounds and restore some of its losses. Integral to this kind of education, Shapiro urges, is its emphasis on possibility itself. Correctly pointing out that "the combination of a fixed view of identity with an undeveloped ability to think critically can . . . be lethal," her essay goes on to outline "an education that will contribute to the creation of peace."

Rachel N. Baum closes Part III with what is arguably the boldest essay in *Anguished Hope*. She dares to imagine a time when the Palestinian-Israeli conflict has been resolved and a just peace is in place. She sets for herself the task of envisioning how Jews (not only Israeli Jews) and Palestinians might rethink their narratives after the peace. How might it be possible, she asks, to move beyond the identities of victim and victimizer to create something new in a land of two peoples?

What is needed after the peace turns out to be related to what is needed for peace to take place. With both needs in mind, Baum draws on her Jewish identity and tradition to offer a reinterpretation of suffering, one that is rooted in the text that Jews read yearly at Passover: "Because you were slaves in Egypt. . . ." Here, suffering places a person, not at the center of sympathetic feeling, but at the center of a moral demand. While people often read these words to mean that because the Jews were slaves they should have sympathy for other slaves and oppressed people, Baum suggests a different reading. The Torah says that because the Jews were slaves in Egypt *and because they were saved by God,* they now are a changed people with new obligations.

At the center of this story of suffering, Baum contends, is not the victimization as much as the redemption. While readers often emphasize the slavery, she suggests that the more correct emphasis would read, "Because you *were* slaves." The Jews were slaves but are so no longer, and because of that redemption (the Torah places this in a religious context, but it need not be) they are now a changed people. Thus, rather than a sympathy that draws comparison between two events, the Torah suggests a moral responsibility of survival that is both affective and ontological. While sympathy is based on identification, this responsibility is based on a changed relationship to oneself and the world — a relationship changed by history. "Because you were slaves" suggests that suffering and redemption from that suffering can change people and present them with new obligations to others and to the world.

Hope abounds in the essays on possibility that appear in Part III. Nevertheless, that hope remains anguished because these four writers, like all of the contributors, remain realistically aware that passions, politics, and events themselves may race ahead in directions very different from the ones these essays envision. Yet the conviction of this book is that Holocaust scholars cannot stand by in silence while the Palestinian-Israeli conflict continues. Furthermore, the contributors believe that their outlooks contain insights without which the Palestinian-Israel conflict will lead to more needless bloodshed and useless suffering. That prospect makes anguish and hope uncomfortable and unsettling partners, but it does so in creative and constructive ways that are as necessary as they are possible.

10. *Beyond Conquest: Post-Shoah Christian Anguish and the Israeli-Palestinian Dilemma*

Henry F. Knight

I come to an invitation to engage the tangled situation of Israeli-Palestinian relations deeply aware of flaws in my own history and perspective. In fact, I fear that I have little or no business entering into this enterprise because I sense my own inadequacies so strongly. Not only do I bring a wounded faith to bear on the task, I do not bring expertise on the strategic issues in contention. In fact, I feel always behind in my understanding of the events and issues under review as I try in my limited way to stay abreast of current news about the region and its ongoing conflict. More important, perhaps, I do not live in the midst of this dilemma, though I face one of my own regarding my relationship to it. I am an outsider who can share his dilemma with others only if I acknowledge that I do not have to risk what those who dwell within Israel and its contested lands have to face on a daily basis. However, precisely because I am so keenly aware of why and how my perspective must be articulated with caution, I cannot do otherwise. If I ask, Who am I to offer something to this important discussion, I can only conclude, Who am I not to? But only with very clearly articulated limits and cautions.

Beyond Supersessionism

The confessional work of a reconfigured identity begins with recognizing the violence inherent in an identity constructed at the expense of another. In the case of Christian supersessionism, the identity against which Christian identity is fashioned is Jewish. The challenge, post-Shoah, is to find a way to claim one's Christian identity that remains faithful to the historical identity one has received as a follower of Christ, while at the same time avoiding being agonistically constructed over against a negated, Jewish other. For me, hospitality, fully embodied in the life and ministry of Jesus, has been an essential feature of that identity.

Through the hospitality articulated in and through the life and work of Jesus, I take my place in the covenantal partnership of creation. I do so as an included one in the household of God by way of the house of Israel — a friendly, but important, amendment to the work of Clark William-son.[1] I am an included one in a reality always, already including me. I experience my place and role in God's household, literally the domain of creation, as a guest, who is asked to accept responsibility for its care and is invited to share that experience as a responsible steward of creation. In other words, my responsibility of including others is always derivative.

Supersessionism has challenged me to reconfigure the Christocentric posture of my faith identity. Despite the universal claims of Christocentric faith, it too easily expresses a supersessionary logic. One truth, one path, one way denies the promise and life affirmations of all others. Facing up to this feature of Christian faith has led me back to the logic of creation and its hermeneutic of abundance expressed in a creation-centered theology of hospitality that I discover embodied in the life and ministry of Jesus. Although it is filled with attendant peril and risk, its logic is the promise that has been present in creation as its gift of life from the very beginning. As a Christian, my return to this dynamic gift remains Christomorphic, however, even if it is not Christocentric.[2] Its promise comes from a fundamental choice to follow the path of plenitude that reflects the very gift of creation and the summons to tend its garden of delight. Thereafter, having chosen the way of life and generosity that is creation's way, there are multiple paths that affirm this fundamental one. Nonetheless, there is still a fundamental choice between creation's logic of abundance, which I believe is embodied in the hospitality and generosity

1. Clark Williamson builds his 1993 work of post-Holocaust theology on the metaphor of being a guest in the house of Israel (*A Guest in the House of Israel: Post-Holocaust Church Theology* [Louisville, Ky.: Westminster John Knox Press, 1993]). For him, Israel is the proper context of Christian theology and ecclesiology.

2. See my work on this material in *Confessing Christ in a Post-Holocaust World: A Midrashic Experiment* (Westport, Conn.: Greenwood Press, 2000), pp. 77-80.

of Jesus' life and work, and the logic of scarcity, which shapes the world
into camps of haves and have-nots.

The Logic of Scarcity and Conquest

I am deeply aware of the danger of triumphalism and conquest in my tradition. Anti-Judaism flourished in its soil and grew into contempt and
competition over who would rightly bear the name "Israel" and "God's
people for the world." As Christianity emerged with institutional stability
and with support by imperial power, Christianity's triumphant spirit became full-blown triumphalism, leaving no room for Judaism's presence as
the living people of Israel in Christianity's master narrative. Triumph led
to contempt as its adversarial spirit laid exclusive claim to the historic
identity of the people Israel. In the process, Judaism, Christianity's contending other, bore little positive significance in its signifying presence in
Christianity's world.

Regina M. Schwartz has characterized this attitude toward the religious other as an inherent danger of monotheistic thinking, seeing it embodied not simply in Christianity but also in Judaism and Islam.[3] She
views it as the seductive flaw that accompanies any claim to be the single
representative people of the one God of all creation. She argues that inherent in the argument that one is God's representative is the assumption that
no one else can embody this identity. Consequently, the identity of such a
people is constructed agonistically, denying the credibility of any other
who might make such a claim.

Schwartz contends that this pervasive attitude in the biblical witness
expresses a logic of scarcity that views the promise of creation as being
limited and scarce, offered in succeeding generations only to one recipient,
beginning with Abel. That legacy continues through favored sons, eventually leading to Jacob/Israel. Similarly, Israel's promise of land is restricted
to Israel as the domain in which Israel dwells in faithfulness and from
which Israel is exiled in judgment. According to Schwartz, obedience to the
one God and the either-or logic restricting the blessing of one parent to a
favored child is the consequence of a pervasive and exclusive mind-set.

3. Regina M. Schwartz, *The Curse of Cain: The Violent Legacy of Monotheism* (Chicago: University of Chicago Press, 1997), pp. 15-16.

Over against this approach she identifies an alternative logic of plenitude, which she acknowledges may be found in Scripture as well.

Whether one adopts Schwartz's terminology ("the logic of scarcity") or uses the more familiar language of triumph and conquest, this attitude is distinguished by an either-or, binary approach to identity that does not allow for fundamental difference and diversity. Rather, the logic of scarcity is a logic of exclusion and violence that insists that identity cannot be shared: if one community is the guardian of truth, then others cannot be. Moreover, such a way of viewing the world extends to claims of truth and power. If one community's perspective of the truth is right, other perspectives are wrong or mistaken; if one has power, then the other cannot. In contrast, what Schwartz calls a logic of plenitude (or abundance) is able to share identity and power; it recognizes that truth can be expressed in diverse and sometimes competing ways. Such a logic is both-and, an inclusive way of valuing and approaching others. Its logic of generosity and grace embraces the presence of the other as other and welcomes the richness of creation as its intended blessing for life and nourished in a covenantal ecology of shared responsibility.

Any confessional movement to reconfigure Christian identity in a nonsupersessionist way must come to terms with its underlying logic of scarcity and move toward some form of the logic of plenitude. To overlook this dynamic is to fail to deal with the funding logic of an agonistically constructed identity, which is the heart of Schwartz's argument. The importance of this hermeneutical observation can be illustrated in the reaction to Rosemary Radford Ruether's publication of *The Wrath of Jonah* in 1989. Along with her husband, Ruether developed a critique of Israel that was based in liberationist political theology and sought to expose the injustice being experienced by the Palestinian people at the hands of the Israeli government. Her argument was met with accusations of anti-semitism, which she and many of her colleagues refuted, citing her exposé of Christian anti-Judaism as the left hand of Christology.[4] In *The Wrath of Jonah* she employed the ideological critique of liberation theology, in effect

---

4. Ruether explores the relationship between Christian identity and anti-Judaic attitudes in her work *Faith and Fratricide: The Theological Roots of Anti-Semitism* (Minneapolis: Seabury Press, 1974). See also chap. 3 in her *To Change the World: Christology and Cultural Criticism* (New York: Crossroad, 1981), pp. 31-43, esp. p. 31, where she focuses on her critique of Christology as "the negative side of the Christian affirmation that Jesus was the Christ." In this context, she identifies antisemitism as the "left hand of Christology."

exercising liberation theology's preferential option for the poor to challenge the violence in the Palestinian-Israeli conflict. By not avoiding the underlying logic of scarcity, however, she fell victim to the either-or dynamic of choosing sides for or against the scarce resource of justice. That is, only one people could be experiencing injustice in this situation. As a result, her critique became an apology for Palestinian justice at the expense of any support for Israel.

On the face of it, liberation theology's preferential option for the poor may appear to articulate a corrective option for moving beyond supersessionism. If the underlying logic of scarcity remains operative, however, the ideological critique will fail to attend to the deeper issue of building an identity at the expense of others. For example, utilizing the same logic, one could conclude, in contrast to Ruether, that post-Shoah Christians are called to embody a preferential option for Israel. While such a claim might have merit if placed in an inclusive context, it too easily overlooks the implications of taking sides when exercising such a preference. If justice is viewed as requiring that one must choose one side against another, then what Schwartz calls the logic of scarcity has not yet been addressed. Indeed, the logic of scarcity can linger and fund future problems, just as it did for the Ruethers as they sought to apply a preferential option for the poor to the Palestinians.

Beyond Conquest

As Post-Shoah Christians, we must come to terms with the logic of conquest and move beyond its claims, otherwise we remain trapped in the logic of scarcity that funds the agonistic identity that has fueled the anti-Judaic tradition we seek to overcome. Any other path fails the test of post-Shoah credibility. For me and many Christians like me, the path beyond conquest is rooted in a larger, more inclusive covenantal project that includes the people Israel. In other words, as a post-Shoah Christian, I am keenly aware that I am an included one in another's covenantal story and witness. Moreover, I take my place in this way of walking through manifest acts of generosity and hospitality that I have come to identify with, but not restrict to, the way of Christ in the world. Indeed, I view them as covenantal gestalts of God's rule and realm. Such moments are manifestations of creation's fundamental intention for life, which I believe were embodied in the life and work of Jesus. But I do not believe that these gardens of delight cannot occur outside the domain of Christian faith. Moreover, as I take my place in them, I accept my own responsibility to welcome others in this rich and abundant vineyard. As a result, I am ever vigilant to the not-yet-included, but never, I trust, at the expense of forgetting that I have been welcomed into an enterprise that has made room for me. In other words, though its relational logic is covenantal, its nature is inclusive and expansive, rooted in the fundamental commitment of creation toward relationship with others. Any preferential option for the not-yet-included is rooted in having been already included by others. And that prior inclusion begins with the house of Israel.

The way beyond conquest has been a confessional journey that has led me to confront the ways conquest has operated in my own identity and to accept personal responsibility for being part of a larger, more inclusive venture that includes the people Israel. Consequently, when I disagree and even contend with others with whom I share this legacy, I do so fully aware that I am a guest in an enterprise that is larger than my own grasp of its significance, even as I am aware that its communion is greater than the community I identify as church. Moreover, any articulation of what this covenantal wholeness might mean will be limited and most probably flawed. In other words, a flawed covenantal wholeness is the context in which any critique is offered. In addition, it necessarily includes the people Israel, even if I must differentiate them from their nation-state. But I can be successful in doing so only to the extent that I draw similar distinctions in my own participation in the peoples called church and nation. The confessional character of this walk extends to these realities as well.

This doubly focused, confessional dynamic cannot be overlooked as Christian leaders attempt to speak to the Israeli-Palestinian dilemma. We will undoubtedly differentiate the people Israel from the nation, seeking to be clear about our context of covenantal wholeness. If American Christians like me, however, also seek to raise questions about the policies and actions of the Israeli government, we must be careful not to raise questions we are not prepared to raise with regard to our own nation. Likewise, we should be alert to similar concerns with regard to the church as we attend to the people Israel. For example, it would be hypocritical for American churches to call for the divestiture of Israeli stocks in protest of Israeli actions when we do not call upon the churches or other nations to divest themselves of American stocks when the United States demonstrates its own propensity to enact the logic of conquest and empire.

We may put the matter more positively. Recognizing that Israel is a wounded people as well as a flawed political entity should not be an act of condemnation but a recognition that Israel is not encountered in an ideal state but in its manifestations as a living people and an actual political entity fully participating in the imperfections of human and cultural existence. In like manner, a similar recognition operates with regard to the reality Christians call church. Its people and cultural manifestations are similarly flawed. In other words, instead of the wounded character of Israel's life being something that could be used against either the people or the political entity, it should be a leveling awareness that reminds us of shared imperfections. That is, in critique as well as expectation, we should not require of Israel, either as a people or as a nation-state, a purity that we would not apply to any other people or state, especially our own. At the same time, we should not avoid raising questions about specific behaviors or policies, but only as we are willing to bring the same questions and concerns to our own differentiated realities of church and nation. And the same logic should guide our critique and expectations regarding the Palestinian people and its leaders.

The confessional nature of these observations is significant. Simply put, the way beyond conquest is necessarily confessional. None of us should tell someone else that he or she must embrace the risk that comes with choosing to follow this path. We may follow another who has chosen it. Or we may choose it for ourselves, however much we might choose it for the sake of others. Any other choice is a usurpation of the other's agency and hence a step, however veiled, on the path of conquest. Or to put the matter in Christomorphic terms, such an enterprise is tantamount to asking others to take up their cross, but not taking it up ourselves. Quite simply, we can undertake this action only for ourselves. Still, we can make room for others to choose this option, articulating its promise and peril as we do. Such hospitality is a mature form of Christian witness. But in providing such hospitality, we should also be providing safe space for moving beyond the logic of conquest while accepting our part of the risk as responsibly as we can. At the same time, we should also warn the other of the risk that accompanies this way of proceeding. Even so, I remain keenly aware that I, and many Christians before me, have used this confessional heritage in triumph and conquest to wound and violate others, turning the cross into a formidable weapon. For this reason, if for no other, I am convinced we must proceed not just confessionally but also with extreme caution.

There are historic examples of the danger of moving beyond conquest for us to ponder. Anwar Sadat and Yitzhak Rabin each sought to move their nations along this path. They were assassinated, however, by adversaries from their own communities. As reconciliation became a tangible possibility, there were significant numbers who preferred to relate to justice and land as scarce resources they wished to control, not share. It should come as no surprise that any Palestinian action in this regard must negotiate the same dynamics. Yet without sacrificial actions like these,[5] the cycle of violence can only spiral into ever more dangerous levels. Nonetheless, the risk is significant.

To move beyond conquest requires not only that those with power find ways to share the basic resources of life while recognizing the danger of living out of a logic of scarcity, but that those who have been the victims of conquest also learn to recognize the danger and to let go of the same logic. Otherwise, they will only seek to obtain a reversal of roles in an ongoing dynamic that holds both victims and victors hostage. Indeed, the continuing investment in the logic of scarcity and conquest can be seen in the actions of suicide bombers, whose activities increase when the potential for rapprochement grows. They act, and in doing their work, their violence breeds contempt and rage, as well as death and mayhem. It is designed not simply to destroy and kill but also to deepen the wedge that separates the parties in conflict. And in this sense, its violence is radioactive. It contaminates all the parties involved, affecting both sides of the issue and leading each to see the other in the most negative ways. Perhaps in this case, the way beyond conquest would have to be some form of Fackenheim's 614th commandment applied to terrorist bombers: Thou shall not give the terrorist a posthumous victory![6] Yet the danger remains, and third parties with strong investments in the conflict will have to act to offer security to those who choose to act on the premises of another way of managing the violence. U.S. support of Israel during the 1991 Gulf War provides an important example of how nations might make it possible for

5. Note well that the meaning of such sacrificial actions lies in the choice to live with others nonviolently. The meaning of sacrifice does not rest in the suffering or death that is risked but in the choice for life that bears the risk.

6. Emil Fackenheim, *God's Presence in History: Jewish Affirmations and Philosophical Reflections* (New York: Harper Torchbooks, 1972), pp. 84ff.

other nations to venture into this perilous territory. Still, such risk cannot be prescribed for another, especially if we should offer such advice in relative safety while doing so.

Mythic Implications

Any responsible encounter with the Palestinian-Israeli dilemma must face up to the mythic character of its conflict. Enemies are often portrayed in biblical categories, which reduce the other to only one way of viewing them — as irreconcilable others. When Palestinians are portrayed as Amalek, or Israelis are portrayed in corresponding terms by Palestinians, the logic of scarcity once again holds the protagonists hostage. People are demonized, and the logic of scarcity prevails in the most absolute terms. Similar dynamics abound when the land is seen as a scarce resource that can be possessed by only one people. When mythic categories harden, the logic of conquest hardens with it. In searching for an alternative logic to speak to such a situation, midrash may provide a way for religious leaders to reconfigure the conflict.

Emil Fackenheim has argued that the midrashic framework provides a post-Shoah way of negotiating the biblically rooted affirmations of Israel's relationship with God and its neighbors. It allows, he argues, for the root experiences of Israel's existence to be affirmed while being challenged and stretched by contemporary experiences of suffering in the world, what he calls a tension between narrative stubbornness and unyielding realism.[7] This midrashic attitude implies a similar dialectic between scarcity and plenitude, in which plenitude is sought in the given realities of our world, no matter how scarcely they embody the resources of life within them. In other words, the imaginative mind-set operating in midrashic logic resists the logic of scarcity by insisting on finding more meaning and opportunity than the logic of scarcity presumes, and often it does so by reconfiguring how one interacts with the given reality being interpreted. The goal is not so much solving a conflict but seeking to find healthier ways to engage it.

For example, if two peoples claim that the land they inhabit is a divinely sanctioned right exclusively granted to them, then they are locked in the logic of scarcity. Only one of the parties can be right. The conflict

7. Ibid., pp. 20-25.

could be reconfigured midrashically, however, reading the situation and the religious mandates through the lens of plenitude, asking, Why would God give land to a people, promising that land to them in perpetuity, if God was fully aware that others already dwelled in the land? The logic of scarcity presumes that the land is Israel's alone; and much of Scripture bears witness to this understanding. If we resist that tradition, however, and read the gift to be one rooted in the recognition that the Promised Land is always identified as the land of someone else, then it may be that the human responsibility accompanying this gift requires that we find ways to share the land with those who already dwell there. In this case, the onus falls on the receivers of the divine gift to share creation with others in the same fashion that God has shared creation with human creatures — practicing a thoroughgoing hospitality to those who are always other.

The Way beyond Conquest

The way beyond conquest does not lead directly to a specific political strategy, no matter how much I might wish that to be so. Nor is the way beyond conquest a plea for political naïveté. Indeed, a strong dose of political realism must guide any attempt to move beyond the logic of triumph and empire. Fundamentally, the way beyond conquest is about the imagination, confessionally embodied and articulated in word and deed. More often than not, such an approach will be expressed in anguished commitment to those held hostage to the narrow confines of a world ruled by subjugation. Equally important, the way forward will lead toward reconfigured conflict so that each of its contending parties may find alternative ways to reshape their struggle and move beyond the logic of scarcity in which their dilemma is currently framed. Any other path, I fear, remains trapped in an endlessly escalating spiral of violence in which we all lose.

Contributors' Questions for Henry F. Knight

You warn us, appropriately, not to apply to Israel what we are not asking from ourselves as nations or civilians within a nation. However, might not looking first to one's own sins paralyze moral discourse about the Israeli-Palestinian conflict? Must I be silent about one people victimizing another (or two peoples victimizing each other) because I live in a country that is itself victimizing others? What happens to the victims of the struggle outside my own home/institutions/nation while I am (perpetually?) in the process of rectifying wrongs at home? Does not the Holocaust teach us that we must speak out?

You argue that the gift by God of an already-occupied land suggests that the human responsibility is to share the land. But as you also note, the biblical tradition (and to an extent, the qur'anic tradition) places the opposite requirement on its readers, namely, to conquer the land and possess it. While your confessional stance may be possible in Christianity, is it possible also in Judaism and Islam? You say that as a post-Shoah Christian you are included in a larger convenantal project. What might be the nature of your inclusion within the Palestinian/Islamic convenantal story?

Response by Henry F. Knight

There are several issues raised by the questions posed to me by my colleagues. The first, the problem of moral paralysis, should be self-evident. I have raised the issues I wanted to discuss in my essay while acknowledging the danger of not confronting the logic of conquest in my own world. That logic operates in my own national and religious traditions, just as it operates in the scriptural traditions of Israel and Islam. The issue is how to address this double and triple bind. Not addressing this bind is no longer an option for me. Having it prevent me from speaking up is likewise not an option. The task, then, is how this may be done. Our collegial enterprise in this project reflects one approach for attending to this matter, committing its participants to dialogue, mutual critique, and an honest engagement of our different interpretations about the problems and possible responses to them. I have tried to incorporate an additional strategy in raising the concerns of my chapter by writing self-consciously in a manner that reflects a different way of confronting the imaginal mind-sets that hold us hostage when we exercise the rhetoric of prophetic discourse.

The problem is not getting one's own house in order *before* looking out for the needs of one's neighbors. To approach the matter this way is to set up a false dichotomy and to miss the point of my critique. The task is to tend to one's own world with the same integrity one uses to reach out to the larger world around it. The logic at work here is not an either-or approach of sequential moral action. Rather, the logic is self-consciously dialectical, searching for a both-and strategy that calls forth the capacity to act publicly and privately, inwardly and outwardly, within one's own household the same way one acts in the increasingly wider domains of the public square in which we have voice and opportunity and for which we share responsibility with others. Whether I have found a way to do that successfully is another matter. But it would be a mistake to read my caution about tending to the logic of conquest in my own domain as an argument for not acting, or for declaring that one must first correct the problems in one's own household before addressing the needs of one's neighbors. Rather, my concern is to find a way to speak and act that actually offers a strategy for facing the dilemma before us with consistency and integrity.

If the Shoah is a reorienting event that causes Christians and Jews to rethink their moral and prophetic rhetoric, as I believe it does, then we should not expect otherwise. We must see ourselves, the world, and our place in it differently. This task will require not simply changing whom we view as perpetrator and victim or enlarging our scope of moral accountability, although such adjustments will inevitably be made. We must recognize that the epistemological reorientation cuts deeper than that. Hence my turn to the notion of a wounded faith, one that has faced the fundamental flaws that twist through the bedrock of my own tradition and through conventional foundations of Christian identity. Coming to terms with foundational problems requires either a new foundation altogether, one that is devoid of flaws (and thereby reinvests in the logic of scarcity), or an alternative way of facing and working with the flaws that are part of who and what I am, as well as who and what the narratives of Scripture tell us we all share when we walk in faith with our brothers and sisters. Hence my commitment to what I call a wounded and hospitable faith — one that limps with humility in its movement forward. Indeed, I am convinced that this same strategy is at work in the narrative logic of the Genesis tradition as it follows the unfolding story of rival siblings who struggle to learn how to share blessing and land.

I am convinced that this struggle attends the world of Palestinians and Israelis and how they dwell in their contested land just as much as it marks my own post-Shoah journey with God and others. Indeed, as I have tried to demonstrate in referring to the work of Regina Schwartz, the logic of conquest runs like a deep fault line through the heart of the Israeli-Palestinian crisis much like the Syrian-African rift cuts through the bedrock of the region underneath the Jordan River Valley. At the mythic level this imaginal divide operates much the same way the geologic fault does. In the most fundamental of ways, the world does not fit together in this holy and contested land, and its subterranean pressures must be faced for what they are — and reconfigured where possible.

I have tried to show that we may find some help by recognizing that the rhetoric of conquest, articulated clearly in the scriptural record, is not the sole voice recounted in its witness. Employing the logic of plenitude embodied in midrash, I have sought to articulate alternative ways of reading the tradition, with the hope of redirecting some of the mythic pressures that contribute to this conflict. In doing so, I am aware that I am acting out of an inclusive logic that I understand, post-Shoah, to be the relational logic of creation — the covenantal project that my post-Shoah grappling with Christian faith has led me to see and embrace as a logic of generosity and hospitality.

The Shoah, in other words, has forced me to face up to the problems that Schwartz identified as the logic of scarcity at work in the exclusivist claims of my own faith tradition. The problem, then, as a post-Shoah Christian, was whether there was a way of claiming my Christian identity that allowed me to be faithful to Christ and the traditions of the church such that I could move beyond the logic of scarcity and conquest manifest in its primary forms. I have tried to articulate that path in this essay as grounded in the divine wager for relationship that the three Abrahamic traditions know as creation. Its path is the way of hospitality. For me, it has unfolded in a postcritical wrestling with my own tradition and its problematic history with Judaism. Furthermore, the inclusive logic of creation that I have discovered by way of a midrashic reading of my own tradition is deeply indebted to Judaism and to Jewish partners in dialogue over the years. Nonetheless, my reading, even when it is dependent on Jewish sources, is Christian. Whether or not my work could be instructive for Jews, not to mention Muslims, must be for them to determine. I do, however, try to write with enough hospitality that others outside my tradition can find room in my rhetoric to explore how they might wrestle with the issues that I have raised. Indeed, it is my hope that I have encouraged this to happen. In the end, though, the claim I make about being included in a larger covenantal project is a claim I make as a Christian who views the covenantal intentionality of creation as being larger than any of the traditions of church or synagogue or mosque. Even so, it is a claim I can make only for myself and venture on behalf of the tradition I represent. Anything more would be an expression of post-Shoah hubris and the logic of conquest that I wish to avoid.

At times, to be sure, the algebra of violence and victimization is much simpler, and the summons to responsible action more clearly discernible. In these cases, the danger of overanalysis can pose a serious obstacle to responsible action. And in many of these circumstances the need for moral and prophetic courage may be more important than getting the subtleties and nuances of the conflict right. But neither of these dangers is the major problem in this dilemma. The situation in which Israelis and Palestinians find themselves is far too complex, especially when we consider the difficult and tangled history that lies behind and within it and the mythic dimensions that underlie and inform it. Consequently, any response to the Israeli-Palestinian conflict must come to terms with how we — and they — configure their conflict and understand the realities they face.

11. *The Holocaust, Israel, and the Future of Jewish-Christian Relations in the United States*

Hubert Locke

The State of Israel, its tumultuous relationships with the Palestinian populace in its midst, and the Holocaust, in the grim history of which its existence is rooted, have long presented difficulties for a serious dialogue between Jews and Christians. The dialogue is made the more problematic by
what has always been a difficult, at times tortured, and, in many respects,
inauthentic relationship — at least in the United States — between the
Jewish world and that of its stepchild, the Christian community. Since
some will find it disturbing to suggest that Jewish-Christian relations have
been marked by inauthenticity, particularly in their American context, it
may be best to start with this consideration and work back to the more
problematic issues to be considered.

In the United States the roots of intentional encounters between
Christians and the Jewish community are to be found in political and social — not theological — concerns. The presidential campaign of 1928 pit-
ted a Roman Catholic candidate, Alfred Smith, against the incumbent
Herbert Hoover and brought nativist "Christian America" forces to the
fore. These were some of the same religious sentiments that a decade earlier produced the Volstead Act and the Eighteenth Amendment to the U.S.
Constitution and, a few years earlier, the reorganized Ku Klux Klan, which
had expanded its antiblack platform to include anti-Catholic and antisemitic positions.

In reaction to this rise of religiously based conservatism in some
Christian quarters and rank bigotry in others, "a group of public-spirited
Protestants, Jews, and Roman Catholics" founded the National Conference

of Christians and Jews in 1928.[1] The NCCJ, as it was popularly called, became a major force in promoting interreligious cooperation between the three major religious bodies, but it did so at the expense of genuine theological discourse. A typical NCCJ program featured a priest, a minister, and a rabbi who each spoke briefly about his tradition and then appealed to those assembled to "reject bigotry" and learn to appreciate other religious traditions.[2] Annual Brotherhood Week observances in an earlier period and contemporary practices of holding seders in Christian churches during Pesach (Passover) and Holy Week are legacies of this historic effort. But serious discussions of two millennia of conflict between Judaism and Christianity or of the Christian roots of antisemitism were not part of this agenda.

Herein lie the roots of a lack of authenticity in Jewish-Christian relations in America. As earnest and sincere as the leaders were in both the Jewish and Christian worlds who established institutions and occasions for encouraging encounters between the two communities, their efforts were motivated far more by considerations of civic courtesy than a desire to overcome the centuries of hostility between the two religious traditions. It was almost as though there was a deliberate attempt to avoid serious theological dialogue, as if that would threaten or possibly shatter this new and fragile alliance between two historically hostile forces. For eight decades, therefore, Christians and Jews in America have been unfailingly polite to one another while meticulously avoiding, except in the rarest of settings and circumstances, discussions of substance about the historical and theological gulf that separates one community from the other.

The events that transpired in Europe between 1933 and 1945 should have provided both an occasion and the incentive for overcoming this unwillingness to engage in honest dialogue. The murder of almost six million Jews in the heart of Christian Europe poses such a monstrous problem for the whole of Western civilization that one would expect to find Christians in the vanguard of those seeking to unravel the sources of this cataclysmic occurrence and its antecedents. To their credit, where such efforts to come to terms with the Shoah are being made, a small cadre of Christian leaders and thinkers is deeply engaged. But their efforts are a distinct departure from the mainstream of post-Holocaust Christianity, which remains con-

---

1. Franklin H. Littell, *Historical Atlas of Christianity* (New York: Continuum, 2001), p. 401.

2. Ibid.

tent either to embrace the Jews eagerly as part of an apocalyptic drama in which Israel is a brief chapter in the end of Christian history or to be satisfied with interfaith conversations and rituals that avoid offending by sidestepping any confrontation of a mutual history of hostility.

To speak of a mutual history of hostility is to suggest that the burden of this current situation does not entirely rest on Christian shoulders. An authentic dialogue between Jews and Christians has been hampered not only by Christian unwillingness to confront what two thousand years of Christian history has meant for the Jewish people but also by the assumption, in significant sectors of the Jewish world, that the Christian community, because of the record of its past failures, should atone for its past by providing unwavering support of the State of Israel. Support for Israel is interpreted, by some voices in the Jewish community, to mean unwavering support for the policies of the various Israeli governments that have guided the affairs of that tiny nation since 1948.

Jews and Christians face a situation, therefore, in which neither group is as prepared for serious dialogue as one might wish. There is, in fact, a dynamic about the issues of the Holocaust, antisemitism, and the State of Israel that is immensely troubling to anyone who values the importance of wholesome and cooperative Jewish-Christian relations. All three are issues on which the perspectives of Jews and Christians appear to be widening, rather than coming closer together.

With respect to the Holocaust, for example, sharply divergent perspectives exist in the Christian and Jewish communities. To most Christians who have given thought to the matter, the experience of Jews in Europe during the Nazi era was an enormous catastrophe of incredibly brutal proportions. It stands foremost but tragically not alone in a steady progression of brutalities inflicted on selected groups of people — the Armenians during the First World War and, after the Second, the Cambodians, the Biafrans, the Bosnians, Muslims in the former Yugoslavia, and the Rwandans. Taken all together, they mark and mar the twentieth century as the century of genocide.

For many in the Jewish community, the Holocaust is a calamity quite unlike that experienced by any other people, either before or since. The Holocaust, from this latter perspective, is not the most horrific example of genocide in modern times; rather, it is a unique occurrence that reflects the singular experiences of the Jewish people in history.[3]

3. Regarding Christian perspectives, see, for example, essays in Carol Rittner, John K.

A similar difference in perspective can be seen in the current concern over the resurgence of antisemitism, particularly in Europe. Christian commentators find this resurgence to be part and parcel of the racism and xenophobia that are becoming widespread on the European continent and that are marked by increasing expressions of hostility against "alien elements" in communities both in and outside of the European Union. For many in the Jewish world, however, antisemitism is a unique phenomenon with a unique history "whose horror would be diminished if it were linked to other forms of bigotry."[4]

For those for whom the Holocaust and anti-Semitism are unique experiences, it is not difficult to understand how Israel, in turn, has become a unique and singular answer to the question of Jewish survival. From this perspective, only to the extent that a secure Jewish future is predicated on Jewish resources and resourcefulness can that future be assured. It is this simple and basic fact, it is argued, that gives the State of Israel its raison d'être.

One might expect Christians to have an especial sympathy with this viewpoint, since it is the experience of Jewish people living in ostensibly Christian nations and societies that has given rise to the fears that form at least part of the foundation of the State of Israel. But two other sentiments that Christians bring to the discussion confound the problem. Both sentiments, unfortunately, reflect and are reinforced by a uniqueness argument as well, but one that works, in one instance, against sympathetic views toward Israel and, in the other, against the interests of Israel and the Jewish people as a whole.

The first sentiment is deeply rooted in both mainstream and evangelical Christianity. Generations of Christians in both camps have been raised, in Sunday schools and from sermons from Christian pulpits, on the idea of Jewish uniqueness — particularly, the idea of the Jewish people as the Chosen of God. Although in conservative Christian circles this idea of the Jewish people as chosen has been trumped by the notion that Chris-

---

Roth, and Wendy Whitworth, eds., *Genocide in Rwanda: Complicity of the Churches?* (St. Paul, Minn.: Paragon House, 2004). Prominent scholars who hold this position include Yehuda Bauer (*Rethinking the Holocaust* [New Haven: Yale University Press, 2001]) and Stephen T. Katz ("The Uniqueness of the Holocaust: The Historical Dimension," in *Is the Holocaust Unique?* ed. Alan S. Rosenbaum [Boulder, Colo.: Westview Press, 1996], pp. 19-38).

4. "Europeans and Americans Seek Answers to Anti-Semitism," *New York Times,* February 20, 2004, A11.

tians now enjoy this special status, the idea nevertheless persists among Christians that the Jewish people somehow — at the least, historically — have had a special place in the divine economy or have been given a more heightened moral grasp of the divine will than that afforded other people in the ancient world.

Accordingly, many Christians have been long convinced that they could look for a different, more elevated moral response to injustice and human conflict from the Jewish people than from other groups, including even themselves! Mainstream Christians came to believe that they saw just such a heightened moral sensitivity in the engagement of the American Jewish community in the struggle for civil rights and liberties in the United States — the prominent role, for example, of Jewish leaders in the founding of the National Association for the Advancement of Colored People (NAACP), the Urban League, and the American Civil Liberties Union (ACLU), among others. Christian leaders hailed the same sentiment when their Jewish colleagues eagerly joined in the establishment of the National Conference of Christians and Jews — even though the NCCJ was a response to essentially a Christian problem, namely, that of bigotry within Christian America!

Similarly, in the creation of the Congress on Racial Equality (CORE), the Committee on a Sane Nuclear Policy, and opposition to the war in Viet Nam, the mainstream Christian community came to take for granted the presence and support of the Jewish community as wholly consistent with the Christian image and understanding of a people who have a special, historic, and unique — even if, for some, superseded — relationship with a God of compassion and justice.

In this context, the establishment of the State of Israel was anticipated, in large parts of the Christian world, as the advent of a modern nation that would reflect this ancient tradition of an elevated, national morality and display it in world affairs. Modern Israel, it was assumed, would be a replica of biblical Israel; its governments would not be guided by principles of self-interest and power politics, like other nation-states, but by the prophetic ideals espoused by Isaiah, Amos, and Micah.

Continuous conflict between Israelis and Palestinians, therefore, has shattered this romanticized notion of Israel that many Christians have harbored. They recoil from the intifada and other eruptions of violence on the part of Hamas, the PLO, and Hezbollah; they are also dismayed when the Israeli government restricts the movement of and imposes curfews on

Palestinians, bulldozes their homes, erects a wall, bombards Lebanon — all in an effort to achieve a secure Jewish state.

In effect, the Christian community has become victim of its own idealized expectations. Its image of a Jewish nation that would be, in biblical terms, a "light to the Gentiles" has been marred by the realization that Israel behaves exactly in the same manner that every other nation does — including and especially the United States — insofar as national security is supreme and national interests are to be advanced and protected above all else.

Both this Christian expectation and its disappointment are compounded by a religious factor that further embroils the possibility of a Jewish-Christian dialogue regarding Israel. A significant (not in numbers but in status) segment of the Palestinian populace is Christian, with close church ties to mainstream Christian bodies in the United States and Europe. Accordingly, those whom many Jews may view as sworn enemies of Israel are viewed by many Christians as those who share a common faith and are the victims of occupation and oppression by Israeli forces.

This relationship produces some marked differences in attitude and perspective on various issues of public policy regarding Israel between some sectors of the Jewish world and that of mainstream Christianity. If, for example, one takes the basic idea of Eretz Israel — of the Land of Israel as having especial significance for the Jewish people — one finds that mainstream Christian bodies take a decidedly neutral stance on this issue or, in some instances, support competing Palestinian claims.[5] A tragically bifurcated collection of sentiments along a Jewish-Christian divide thus erupts whenever Israel is under discussion. In its essence, this schism is be-

5. See, for example, the 1990 declaration of the United Church of Christ: "We appreciate the compelling argument for the creation of modern Israel as a vehicle for self-determination and as a haven for victimized people; we also recognize that this event has entailed the dispossession of Palestinians from their homes and the denial of human rights." American Lutherans similarly state that "it seems clear that there is no consensus among Lutherans with respect to the relationship between the 'chosen people' and the territory comprising the present State of Israel," while the Anglican communion, as recently as 2003, reaffirmed its long-standing position, which condemns "violence on all sides and seek[s] peace and justice for all Holy Land residents." The citations are from F. Michael Perko, S.J., "'Jerusalem in Slavery': Christians, the Bible, and Contemporary Israeli/Palestinian Politics" (paper presented at the Annual Meeting of the Association for Israel Studies, May 2003), available online at http://www.bc.edu/research/cjl/meta-elements/texts/cjrelations/resources/articlesperko03.htm.

tween people who share nearly everything of importance — a common religious heritage, a shared political commitment to democratic ideals, and common values deeply rooted in the Western tradition — all except a history that permits Christians and Jews to see the contemporary world through one another's eyes.

The second sentiment that confounds discussions between Jews and Christians is found among the Christian Right and is far less benign toward the Jewish people. Because of this sentiment, it is especially ironic that there are closer, more collaborative relationships currently between some quarters of the Jewish establishment and that of the Christian Right than that between Jewish leaders and their mainstream Christian counterparts.

For the segment of the Christian Right that has a peculiar, apocalyptic vision of what are called the end times, the founding of the State of Israel has an especial, theological significance. In such a view, the return of the Jewish people to the Land of Israel is only a prelude to the return of Christ to earth and the beginning of his final reign. In this theological calculus, the Jewish people are but pawns in a Christian drama in which the Jews will, in the end, disappear. Matthew Engel has graphically described this theological sentiment (known as dispensationalism), pointing out that it centers on "the Rapture, the Second Coming of Christ which will presage the end of the world. A happy ending depends on the conversion of the Jews. And that . . . can only happen if the Jews are in possession of all the lands given to them by God. In other words, these Christians are supporting the Jews in order to abolish them."[6]

It is perhaps a measure of the current estrangement between Jews and Christians that portions of the Jewish community, anxious to secure support for the State of Israel, find it more advantageous to make common political cause with a segment of the Christian world that theologically envisions the end of the Jewish people than with those Christians who theologically affirm Judaism and the Jewish people as equally valid expressions of God's creation but who have political reservations about Israeli government policies. It is but one of several reasons that a Jewish-Christian dialogue, reestablished on a more realistic and candid basis, is one of the imperatives of our time.

Such a dialogue may be difficult to initiate, as many Jews and many

---

6. Michael Engel, "Meet the New Zionists," *Guardian*, October 28, 2002, p. 2.

Christians outside the evangelical fold find themselves presently at an impasse. For those who are Jewish and for whom Israel is the only guarantor against a madness like the Holocaust reoccurring, the existence of that tiny nation in the midst of a sea of Islamic hostility must be defended at all costs. It frequently means defending policies of an Israeli government that others find oppressive or abhorrent. For Christians who view the Holocaust as one of, if not the greatest of, the moral failures of modern history, the massacre of the Jews of Europe does not provide the government of Israel with a cloak of immunity from criticism of its policies. Somewhere between what to each side are rational, defensible positions, dialogue has ceased, being replaced by varying levels of distrust and recrimination.

Jews and Christians perhaps should proceed with discussions neither of the Holocaust nor of Israel but with the enduring problem of antisemitism. With respect to the Holocaust, we have entered an age in which nearly everyone has a saga of victimization — even modern German writers now recount the firebombing of Dresden and other wartime atrocities with the lament that Germans were victims too! Perhaps we shall have to get beyond a generation of self-absorption and self-pity before we can rediscover the true foundations of moral outrage. As for Israel, for reasons already suggested it is not the place to launch conversations between Jews and Christians. Hopefully, Israel is a point toward which those conversations can progress, once more basic issues have been addressed.

Of all the issues, antisemitism is the most basic — not simply because it precedes the Holocaust and the State of Israel, but because it is fundamental, lying at the core of the hostility of non-Jews toward Jews, including the hostility of some Christians, and because it often serves as a self-imposed barrier among Jews to candid conversations with the non-Jewish world.

A serious examination of antisemitism, however, if it is to occur among other than the Jewish people themselves, requires abandoning the notion of its uniqueness. Antisemitism is unique only to the extent that it is a label given to (frightfully widespread) attitudes or behavior directed against Jews. Whether displayed toward Jewish people or more generally, however, the attitudes and behaviors are of the same character and quality as that of all other racial hostility; the same instincts and convictions drive them. All such attitudes and behaviors have in common, and rest on, the social artifact of *race;* only in acknowledging this fact do we begin to fathom the nature of the problem with which we must deal.

In a curiously tragic sense, tens of thousands of German Jews were trapped in Germany after the war broke out in 1939 because they could not bring themselves to acknowledge that race was the way in which the Nazis were defining their presence and their nonplace in German society. These were Jewish people who, to a remarkable degree, were well-established among the German middle and upper classes. They thought of themselves in every respect as good Germans and were utterly devastated not to be seen and accepted as such.

But National Socialism was fixated on what it considered to be German society's race problem. German Jews were deemed to be the most prominent feature of that problem. It mattered not that the Jews did not think of themselves as a race — the Nazis did, and that conviction ultimately required, in Nazi terms, a "final solution" to the society's imagined racial crisis.

Antisemitism is the application to Jews of notions about race, racial superiority, and racial inferiority that in other ethnic and social contexts are applied to other peoples in equal measure. Coming to terms with this wider phenomenon gives Jews, Christians, and a good portion of the rest of the world a common problem to be recognized and addressed.

Addressing the problem of race in the modern world places an equal burden on Christians and Jews. As the history of Christianity is marred by its moral blindness whenever the issue of race has been paramount — slavery in the seventeenth and eighteenth centuries and colonialism in the nineteenth are two prominent examples — it should require no more than a reminder of this tragic feature of the Christian record to underscore its urgency for the Christian community in the present era.

The challenge for Jews is more complex but no less urgent. It is undoubtedly difficult for a people who, however much they might resist the designation, have themselves been seen as a distinct racial group to see themselves as capable of racial bias. Jews who have been in the forefront of efforts to eradicate racial prejudice and its impact may especially recoil at the suggestion that racial bias might be a problem within their own community. For a people who suffered the ultimate in racial hatred, this suggestion is likely to be particularly offensive.

Nevertheless, the very fact of the Holocaust, which serves as a grim reminder of the worst experience of racial antipathy on record, obliges Jews to inquire about the extent to which some members of the Jewish community might be participants in the problem of race, as well as its victims. Public opinion polls, media reports, and academic studies suggest that the Jewish world — especially in segments of Israeli society — faces a problem of no small consequence in this regard.[7]

If it is possible, at some future point, to look back on this era as one in which communities that harbored historic hostilities toward one another moved instead toward accord and harmonious relations, it will be in no small measure because Jews, Christians, and Muslims worked assiduously to overcome centuries of racial hostility between and among them. The Holocaust should warn all three religious traditions about the incalculable cost of failure.

7. See, for example, "Attitudes regarding Israeli Arabs," in Asher Arian, *Israeli Public Opinion on National Security, 2003* (Tel Aviv: Tel Aviv University, Jaffee Center for Strategic Studies, 2003), pp. 31-32. The report is available at http://www.tau.ac.il/jcss/memoranda/ memo67.pdf.

Contributors' Questions for Hubert Locke

You note that the ice of Christian-Jewish harmony is thin and hardly covers the underlying sea of prejudice. You suggest starting anew with a discussion of antisemitism as racism. But does this discussion manage to overcome old paths of politically correct Jewish-Christian dialogue, or is it not itself one of these paths? You argue that antisemitism is a subspecies of racism shared by both Jews and Christians. Yet is it not the case that Christian antisemitism — rooted in the theological claim of the "disconfirming other" — is so distinctive that the issue of the uniqueness of this particular bigotry will inevitably arise early on?

You write: "For those for whom the Holocaust and antisemitism are unique experiences, it is not difficult to understand how Israel, in turn, has become a unique and singular answer to the question of Jewish survival." Given that your essay positions the Holocaust and antisemitism within larger contexts, would you further argue that Jewish survival does *not* rest upon the survival of Israel? Does your essay imply that Jews need to trust non-Jews more for their survival?

Response by Hubert Locke

Given the realities of Jewish history, the tendency to consider antisemitism as a unique form of antipathy quite unlike that which any other group of people has experienced is understandable. Antisemitism is not, however, so distinctive as to warrant its treatment as a special case in the interminable list of racial hatreds that have marked and marred Western societies, virtually since their inception.

Two realities would seem to belie this assertion. One is the Holocaust itself — a genocidal act so enormous in its reach and barbaric in its result as to appear incomparable. The debate among scholars regarding the uniqueness of the Holocaust continues unabated; by and large, that debate is not germane here except to note that even if one were to grant the uniqueness of the Holocaust, it would not, per se, validate the uniqueness of antisemitism but only the exceptional features of one antisemitic experience.

The basic problem with the position of those who point to the Holocaust as an indication of the uniqueness of antisemitism is that it inadvertently endorses the very position that Hitler and the Nazis took regarding Jews. Their racial policy was disdainful of everyone who was not of Teutonic ancestry — there was no room in the Third Reich for Slavs, except as a racially inferior, subservient populace, or for the Sinti, who were viewed as an antisocial, criminal class, or even for persons of mixed racial backgrounds because, it was alleged, they might pollute the pure Teutonic stock. Only for Jews, however, was a special racial category reserved. And the antisemitism-as-unique position, carried to its logical end, comes to the same conclusion: the Jews are a special group of humanity!

It is one matter to consider uniqueness as attributable to positive traits; it is obviously another matter entirely if uniqueness is seen in wholly negative attributes. Either way, when unique attributes — either positive or negative — are applied to groups rather than to individuals, they are tantamount to stereotypes and, as such, reflect habits of mind we should all like to see disappear.

The other reality that would seem to confirm the uniqueness of antisemitism is older and more extended. It is the antipathy toward Jews that arises out of distinctly Christian sources — theological in some instances, cultural and national in others, or a combination of all three in yet other settings and situations. It is fundamentally important that this historic reality is acknowledged; it is equally important, in this first part of the twenty-first century, to recognize that the curse of Christian antisemitism currently does not have the currency it had in the past. To continue to treat Christian antisemitism as though it were the plague it undeniably represented in the Western world up until and including World War II is to dismiss, out of hand, much that has transpired in the past half century.

Clarity and precision are important here. Before us is only the issue of Christian antisemitism — not the forms and features of anti-Jewish hatred that find their impetus and expression in an assortment of other phobias (economic, intellectual, professional, etc.). The history of Christian antisemitism is traceable back to the Church Fathers, and for some scholars to portions of the Christian New Testament itself, but unless that history takes into consideration intensive and extended efforts in nearly all of the mainstream Christian bodies — both Roman Catholic and Protestant — to own up to this tragic legacy, to renounce its roots and its consequences, and to undertake tasks aimed at its eradication, it is incomplete. Even worse, it risks becoming suspect, as though there is something to be gained by continuing to claim that which circumstances no longer warrant.

No one can claim, however, that Christian antisemitism is a thing of the past. Pockets of ignorance and bigotry remain in some segments of the Christian world, untouched by the efforts of the past half century. Some people who profess to be Christians still cling to a hatred of Jews, in many instances together with a hatred of all "others" not like themselves — including blacks, Muslims, gays, and lesbians. This is the primary reason that enlightened Christians and Jews ought to take up jointly the task of addressing the larger phobia of race (and its sexual derivative) that infects the modern world, rather than remain absorbed in its more specific manifestations.

For anyone who is not Jewish, to opine on the problematics of Jewish survival and the State of Israel is, to a considerable extent, presumptuous. Several dimensions of the question, however, are of interest to non-Jews, as well as to the Jewish world. First, the history of the past two millennia has been that of a period in which the Jewish people have existed in every continent on the globe. Only for a very brief period during this time has the State of Israel been in existence. Clearly, therefore, Jewish survival has not, for most of the past two thousand years, rested on the existence of the State of Israel. Furthermore, and for those who are inclined to consider the question theologically, the covenant between God and the people of Israel is the ultimate assurance of Jewish survival — that assurance transcends any secular or political arrangements that might exist, whatever importance is attached to them.

The underlying issue here is the secular and political arrangement that constitutes the Jewish state that came into existence in 1948. Essentially, we are being asked whether the Jewish people need to trust non-Jews, not for their survival as a people, but for the survival of the State of Israel. Jews — especially Israelis — have ample reasons to reject this question out of hand. One of the major reasons for Israel's creation as a nation-state, as is well-known, arose from the general indifference of the non-Jewish world to the virtual annihilation of the Jewish populace of Europe in the middle of the last century.

Precisely because Israel is a modern nation-state, it behaves like every other nation-state, including its need to make alliances, have allies, and seek support for its interests. (It does so even in such unlikely quarters as the Christian Right, many of whose adherents consider the existence of Israel as a brief, passing, and ultimately dispensable phase in the final drama of history.) Israel therefore has no choice but to look to others outside its borders in order to secure its survival, notwithstanding the legendary record of the Israeli military. If Israel behaves, at times, as though its future were solely in its own hands, it is undoubtedly because of the tragedies of the Jewish past. That Israel's behavior, in part because of this past, is sometimes as problematic as that of its putative friends and allies is part of the tragic reality of geopolitics in the modern era.

12. Critical Thinking and Self-Identity: Educating for Peace between Israelis and Palestinians

Amy H. Shapiro

If I had lived through the Holocaust or grown up in the 1930s in Nazi Germany, I believe I would have been more Jewish-identified than I am today. Had I been the same person I am today, which I would most decidedly not have been, I believe I would have felt compelled to identify myself as Jewish in response to Nazi oppression. I also would have known myself through an identity instilled in me through the categories determined by my social milieu. Perhaps to this day my long-term research into the philosophy of the genocide of Europe's Jews is my means of identifying myself as Jewish. And perhaps, if the Holocaust had never happened, my sense of myself as Jewish would be relegated to family history.

How, I ask myself, would I have seen myself, had I been born and raised in Israel? Who would I have seen in the mirror? Attempting to answer these kinds of questions is akin to saying, "If your grandma had a beard, she'd be your grandpa."[1] Such questions assume matters of nature and seem to operate without doubt. That is, the assumption is that being born Jewish in this life, I would have been born Jewish in another because being Jewish is something essential about my being. I would not be able to look in the mirror and see an Arab looking back at me because, as a Jew,

1. Barbara Lebow, *A Shayna Maidel* (New York: New American Library, 1985), p. 75.

I especially wish to thank Donna Engelmann, without whom I could not have written this article. I want to thank as well the following people for their helpful feedback: Catherine Dupar, Tim Riordan, Kelly Birmingham, Sadiqa Issa, Rachael Hoffman, Tara Mitchell, and Karen van Hoof. — Amy Shapiro

that is precisely *not* what I am. And I certainly would not be able to look in a mirror and see a Palestinian looking back at me because, from a Jewish perspective, to be Palestinian — by definition — is essential to the existence of those particular Arabs.

In his book *Arab and Jew,* David K. Shipler quotes Elhanan Naeh, a Talmudic scholar: "To educate people to be more humanistic is to tell them to live with ambiguity and to like ambiguity — not only to live with it as an accident but to understand human nature as ambiguous."[2] Naeh goes on to point out that such teaching is particularly difficult in wartime. On the surface, his statement may seem benign, a passing remark by an educator who believes he has something to tell his students. But deconstructing Naeh's remark reveals significant issues embedded in educational theory and practice. Understanding these issues can lead us to a way of thinking that might help harvest a long-lasting peace between Israelis and Palestinians.

Naeh's emphasis on ambiguity — our ability not only to tolerate it but also to appreciate it — is provocative. Why ambiguity? one might ask. What do people need to be told about ambiguity? What does it mean "to understand human nature as ambiguous"? What does it mean to teach someone to be more humanistic? This notion of ambiguity radically challenges essentialist understandings of human nature. Although we may behave as if there is certainty in our identity, we live our lives in ambiguity. To say human nature is ambiguous is apparently contradictory. How do we help students understand this paradox?

Naeh's comments use the word "tell." The idea that students will learn something by having it "told" to them is an idea about educational methodology that has long been fostered in public education. It stresses the *content* of learning rather than its *processes.* It speaks to a particular way in which societal values are instilled through education and emphasizes education that is content-based rather than classroom-based.[3] It also speaks to the assumed authority of the educator as the "teller" of knowledge.[4] This methodology potentially implies a tyranny that emerges from presuming, rather than reinforcing, a democratic process of learning. As

2. David K. Shipler, *Arab and Jew: Wounded Spirits in a Promised Land* (New York: Times Books, 1986), pp. 27-28.

3. See Parker Palmer, *The Courage to Teach* (San Francisco: Jossey-Bass, 1998).

4. See, for example, bell hooks, *Teaching to Transgress: Education as the Practice of Freedom* (New York: Routledge, 1994); and Paulo Freire, *Education for Critical Consciousness,* (New York: Continuum, 1994).

long as we only *presume* that a democratic process of learning is taking place, education cannot promote peace between peoples in conflict such as Israelis and Palestinians.

In this essay, I propose a method of education that fosters identity beyond the given social narratives in which individuals have been taught to have a stake and through which they come to recognize themselves as individuals and, hence, as human. Focusing on the development of critical-thinking abilities in education is crucial to the development of identity formation and to the promotion of democracy and peace. Instilling exclusive identities by reifying disciplinary content and the contexts that allow those contents to be expressed will only continue to undermine the potential for peace between Palestinians and Israelis. Though disciplinary content may masquerade as objective, in reality it is ideologically loaded, thus leading to notions of certainty rather than to the appreciation of the ambiguity of human nature (and all that this ambiguity may mean).

The Israeli-Palestinian conflict is no doubt a conflict between socially constructed realities. The best kind of education can reveal this construction and promote peace. Through what is taught in schools (including religious schools) and through the norms of the accepted order (including the perceived nonambiguity of human nature), learners come to believe a set of premises about themselves: what they are and what they are not. Students learn to perceive their identities as certain or fixed, as opposed to ambiguous. Examination of the premises of traditional education is rarely encouraged. Appreciation of ambiguity comes through a different set of strategies employed to teach individuals.

Here I address two aspects of educational theory and practice. The first involves context: the role of the educator and the educational institution as potentially democratizing forces. The second involves the perceptions of the individual who is to be educated. Education that fosters peace involves both of these aspects. An examination of the assumptions at work in our presumed democratic educational processes will bring us closer to creating a truly democratic education.

Educational Values as Context

An examination of curricula within a totalitarian state reveals that education in this context is used to manipulate the narrative identities of its populace to support not only the values (which are not necessarily humanitarian or just) of the state but also the enhancement of its enterprises — even if, or especially if, those enterprises are repressive. Nazi Germany provides a prototype of how a totalitarian state can employ the established disciplines of the university to support its endeavors. Nazi education fostered an identity with the dominant group (the *Volk*) and a rejection of those who were not its accepted members (Jews, for example, and the disabled).[5] Early schooling in Nazi culture reinforced pan-German ideals, the rote learning of Nazi tenets, and loyalty to the state. Education of individuals was an education of national identity.

Examination of curricula in democratic societies also reveals the role of education as a means of cultivating a fixed identity among its citizens. Present democratic systems of education are designed (though not necessarily intended) to reify the values of a given society and strongly dominant groups within that society. In its original intent, the idea of the university in a democracy could be understood to foster an appreciation of the self as citizen (a national identification) and to instill the values of society as a way to produce statesmen — members of the polity who would contribute to the national agenda.[6] A democracy that provides the university's context is understood to provide the framework for liberal thinking. But the agenda of the university in a democracy, not unlike that of the agenda of the university in a totalitarian state, often merely reinforces the values of dominant groups within the society that maintains it.[7] And the academy may also help to reify the positions of these groups within the power structures of the society.

As members of marginalized groups have campaigned for the opportunity to participate more fully in the academy, they have revealed the nature of these power structures and have even served to dismantle many of them. For example, both Nancy Goldberger and Florence Howe exam-

5. See Karl Jaspers, *The Idea of the University*, ed. Karl W. Deutsch, trans. H. A. T. Reiche and H. F. Vanderschmidt (Boston: Beacon Press, 1959); George L. Mosse, *The Crisis of German Ideology: Intellectual Origins of the Third Reich* (New York: Grossett & Dunlap, 1964); and Fritz K. Ringer, *The Decline of the German Mandarins: The German Academic Community, 1890-1933* (Cambridge, Mass.: Harvard University Press, 1964).

6. See Henry Adams, *The Education of Henry Adams* (Boston: Houghton Mifflin, 1918).

7. See Jane Roland Martin, *Changing the Educational Landscape: Philosophy, Women, and Curriculum* (New York: Routledge, 1994).

ine how educational instruction has marginalized women;[8] Patricia Collins and bell hooks identify how educational instruction has marginalized people of color, especially women of color.[9] One might say that theorists have identified contexts in which there is no room to develop notions of the ambiguity of human nature. Through the reinforcement of dominant societal values, which has resulted in delimiting the potential of competing identities, colleges and universities were able to minimize the effect of marginalized people on academic studies. To their credit, democratic educational systems have allowed for a discourse that has yielded ground to new disciplines and fields of study — women's studies, African studies, and Holocaust and genocide studies not least among them.

There are vast differences between the general practice of teaching the content of disciplines versus teaching students to examine the cognitive and critical processes that allow one to think the way one does.[10] Engaging in such examination reveals the influence of these processes on the content and culture of the disciplines. Contextualizing one's own sense of identity within the idea of the ambiguity of human nature cannot really happen without examining the social stratification and individual experiences that have led to development of fixed identities.

When one learns disciplinary content, one learns to "know" what is (already) believed by others, whereas study of the epistemology underlying disciplines involves examining the strategies that are used to "know." The latter involves an examination both of what is believed and of the processes that have led one to believe it. When education is at its best, it engages with both types of examination.

These approaches to education relate to differences in passive versus active learning. Through passive learning, students learn the content of disciplines. Understanding how disciplines engage frameworks and strategies constitutes active learning. Rarely do pedagogical practices in colleges and universities systematically teach epistemology as a critically important

8. Nancy Goldberger, Jill Tarule, Blythe Clinchy, and Mary Belenky, eds., *Knowledge, Difference, and Power: Essays Inspired by Women's Ways of Knowing* (New York: Basic Books, 1996); Florence Howe, *Myths of Coeducation* (Bloomington: Indiana University Press, 1984).

9. Patricia Hill Collins, "Learning from the Outsider Within: The Sociological Significance of Black Feminist Thought," *Social Problems* 33, no. 6 (1986): 14-32; hooks, *Teaching to Transgress.*

10. Marcia Mentkowski and Associates, *Learning That Lasts: Integrating Learning, Development, and Performance in College and Beyond* (San Francisco: Jossey-Bass, 2000).

educational methodology.[11] Democratic educational systems lack the ability to imagine the pedagogical practices that would teach us that contents are related to epistemological frameworks that impose ways of thinking on our approaches to the world.[12]

The absence of an active approach to teaching may contribute to conditions that potentially foster the kind of thinking that produced and maintained the support of Nazi Germany and that today produces and supports fixed Israeli perceptions of Palestinians and vice versa. Democratic education fosters the idea of the individual without necessarily providing the tools that prompt an individual to examine how his or her own beliefs and identity were formed. Before I propose the kind of education that I believe can foster peace, it is important to understand the factors that reinforce identity formation in educational realms.

Development of Self-Identities

Bat-Ami Bar On illustrates the results of social inculcation of identity by referring to an eighteen-year-old Jewish Israeli soldier visiting the Ghetto Fighters Museum: "Walking around the museum aware of himself as a member of a military now heavily engaged with 'policing' the Palestinians, he sensed something and was struggling with the lesson that he was supposed to learn about the importance of his role as a Jewish Israeli soldier. What he was supposed to do is identify with the self-sacrificing Jewish Resistance to Nazi victimization of Jews. He was not expected to see himself reflected in a mirror that implicated him as a perpetrator, perhaps not unlike the Nazis, with the victimization of the Palestinians."[13] The Jewish Israeli soldier was learning to see himself as a Jewish victim, identified with the victims of the Holocaust and, by extension, with the victims of the Jewish Diaspora, subject to a long history of oppression by inhospitable adopted coun-

---

11. James Roth, "Common Ground: How History Professors and Undergraduate Students Learn through History," in *Disciplines as Frameworks for Student Learning*, ed. T. Riordan and J. Roth (Sterling, Va.: Stylus Publishing, 2005), pp. 3-20.

12. Colleges and universities serve a very wide range of students, many of whom are unprepared for college, partly because of this emphasis on content. To develop education that fosters peace, we must keep in mind that we have to educate everyone.

13. Bat-Ami Bar On, *The Subject of Violence* (Lanham, Md.: Rowman & Littlefield, 2002), pp. 34-35.

tries. This identity has been well taught. There is no room for ambiguity of identity when one is required to police or inflict harm on an enemy.

Embedded in Bar On's account is the "teaching" that is taking place at the Ghetto Fighters Museum. This teaching is largely subliminal and therefore reckless. It is meant to help the individual (whom we now recognize as "the soldier") identify himself as human through his Jewish identity. Merely telling him that human nature is ambiguous would mean little.

The example suggests how perfunctorily identity can become fixed, certain, and without ambiguity. Through a lack of critical examination, human nature becomes seen in an essentialist mode. The point is not that one should have no identity, for this would be impossible, but that we dangerously treat our identities as essential when we fail to consider how such identities are learned.

If I am a Palestinian and my understanding of myself as Palestinian is certain and fixed ideologically, the consequences of such thinking have the potential to be, and in reality have been, truly deadly for me and for the other. Presumed in such a sense of self as Palestinian is a definition of what it means to be human. In so defining myself, I am determining, as part of that definition, what I am not.

What is not a Palestinian, however that is defined, is outside the realm of my identity, which puts it outside the realm of my notion of humanness. Because it is treated as a given, being Palestinian becomes essential. As a result, it then does not occur to me to ask what it means to construct such a notion of the self. If my definition of my self is equivalent to my notion of humanness, I have created a tautology. The Nazi ideology of identity teaches us this lesson. To equate state identity with humanness allows one to reason in the moral realm with deadly consequences.

One of my former students, a Palestinian, reflected on her initial response to discussions about the Israeli-Palestinian conflict that had taken place at the beginning of her junior year. In an e-mail message, she wrote: "My beliefs about Israelis at that time had shaped where I felt I needed to be in that conversation, and that was on the Palestinian side. I am also slowly beginning to learn that a lot of it was because I had inferiority issues (I didn't think that a Jew could see me as a human being)." Curiously, she placed the most significant part of her statement in parentheses. Belief that a Jew could not see her as a human being was part of her assumed identity. Her perception of an Israeli or a Jew rested on the idea that the Israeli or Jew saw being Israeli or Jewish as essential to his or her identity as a human being, whereas her identity as a human being was dependent on her identity as a Palestinian.

My student's e-mail message suggests the power of examining perceptions critically. Awareness of thinking processes informed the student's sense of what it is to be human and, consequently, allowed her to see human nature as ambiguous. How she arrived at this juncture is significant for the way we need to construct education to foster a notion of ambiguity of identity, thus creating tools for individuals to become more humanistic.

Critical Thinking

The combination of a fixed view of identity with an undeveloped ability to think critically can, as we have seen, be lethal. Though ethical decision-making may be a form of critical thinking, it is not the whole of that process. As we know from the rationalizations of terrorists, Nazi doctors, and SS officers, one can easily justify one's ethics. Critical thinking calls upon one to reason about the lives of those who are not identified with one's own constructed narratives of the self.

Perhaps it will seem too simple to say that teaching critical thinking will lead to development of a complex notion of identity, one that includes ways to appreciate and even to like ambiguity. But once we realize that the teaching of critical thinking does double duty, this task will not seem so simple. On the one hand, critical thinking is intended to help individuals understand what leads to their identities as human. On the other hand, it is designed to give people the tools to reflect before acting out of presumed identities and to tolerate the complexity of such identities that emerges as a consequence.

Once I realize that my way of viewing myself is reflected in how everyone else views me, I realize I am viewing others to affirm my own identity. This view of the self is tyrannical; it compels me to maintain my place at the center of what it means to be human. Analysis of identity, particularly my own, can free me of this tyranny.

When the strategies used to educate include formal critical-thinking abilities, the student is able to view the self in the context of how he or she has developed identity. Educating for conflict resolution or peaceful coexistence is not simply a matter of teaching individuals about the world around them, learning the techniques of conflict resolution, or putting two people together in the same room and letting them "get to know one another."

To tell Israelis about the experiences of Palestinians and vice versa will only serendipitously lead to change in awareness of the other. But if one teaches Israelis how beliefs about the other have served to identify them within a set narrative, they can question how perceptions of Palestinians have helped maintain their identity as Israelis. The capacity to question and analyze, to consider ambiguity, rather than relying on assumed self-identity, is transformational. This process involves understanding the disciplinary techniques available for analysis of the narratives that construct those identities.

I had a first-year traditional-aged student who identified with her Muslim-Arab father. She expressed apprehension at the possibility that she could learn something from a teacher who was a Jew. Being my student further amplified her awareness of her identity as a Muslim-Arab, causing her to reiterate many negative ideas about Jews. Had I dealt with this situation only by modeling a content approach to education, I doubt that much good would have come of it. Had I dealt with the situation through anger, there would have been no possibility of learning. Instead I emphasized self-assessment. On appropriate occasions in class, I shared examples of the role that false notions had played in my perceptions of others, including examples of negative stereotyping of Arabs. (Heaven forbid I should expect more honesty of my students than of myself!) I also taught methods of analysis related to the educational aims articulated above.

As part of the method of developing critical thinking, I teach students to question the origins of their ideas — exploring both the content of their beliefs and the methods they use to produce and sustain them. Through self-assessment, this particular student began to examine assumptions about Jews. Having learned what it means to make assumptions, she independently reflected on the origin of her perceptions. She was able to place herself outside of the dominant narrative of her identity with her father and to include an identity as student, thinker, and active learner — an approach that fostered an understanding of ambiguity.[14]

This process had its difficulties. The student's sense of security in her

14. One can only begin to imagine how this process affected her sense of the power of her father and how it allowed her to consider the significance of her mother, who was Filipina, in the formation of her identity.

identity was disrupted. Instead of abating, her anger became more intense, at least for a time. She struggled to replace concrete thought with abstract reasoning and ambiguity. However, as she became more aware that her identity was dependent on a limited perspective, her perception of her world shifted. Without any content-prodding from me or others around her, she employed analytic strategies to reflect on her perspective. The student realized that her father's religion and culture (as one framework) might impose a perspective that limited her view of herself in the world.

In her final oral self-assessment, the student shared with the class how analysis had prompted her to reflect on the sources of her knowledge and the assumptions she had carried with her. She affirmed that she hoped to work as a biologist in a Third World country and contribute to the betterment of others.

Conclusion

The best teaching ultimately starts with the student. Good education is about individuals, and it is based on awareness that education left uncriticized can become a tool of power that inculcates problematic societal values or manipulates social identities. We have seen how assumed identity influences how we view others. In this chapter, I have offered an approach but purposely chosen not to give details and examples of what it would mean to educate for peace between Palestinians and Israelis. A teacher must begin with the question of who one's students are, what their contexts are, and what specific strategies they need to learn to gain a sense of the ambiguity of human nature.

If all participants are fairly treated in the classroom (I am not suggesting here that the instructor relinquish all responsibility), then the competing and dissenting voices that emerge as expressions of identity will find a context that can allow them all an equal footing. This will ultimately result in more all-embracing attitudes toward others. Identities are important, but they remain fluid and ambiguous and are never finally fixed or essentialistic. Why emphasize Israeli or Palestinian? Why not men and women, power and powerless, straight and gay, straight and lesbian, white and black, Christian and Muslim and Jew, or even political and philosophical? *Who* emphasizes and *what* gets emphasized usually allow us to avoid multiple identities within an ambiguous narrative. Good educational instruction teaches critical thinking that promotes imagining the other through an examination of the construction of self-identity. Using analysis of disciplinary frameworks, a paradigm of competing identities, and the idea of human nature as ambiguous can provide an education that will contribute to the creation of peace.

Contributors' Questions for Amy H. Shapiro

You critique the essentialist assumption that being an Israeli (or a Palestinian) is equivalent to being human. It is clearly dangerous to identify oneself with any fixed narrative at the expense of seeing the full range of humanity. But do strong religious and ethnic identities necessarily close us off to "the human"? Might it not be the case that well-formed identities can serve as the foundation for a concern with others, allowing us to engage fully with their struggles? How might Israelis and Palestinians be educated so as to create both a strong personal identity and a concern for the other?

Your philosophy supports critical processes that call into question the dominant narratives within which self-identity is constructed. But does this approach not presuppose a peculiarly Western embrace of the values of the individual and of rational thought? How is this solution appropriate for the Middle East — especially for those Muslim nations in which the value of community takes precedence over the individual? Is your solution not ethnocentric in the sense that the Muslims should become like me (an American or European Christian) — namely, individualistic and rational? Might there not be as many ways to educate toward ambiguity as there are peoples?

Response by Amy H. Shapiro

Why is it that when a family member batters a child in the United States, the family member is rarely, if ever, prosecuted? The answer presumably lies in the fact that the beating of a child falls under certain privacy issues that have a long, drawn-out history and that are based on the sovereignty of the family or the community. If I were to beat a child not my own, I would most likely be prosecuted and end up in jail. It is not so long ago that it was still legal in the United States for a man to beat or rape his wife. And it was not so long ago that on account of national sovereignty, the world lacked the word "genocide" to name the crime that this term now denotes.[1]

Who falls under the law is very much determined by the sovereignty of groups, an idea that did not escape Raphael Lemkin's understanding when he coined the term "genocide" in the 1940s. Identity is very much premised on the idea of belonging to a group or set of groups. To be human is premised on such belonging. Studies of feral children reared in the wild and without human contact reveal that the development of human identity is very much a matter of socialization through group interaction. Both Ludwig Wittgenstein and Lev Vygotsky understood the social nature of language learning and the significance of identity formation in such a process. Our identities and hence our understanding of what it means to be human are deeply connected to our identification within groups and

1. For more detail on this topic, see Samantha Power, *"A Problem from Hell": America and the Age of Genocide* (New York: Basic Books, 2002).

the ways in which those groups articulate their understanding of what it means to be human.

My critique of the essentialist position is not a critique of identification as Israeli or Palestinian per se. It is a critique of the way these identifications are used when they are assumed to have fixed natures and meanings. It is as if being Israeli or Palestinian, Jewish or Muslim, is definitive to what it means to be human. By virtue of their unexamined ideologies, such self-identities not only exclude competing or alternate views of what it means to be human but also often lead individuals to define themselves and their definition of humanness in opposition to competing or alternate views. For example, I was taught as a child that the Arabs ran away from the Jews during the fight for the State of Israel. I need not explain further what that assumption implied about the power of the Jew and his representation of the human in contrast to the fearful, ineffective objectified Arab, let alone what it implied for the role of generalization as the means for maintaining an ideology.

Often such narrative ideologies even exclude individual members within a given group. The example of beating one's own child with impunity serves as an analogy to significant attitudes that exist both among as well as within identity communities.

Although I did not directly discuss a feminist standpoint in my essay, it is active throughout, and it bears on the questions asked of me. It is rarely the case that the articulation of what it means to be a Jew or what it means to be a Muslim, what it means to be Israeli or what it means to be Palestinian, engages *as central* the experiences of women and children within the narrative groupings. They are more often excluded altogether.

The concept of community as it is articulated throughout the world is often expressed through male hegemony; such an outlook gives sovereign expression to the experiences of the male within the community. The point is not to critique any of these communities but to acknowledge how most expressions of the meaning of any community's narrative identity will fail to come even close to actually expressing how its members diverge from any fixed norm. When the community behaves as if it is defining what it means to be human through a male hegemonic stance — whether this is done explicitly or implicitly — it ceases to include women and children as fully human. A look at much of the Muslim world and its master narratives reveals that male hegemony defines females as other than fully human through its failure to provide them with rights and protections equivalent to those belonging to males. In some of these communities, males can murder females with impunity. A less apparently lethal articulation in the Jewish world can be found in the suffering of battered women in the Orthodox community. Or in another instance, Emmanuel Levinas, who wrote so extensively about the face of the other, used the female in a less than gracious relation to the male, who was identified as subject (the defining human?).

Although I have no doubt that my view may convey a "peculiarly Western embrace of the values of the individual and of rational thought," I think it may also lend itself to viewing the role of narratives as they play out within communities. To make a claim that religious or ethnic communities contain within them healthy competing narratives that help to provide ambiguous and complex definitions, and to suggest that such narratives are needed to challenge the master narratives, is not necessarily an embrace of specifically Western values. It is simply an observation that lends itself to a form of critical education that employs awareness of a range of narratives for furthering peace both among and within these communities.

When hegemonic attitudes within a community are unchecked, they can easily be deployed against other communities. Just as the narrative identity that excluded the voice of the Holocaust survivor from the formation of early Israeli identity may have conveyed a powerful notion of communal renewal and power over the land, that same narrative might be seen as legitimating Jewish-Israeli attitudes that excluded, for instance, the self-expression of Arab-Israeli identity because it fell outside of the master narrative.

Some of the hallmarks of critical thinking are a tolerance for ambiguity, the ability to engage different perspectives, and the capacity to observe and analyze multiple dimensions of what is happening around one. Yes, one might see these ideas as specifically Western in nature. It will not escape the reader, however, that whether or not one wants to acknowledge the reality of dissenting opinions within a community, they exist by virtue of the actual differing perspectives of its members.

The critical thinking I want to teach and encourage does not impose values but acknowledges different valuing perspectives as a dimension within and among human communities. To be a community at all suggests that a community is made up of a group of people. Although it may share a great number of beliefs and values, any group of people also has different perspectives simply by virtue of the roles and duties its members perform. Development of critical thinking engages this aspect of the community, potentially enriching the community through the comprehension of potential narratives that can be claimed and nurtured.

For example, there is no denying the hegemony of antagonistic power that is at work in both Israeli and Palestinian narratives of identity. Narrative values of losing face, owning the land, and showing strength by force are powerfully represented in both communities. But within these communities, there are also deeply articulated concepts of what it means to love the other, notions that hold all humans in high regard and express awareness of living in a world that is complex and full of suffering. There are also narratives that reject these latter beliefs or ideas. When the latter narratives gain ground, they diminish the complexity of narrative identity while authorizing their own narratives as defining what it means to be human. If this were not so, then we would not have Palestinian suicide bombers or Israeli settlers in the West Bank who think in absolutes, failing to use critical-thinking processes to reflect on who is not only outside but also within their own communities.

13. *After the Peace: The Moral*
    Responsibility of Survival

Rachel N. Baum

My title is a leap of faith, my own *ani ma'amin* — I believe — toward the redemption of peace. After the peace. *After.* The word bears such resonance, particularly for those of us who study the Holocaust, who know that what remains after conflict is not necessarily peace. Yet even asserted hesitantly, the word whispers of something different, a new vision: *After.*

After the peace is, of course, not a destination as much as an ever-negotiated foothold. Even when the struggle over the land has ended, there undoubtedly will still be conflict between Palestinians and Israelis. Indeed, as several contributors to this volume point out, the fighting in the Middle East has been narrative as well as physical, a struggle to control how the story of the conflict will be told. The Holocaust has loomed large in this struggle, with each side attempting to show itself as the victim of an aggressor seeking its destruction, like the Jews in the Holocaust. What is at stake in this narrative struggle is nothing less than the future of the conflict, as both sides attempt to garner the support that will produce favorable results for its people.

Even after the peace, this jockeying for sympathy will likely continue. Who will be portrayed in the history books as the victim, and who as the aggressor? Whose stories will garner sympathy, and whose revulsion? Like the conflict itself, this issue seems without resolution, and one can easily imagine the retelling of the events becoming fodder for competing narratives of endurance and triumph. Yet if there is indeed going to be a lasting peace, Palestinians and Israelis will need to find different ways to tell of their suffering, ways that move beyond the simple narrative lines of allegiance and sympathy.

Sympathy is a powerful force, for many of us turn to sympathy and identification as moral guides. Imagining ourselves on one side or the other, we look for resemblance between their experiences and our own. With whom do I identify — Palestinian or Israeli? With whom does my sympathy lie? Yet such efforts may not elucidate this conflict because the complexity of the situation forces us to choose which parts of our experiences to highlight and which to push to the background.

Let me offer an example. Not long ago, I was speaking with an older German man who was expressing his negative opinions about Israel and its policies. "Perhaps I feel sympathy for the Palestinians," he said, "because I too know what it feels like to be forced to leave your home." He is from Silesia, German land before World War II, now Polish, and I am not sure whether he meant the literal loss of his home or the loss of his homeland. Either way, I was stunned at the comparison, although I could not initially say why. Surely the man, a boy at the time, did suffer when the advancing Russians caused his family to leave their home, and surely Palestinians have been forced out of their homes. It seems wrong to argue with the man's feelings, as if I am trying to take away part of his experience. Yet upon further thought I realize what has bothered me: His statement has effectively erased Jewish suffering both in the Holocaust and in Israel. Why do his experiences not bring him closer to the Jews who lost not only their homes but their very lives in the Holocaust? Why does his memory of the Holocaust not bring him closer to understanding the Jewish need for a safe haven in the world?

The problem is that while the displacement of a young German boy from his home is an essential part of the narrative of that child's life, it is not a central part of the Holocaust story and thus does not bring that boy (now a man) closer to understanding the dimensions of *that* story. In fact, the pull of his own story might actually lead him away from the story of others. Had I had the presence of mind to think through this implication during our conversation, this is what I would have wanted to tell my companion: that by focusing so exclusively on his own story, he had lost the larger narrative frame, and that without that frame, he could not fully understand the situation of the Jews.

My thoughts on this incident forced me to wonder about my own sympathies: Whose story do I not see because the pull of my own story leads me away from them? Whom do I not see because the boundaries of my sympathy leave them outside? It is difficult to feel sympathy for both sides of a conflict. To have one's sympathies lie with one party suggests, by extension, that they do not lie with the other. When I feel sympathy for the Israelis, that sympathy comes close to justifying the violence against the Palestinians. When I feel sympathy for the Palestinians, I feel as if I am betraying my people and ignoring their suffering. Yet to express a general sympathy for the situation feels morally vacuous, as if I am simply sidestepping its difficult questions about good and evil, violence and suffering.

The difficulty of feeling sympathy for both sides arises in part because of the connection between sympathy and story. In the best literature the lines between protagonist and antagonist may be blurred because the narrative elucidates something complex about the human condition. Political narrative, though, is not nearly as nuanced. However sophisticated a given analysis of a political situation, sympathy demands clearer lines because we look to sympathy to guide our actions. To be the object of political sympathy has real effects — money, food, medicine, land. To lie outside of such sympathy is to be cut off from such support.

In drawing the lines of our sympathy, we sometimes turn to the past as a guide. The German man in my example was drawing from his experience of suffering in order to shape his contemporary politics. To some extent, we all do this, learning from the anguishes in our histories in order to determine our contemporary identities and passions.

Yet the work of creating analogies and drawing connections between two distinct events reveals that there is no simple linking of one experience to another. Such an act requires its own layers of story and interpretation that depend in part on how we want to see ourselves. For example, the German man whose story I tell might have drawn the lines of his sympathy differently. One would understand had he said, vis-à-vis Israel, "Perhaps I feel for the Jews because I saw firsthand what was done to them during the Holocaust." Yet his interpretation of his own experience led him to identify with the Palestinians — not because his story of being a German citizen during World War II necessarily lends itself to a comparison with contemporary Palestinians, but because he chose to narrate his story through these lines of sympathy. Thus, to draw connections between two historical events, or between two experiences, is to define the edges of *both* narratives. This is what makes such connections so powerful: by drawing the lines of sympathy, we shape the telling of both stories.

Not only, then, does our sympathy shape who we are. More to the point, how we *already* see ourselves, or want to see ourselves, shapes the paths of our sympathies and potentially strengthens our self-identity. Sympathy is thus not a simple affective response; rather, it is a complex drawing of lines of similarity and affiliation. By comparing his story to that of the Palestinians, my German companion simultaneously narrated his own story as one of victimhood and loss. Had he focused instead on comparing his story to that of the Jews, he would have been in the more uncomfortable position of seeing the ways in which he was not a victim.

Jews also have had a stake in maintaining a narrative that focuses on victimhood, one that sees the situation in Israel through a historical narrative of the oppression of Jews. Some Jews have used Holocaust language to decry Israel's security fence,[1] while others have protested Israel's disengagement plan with calls to stop the deportation of Jews.[2] While such rhetoric is more extreme than most mainstream Jewish language, its emphasis on Jews as victims or potential victims can be seen (albeit less virulently) in much pro-Israel Jewish discourse. It has been harder for Jews to wrestle with the tension between the simultaneous realities of historical and contemporary oppression of Jews and the level of Jewish power in Israel.

Each example reveals the power of shaping a narrative through the lens of the victim — namely, the supposed moral force of being the victim. To be the one initially attacked is, by definition, to be in the right about a situation, to be the object of violence rather than its perpetrator. This sense of the moral force of victimization has shaped much of the discourse around the Palestinian-Israeli conflict, as each side tries to maintain its primary role as defender rather than attacker. In this model, the past elucidates the present by providing the historical basis for the claim to victim status. After the peace, one can easily imagine the debate turning into an

1. Jerome S. Kaufman of the Zionist Organization of America writes: "Does a fence make any military sense? If one has an enemy dedicated to his destruction, does one hide in the cellar like the Jews of the shtetels of Poland and Russia? Was that effective against the Cossacks pounding on the cellar door? Does one build a ghetto along a slender Mediterranean corridor packed with more Jews per square inch than any other place in the world, in order to isolate these Jews from their enemies? Yes, the Germans did that to the Jews of Warsaw and that ghetto wall was very effective. The only problem was that ghetto wall was effective in killing Jews rather than saving them" ("Israel's 'Fence': The Continuation of a Dangerous Lie," Zionist Organization of America, online at http://www.zoa.org/2003/10/israels_fence_t.htm).

2. "ADL Distressed by Continued Use of Holocaust Analogies Related to Israeli Disengagement Plan," Anti-Defamation League, online at http://www.adl.org/PresRele/IslME_62/4657_62.htm.

argument about who has suffered more, and hence, whose triumph is greater.

I offer here a different model of how the past can be used to understand and shape the present. It is a narration of suffering, but one that does not invite jockeying for victimhood. Jews read it yearly at Passover, in the Haggadah's retelling of the exodus from Egypt: "Because you were slaves in Egypt. . . ." It is a formula repeated several times in Deuteronomy, an admonition to care for the most vulnerable members of society: "You shall not subvert the rights of the stranger or the fatherless; you shall not take a widow's garment in pawn. Remember that you were a slave in Egypt and that the LORD your God redeemed you from there; therefore do I enjoin you to observe this commandment" (Deut. 24:17-18).

Often this precept to "remember that you were a slave" is understood as a call to use the memory of slavery to imagine the heart of another. Indeed, there are passages in the Torah that emphasize this reading: "You shall not oppress a stranger, for you know the feelings of the stranger, having yourselves been strangers in the land of Egypt" (Exod. 23:9). Yet while using memory to empathize with the experience of another is central to moral imagination, my initial example suggests that our decisions over which aspects of our memory to uncover are laden with complexity. We are potentially still in the morass of comparative suffering. Any way out of such a morass, after the peace, will need to include not only the experience of slavery but also the experience of freedom.

I suggest an alternative reading of the Torah precept, one that emphasizes survival over victimhood: In the place of "because you were *slaves*," let us emphasize, "because you *were* slaves." The Torah says that because the Jews were slaves in Egypt *and because they were saved by God,* they now are a changed people with new obligations. At the center of this story of suffering is not so much the victimization as the redemption.[3]

In the place of a sympathetic comparison between two events, this

---

3. Several readers have suggested to me that this is indeed the lesson of the Haggadah already, that the Jewish tradition already emphasizes freedom over slavery. Surely freedom is always present at the Passover Seder, the memory of slavery set against our current (albeit imperfect) freedom. Yet the moral force of the Haggadah stems from the knowledge that slavery affords. Because we were slaves, we know what it is to be oppressed, and we are called to help other oppressed people. There is nothing wrong with such a stance; it is indeed a central part of the moral imagination. What I am offering is simply another way to conceptualize our responsibility, after slavery — one that focuses not on the other but on ourselves.

reading suggests a moral responsibility of survival that is both affective and ontological. Rather than identification with the suffering of another, this responsibility is based on a changed relationship to oneself and the world — a relationship changed by history. "Because you *were* slaves" suggests that suffering and redemption from that suffering changes us and presents us with new obligations to others and to the world around us.

The emotional component of such a responsibility is not sympathy but compassion. Compassion includes both the recognition of suffering and, significantly, the desire to end such suffering. Because we were slaves *and because we are not now,* we must pursue justice. Such compassion has one foot in the memory of slavery and one foot in the moral demands of redemption. We must end suffering because we have been spared; our lives gain meaning when we use them to end the suffering of others. Here our work is not only to imagine the stranger's heart but to reimagine our own.

With this reading, we can start to understand why justice has been so difficult to achieve in Israel. Jewish Israelis never felt the expansiveness of redemption, the safety of survival from the Shoah. From the very beginning, Israel had to defend itself against those who sought its destruction. If they are to get beyond claims of who has suffered more, both sides must truly be safe. Only then may they both say that they were victims but are no longer, and because of their having been saved, they are changed.

Yet to speak of redemption in the context of Israel is fraught with difficulties. In one Jewish narrative about Israel, redemption signifies that the answer to the question about Israel is already decided — by God. Survival here is religious destiny on one hand, or political destiny on the other. For those who favor political destiny, Israel provides the redemption of Auschwitz, imbuing Auschwitz with a meaning that cannot help but carry the tinge of destiny itself.[4]

---

4. Consider Joseph Soloveitchik's essay "Kol Dodi Dofek" (Hark, My Beloved Knocketh), reprinted as *Fate and Destiny: From Holocaust to the State of Israel* (Hoboken, N.J.: Ktav, 2000). Drawing imagery from the Song of Songs, Soloveitchik imagines the Jewish people as the maiden who longs for the return of her beloved, yet fails to get up from her bed to greet him when he does return. Arguing that Jews did not do enough to stop the slaughter of the Holocaust, Soloveitchik calls upon Jews to answer God's call by supporting the State of Israel. He writes:

> Eight years ago, in the midst of a night of terror filled with the horrors of Maidanek, Treblinka, and Buchenwald, in a night of gas chambers and crematoria, in a night of absolute divine self-concealment *(hester panim muhlat)* . . . in a

Yet this is not the dominant lesson of Holocaust narratives. While each narrative is distinct, the testimonies of Holocaust survivors again and again point to the luck that they survived. Where survivors seek to find meaning (even divine meaning) in their survival, they are careful not to find this meaning in contrast to those who died. Survival in Holocaust narratives is not triumphalist. It is marked by humility and often by wonder or incredulity: Why me? Why was I spared? It is phrased more often as question, rather than answer.

Bringing this kind of questioning wonder into the Palestinian-Israeli conflict would force each side to narrate its story in such a way that emphasizes the surprise of survival rather than the supposed moral force of victimhood. Consider my original example. While the German man sought to connect his experience to that of the Palestinians, a perspective founded on survival would have caused him to consider not only that he was a victim but also the ways in which he was emphatically not a victim. This identification with his own good fortune (the fortune of having been born a Christian rather than a Jewish German) might provide the basis of a moral responsibility fueled by compassion and justice.

A focus on survival places one's identity in the shadow of those who did not survive. This is the basis of Primo Levi's distinction between the drowned and the saved. While all Holocaust survivors are victims, Levi reminds us that ultimately, they are among the saved and therefore do not bear the truth of the horror in the same way as the drowned. Levi writes of a friend who came to visit him after liberation, who insisted that Levi's survival could not have been chance, that it was providential. Levi responds: "Such an opinion seemed monstrous to me. It pained me as when one touches an exposed nerve, and kindled the doubt I spoke of before: I

---

night of continuous searching, of questing for the Beloved — in that very night the Beloved appeared. "God who conceals Himself in His dazzling hiddenness" suddenly manifested Himself and began to knock at the tent of His despondent and disconsolate love, twisting convulsively on her bed, suffering the pains of hell. *As a result of the knocks on the door of the maiden, wrapped in mourning, the State of Israel was born!* (p. 25, italics in original)

While Soloveitchik does not go so far as to posit a divine meaning to Auschwitz, rejecting theodicy entirely, his vision of the creation of the State of Israel as a kind of divine response to the suffering of the Jews comes close to suggesting that the Holocaust and Israel are part of the same destiny. Indeed, the new title of Soloveitchik's essay would encourage such a reading.

might be alive in the place of another, at the expense of another; I might have usurped, that is, in fact, killed. The 'saved' of the Lager were not the best, those predestined to do good, the bearers of a message: what I had seen and lived through proved the exact contrary. Preferably the worst survived, the selfish, the violent, the insensitive, the collaborators of the 'gray zone,' the spies."[5]

Here, we seem far from the moral force of the exodus. There was no moral force to Auschwitz. Yet the very wrestlings of Levi's writing, with their anguish, reveal an insistence that survival should neither be taken for granted nor seen as destiny. The moral force of survival comes from the recognition of the costs of survival, from the memory of those who did not survive. This is the ultimate boundary against any kind of triumphalist reading. Who would be arrogant enough to assert his or her own providential survival against that of another?

Brought to the Palestinian-Israeli conflict, Levi's words might translate into an acknowledgment that survival came at a price for each side. Each side has done terrible things (this is not to draw equivalencies; my point is that after the peace, we must stop weighing). Each side has survived despite the odds against it. Each side has paid the terrible price of loss of life.

Or more to the point, each individual will need to say, "I survived" — not only "we survived," which might slide again into nationalist, triumphalist narratives. This is, after all, the point of the Passover Haggadah; each Jew must see himself or herself as personally saved from Mitzrayim (Egypt). This emphasis on individual survival forces each person to take on the moral responsibility of survival.

The Haggadah story is also a story of identity. How will we see ourselves after being slaves for so long? This question haunts Holocaust memoirs as well. What does it mean to know yourself anew after knowing yourself as a slave, as a victim? In terms of the Palestinian-Israeli conflict, this might mean acknowledging that we were victims, we were victimizers . . . *but we are no longer.* We take our memories of the past with us, but we also open a space where we might be different. And in that space, however small, between the old world and the new, perhaps a tentative peace can grow.

5. Primo Levi, *The Drowned and the Saved,* trans. Raymond Rosenthal (New York: Random House, 1989), p. 82.

228

Contributors' Questions for Rachel N. Baum

Your chapter calls for a new rhetoric between Palestinians and Israelis, one that does not produce war through comparative victimhood, but one that can sustain peace by shared joy in survival. But the trope of slavery and freedom is part of a Jewish narrative, as is made clear in the Haggadah. Will this rhetoric make sense for a Muslim? What is the analogous narrative in the Muslim tradition, one that Arab Muslims can turn to in order to reshape the existing discourse of Jew hatred? And if there is none, how do you get a culture to change its narrative?

You argue that having sympathy with the experience of the other will help forge links between us. But what makes it possible to have sympathy for one who is radically different from me because of our conflicting narratives? Is an ethics based on sympathy adequate to the task? Might an ethics based on sympathy have to be grounded in an ethics based on respect? Must I not feel commanded to respect the radically different other — the other whom I may not even like or sympathize with? Is not the command to *respect* a precondition for developing *sympathy*?

Response by Rachel N. Baum

The thoughtful questions posed to me by my colleagues vibrate with concern for reality: Can what you are suggesting *actually* happen? How will such change of narratives be initiated and sustained? Is there any evidence that a new story is possible in this region, between these peoples?

Part of the difficulty in responding to these questions is that my charge was to envision a world *after* the peace, to consider what changes might need to occur to move each side beyond a triumphalist stance. It is a peculiar exercise, envisioning the world after peace in Palestine and Israel. That *after* will not come without significant shifts in the Palestinian and Israeli worldviews, and of course the existence of a peace agreement will itself change the internal narratives of each side. I thus am joining a conversation that does not yet exist and whose reality I cannot fully imagine.

Yet it is clear to me that the emphasis on sympathy will only contribute to the problem, and thus I propose a movement away from an ethics of sympathy toward a postconflict stance that does not depend on identification with the other. The question I posed was whether it was possible to survive a conflict without imbuing one's survival with triumph. How, I asked, might one narrate one's own survival outside of the paradigm of victim and victor?

The first question posed to me speaks of a shared joy in survival, yet the postconflict emotion I am envisioning is more complex than joy, for it lives in the shadow of the destruction of one's friends and family. Were the survivors of the Holocaust joyful to be alive? I imagine that many were, at least for a time. Yet surely for many survivors the joy of having survived was overshadowed by the grief and loneliness of being only *one* who survived. The emotion I am trying to articulate is a humble one; it is a mixture of gratitude and wonder. "Why me?" it asks. "Why did I survive?"

I use the Jewish narrative of the exodus to demonstrate how one might — within the same narrative — choose to emphasize one's slavery or one's survival. Yet I do not mean to suggest that Jews are more likely to embrace the responsibility of survival than their Muslim counterparts. Indeed, while the majority of American Jews relive the exodus each year at a Passover seder, the American Jewish community is still dominated by what Jacob Neusner has called the "Judaism of Holocaust and Redemption," whereby the horror of the Holocaust is given meaning through the redemption offered by a Jewish state. While the Torah represents the Jewish people as different from non-Jews in terms of their obligations, the Judaism of Holocaust and Redemption says that Jews are different from non-Jews in their status as potential victims. Such a perspective cannot help but emphasize slavery over survival. Neusner writes: "While only some Jews find a correspondence between covenant and imagined status as God's holy people, all Jews see themselves on a continuum with the Holocaust: if I had been there, I too would have been gassed and cremated."[1] So while one might ask how an Arab Muslim would find his or her way into a narrative that foregrounds the responsibility of survival, one might equally ask how Israeli and American Jews will relinquish their identity as victims in order to consider the responsibility of survival in Israel *beyond* the responsibility to other Jews.[2]

Still, the question of how a culture rethinks its own narratives is an important one. I do not think that outsiders can "get" other cultures to change their narratives; rather, there are always competing narratives within a culture. Lest we risk isolating Islam entirely from Judaism and Christianity, we would do well to remember that it was not so long ago his-

1. Jacob Neusner, *Fortress Introduction to American Judaism* (Minneapolis: Fortress Press, 1994), p. 115.

2. In no way do I mean to suggest that American Jews are concerned only for other Jews after the Holocaust. Indeed, Judaism's tradition of social justice has led many Jews to care generously for the needy outside of their own communities. Yet vis-à-vis Israel, many American Jews see the relevance of the Holocaust only in terms of the Jewish community. Indeed, it is the very persistence of this narrow perspective *in the face of other powerful and compelling Jewish narratives of social justice* that reveals the difficulty of reshaping narratives about Israel — narratives held by Jews, Muslims, and Christians alike.

torically that Christianity was itself guilty of pervasive Jew hatred. Surely, during the majority of Christian-Jewish history, it would have been nearly impossible to imagine Christians as a dialogue partner for Jews. One might ask, What encouraged Christians to change their understanding of Jews? Certainly, Christians do not speak with a single voice, and there remain Christians who hold steadfast to the idea that Jews are eternally damned. But there are many other voices — including that of the Catholic Church — who now say that Judaism is a sister religion to Christianity and that Jews should be left to worship their God in peace.

Was it the confrontation with Jews — particularly the Jewish victims of the Holocaust — that encouraged this new narrative? Undoubtedly. Yet this alone would not have been enough to instill the changes in Christian belief. There was a confluence of factors both within and outside of the Catholic Church that enabled new narratives to take root. Notably, the theologians who work on rethinking the Christian relationship to Jews and Judaism write not only about improving Jewish-Christian relations but, more significantly, about refining Christianity itself.[3] In other words, such Christians understand their Christian identity *through* their treatment of non-Christians, rather than in opposition to non-Christians. The revision of narratives about Jews has thus taken place within a larger context of reimagining Christianity.

Such a new understanding of Christianity and its relationship to Judaism has depended in part on the polyvocal tradition of Christianity. The Reformation initiated a history of dissent and change within the religion that opened up a space through which Christians might reimagine their faith. Islam has not undergone such a reformation, and thus it is more difficult to discern the voices of dissent. Yet while Islam looks to some as unredeemably absolutist, journalist Reza Aslan argues that the battle over

3. This is also true of the Catholic Church's *Nostra aetate* (Declaration on the Relation of the Church to Non-Christian Religions), the Vatican II document that says, in part: "Although the Church is the new people of God, the Jews should not be presented as rejected or accursed by God, as if this followed from the Holy Scriptures. All should see to it, then, that in catechetical work or in the preaching of the word of God they do not teach anything that does not conform to the truth of the Gospel and the spirit of Christ" (§4.6, online at http://www.ewtn.com/library/councils/v2non.htm). *Nostre aetate* expresses the Christian relationship toward Jews through a desire to live the word of Jesus more fully. While this document is far from the final word on Christian-Jewish relations, it marks an effort to narrate Christian obligation differently.

Islam follows in the footsteps of Christian reform, footsteps that were fierce and often murderous. He writes:

> What followed that awful war [the Thirty Years' War] during which nearly a third of the population of Germany perished was a gradual progression in Christian theology from the doctrinal absolutism of the pre-Reformation era to the doctrinal pluralism of the early modern period and, ultimately, to the doctrinal relativism of the Enlightenment. This remarkable evolution in Christianity from its inception to its Reformation took fifteen vicious, bloody, and occasionally apocalyptic centuries.
>
> Fourteen hundred years of rabid debate over what it means to be a Muslim; of passionate arguments over the interpretation of the Qur'an and the application of Islamic law; of trying to reconcile a fractured community through appeals to Divine Unity; of tribal feuds, crusades, and world wars — and Islam has finally begun its fifteenth century.[4]

Like the Christian thinkers who see Christianity's openness to other religions as part of Christ's message, Aslan argues that an Islamic reformation will ultimately return Islam to the vision of the prophet Muhammad:

> When fifteen centuries ago Muhammad launched a revolution in Mecca to replace the archaic, rigid, and inequitable strictures of tribal society with a radically new vision of divine morality and social egalitarianism, he tore apart the fabric of traditional Arab society. It took many years of violence and devastation to cleanse the Hijaz [Arabia] of its "false idols." It will take many more to cleanse Islam of its new false idols — bigotry and fanaticism — worshipped by those who have replaced Muhammad's original vision of tolerance and unity with their own ideals of hatred and discord. But the cleansing is inevitable, and the tide of reform cannot be stopped. The Islamic Reformation is already here. We are all living in it.[5]

Aslan may be overly optimistic about the future of Islam — I cannot say. Yet in imagining an existence after the peace, my essay is, by its very nature, a hopeful one. I know that envisioning a different narrative will not make

4. Reza Aslan, *No God but God: The Origins, Evolution, and Future of Islam* (New York: Random House, 2005), p. 248.

5. Ibid., p. 266.

it so; I also know that a new reality will not come without people to first dream it.

My shift from sympathy to compassion is an effort to draw attention to, and name, the changing emotional landscape of the region. It is not simply that after the peace, one must take the "other side" of the preexisting emotions (love rather than hate, peace rather than war). Rather, I am suggesting that the *emotional narrative* of the region will undergo revision as part and parcel of the rewriting of political and social narratives. Each side will need to reconsider not only who it is but who it wants to be. This may be, after all, the most powerful force to enable new narratives to take root — the desire to be a better Jew, a better Christian, a better Muslim.

Compassion is a virtue to Jews, Christians, and Muslims, who understand it as a quality of God, a quality that humans are called to emulate. As I noted, compassion is marked by a deep awareness of the suffering of another, coupled with the desire to relieve that suffering. The other I imagine is not only the "other side" but the dead of one's own people. Having seen the suffering of one's own people, compassion moves a person to try to end that suffering — in this case, to prevent it from happening again. It is in this context that the post-Holocaust cry "Never again!" might bear the most resonance.

EPILOGUE: *What Else?*

Leonard Grob and John K. Roth

History could make a stone weep.

Marilynne Robinson, *Gilead*

While the penultimate editorial work on this book was under way during the summer of 2006, *New York Times* editorialist Nicholas D. Kristof made a wise observation. "A rule of thumb in the Middle East," he wrote on that July 18, "is that anyone who makes confident predictions is too dogmatic to be worth listening to."[1] Kristof offered that counsel in the midst of violence that made the hope expressed in these pages more anguished than ever. Provoked by the kidnapping of Israeli soldiers by Hamas and Hezbollah earlier that summer, tensions between Israel and its Middle Eastern neighbors, especially in Gaza and southern Lebanon, escalated into violence that seemed to dash — at least for the foreseeable future — realistic hope for a resolution of the Palestinian-Israeli conflict that would bring a just and lasting peace. As Hezbollah rained rockets on Israeli towns and cities and Israel battered Lebanon with air and artillery strikes that attempted to destroy Hezbollah's Lebanese strongholds and their supply lines to Syria and Iran, no one knew what the end game and its aftereffects would be. Those chapters, in fact, are still being written.

Where Palestinian-Israeli relationships are concerned, this book's

---

1. Nicholas D. Kristof, "Feeding the Enemy," *New York Times*, July 18, 2006, http://select .nytimes.com/2006/07/18/opinion/18kristof.html.

writers and readers know that uncertainty remains. Events may take those relationships from bad to worse. They may also turn them in more hopeful directions, for Kristof's apt observation indicates that the future is still unsettled. If so, then the hopes expressed in these pages, anguished though they must be because of the Holocaust and destructive events that have occurred more than half a century later, still have a place that can make a constructive difference. How can and should we — the writers and readers of this book — continue to inhabit such a world? As this book's governing epigraph reminds us, it is not our task to answer that question finally and completely, but it is our responsibility to keep addressing it as thoughtfully and as well as we can.

The philosopher Philip Hallie, a great teacher at Wesleyan University, in Middletown, Connecticut, was a World War II veteran who wrote about cruelty and the Holocaust. He often recalled the hurricane that once had reached his Connecticut home. That experience gave him a metaphor for human existence and for Middle Eastern circumstances in particular. "It's the hurricane we're in," Hallie would say, and then he would add the admonition, "Don't forget it!"[2]

Hallie's sound realism relates to themes from another source that also sheds important light on hope and its anguish. *Gilead,* Marilynne Robinson's Pulitzer Prize–winning novel, was on American best-seller lists as work on this book concluded. Robinson situated her story in the small fictional town of Gilead in the Midwestern state of Iowa. The name she gave to that place has roots in Scripture and song. For example, in the sixth century B.C.E. the Hebrew prophet Jeremiah, who saw ancient violence in what is today's Middle East, asked a lamenting question: "Is there," he wondered, "no balm in Gilead?" (Jer. 8:22). As though in response, a spiritual from the African-American tradition, which also knows plenty about violence, affirms, amazingly, that "there is a balm in Gilead to make the wounded whole . . . [and] to heal the sin-sick soul."

The story that takes place in Gilead, Iowa, focuses on Rev. John Ames, an aging and dying minister who has served his Protestant congregation in that obscure place for a long time. He is intelligent, educated, sensitive, thoughtful, and literate; every week, for years, study and writing

---

2. Philip Hallie, "Cruelty: The Empirical Evil," in *Facing Evil: Confronting the Dreadful Power behind Genocide, Terrorism, and Cruelty,* ed. Paul Woodruff and Harry A. Wilmer (LaSalle, Ill.: Open Court, 2001), p. 128.

to foster compassion, respect, ethical concern, and social responsibility in an ever-changing world have been key parts of his life and work.

Ames knows the force of Jeremiah's lamentations, for he has seen a lot of suffering and grief in Gilead. His own life has included sorrow, which touched him deeply and forever when childbirth took his wife and then his newborn daughter as well. And yet Ames knows, too, that there can be a balm in Gilead, for late in life he has again found love and marriage. He has a child, too, a seven-year old boy. The father knows that he will be gone before his son has really gotten to know him. He wonders if his son, whom Ames calls "God's grace to me," will remember him much at all.[3] So the old man tries to leave behind a written account that one day may help to fill the absence, but he never knows for sure that it has or even that it can.

Early in the narrative that he writes for his son, Ames records where and when he, Ames, was born. Ames also writes down the names of his parents and grandparents, and then he pauses to ask, "And what else should I tell you?" (p. 9). One of the things that he wants his son to understand is that "we human beings do real harm. History," says Ames, "could make a stone weep" (p. 190). That is part of what he has in mind when he adds that "I could never have imagined this world if I hadn't spent almost eight decades walking around in it" (p. 66).

At the same time, John Ames wants his son to see that this world of ours, full of stones that would weep if they could, is also full of "more beauty than our eyes can bear" (p. 246). He observes further that the darkness that loads down the world often requires us to have great courage to see that beauty, to defend and honor it. Recalling that he "could never thank God sufficiently for the splendor He has . . . revealed to me in your sweetly ordinary face," Ames also tells his son that "precious things have been put into our hands and to do nothing to honor them is to do great harm" (pp. 237, 246). Among the last words that Marilynne Robinson has Ames write to and for his son are these: "I'll pray that you grow up a brave man in a brave country. I will pray you find a way to be useful" (p. 247).

What else? Eastward in Connecticut, when Philip Hallie had his hurricane experience, his thinking was moving in currents akin to those of John Ames. Havoc was not all that Hallie saw. Even while the menacing

---

3. Marilynne Robinson, *Gilead* (New York: Farrar, Straus & Giroux, 2004), p. 52. Page numbers in the text refer to this work.

storm raged all around, there was space for calm and quiet within the hurricane's eye. Hallie's eye, moreover, was drawn to the pale blue sky overhead. Probably that blue became his favorite color, for Hallie's passion, as he put it, was to "expand the blue." He recognized and urged that some persons can "make a larger space for blue, for peace, for love." Such work, Hallie insisted, "takes power as well as love. It takes force of will. It takes assertion and commitment."[4]

Such outlooks augment and perhaps sum up many of the insights that *Anguished Hope* has to offer. Especially in the Middle East, it is the hurricane that all of us are in, not only Palestinians, Israelis, and their immediate neighbors. Yet it is possible to expand the blue and to care for the precious things that have been put into our hands. It is possible to use the leverage that is ours to be brave and useful, to make our lives to be a balm in Gilead so that history will be less likely to make stones weep if they could. *Anguished Hope,* a series of shared yearnings and analyses, probes and visions, points in these directions.

4. Hallie, "Cruelty," pp. 128-29.

Select Bibliography

As events, borders, and interpretations of Middle Eastern history have changed and continue to develop in Palestinian-Israeli relations, the editors struggled with decisions about timelines and maps that *Anguished Hope* might helpfully include. In keeping with the book's emphasis on dialogue about differences, we decided neither to publish a single timeline of events, because the entry selection could not be sufficiently inclusive, nor to reproduce the unavoidably small number of maps that a book of this kind could include, for arguably that selection would also be too confining or even biased. Instead, this select bibliography begins by identifying significant Internet sites that provide a wealth of information, including timelines, maps, links to documents that are crucial in the Palestinian-Israeli conflict, and sources for further reading.

At MidEastWeb (http://www.mideastweb.org/), a diverse group of scholars — Arabs, Jews, and others who are committed to peace efforts and dialogue — maintains a major information site about the Palestinian-Israeli conflict. The American Friends Service Committee provides a similar service at http://www.afsc.org/israel-palestine/learn/timeline.htm. Although not completely up to date, the American Public Broadcasting Service (PBS) site at http://www.pbs.org/pov/pov2001/promises/timeline.html helpfully documents how Palestinian and Israeli interpretations of the conflict have differed. The site http://www.hrcr.org/hottopics/palestinian.html, maintained by the Arthur W. Diamond Law Library at the Columbia University Law School, includes links to key documents in the Palestinian-Israeli conflict. There are many other Internet sites, some far more reliable than others, that

focus on the Middle East, but one more to recommend is http://www
.besthistorysites.net/20thCentury_MiddleEast.shtml. It offers useful anno-
tation and guidance regarding numerous informational Internet sites, including entries on the Palestinian-Israeli conflict.

As this book's footnotes indicate, many sources informed the contributions to *Anguished Hope*. Listed below are some of the books that have
most influenced its reflections.

Aslan, Reza. *No God but God: The Origins, Evolution, and Future of Islam*. New
York: Random House, 2005.

Bauer, Yehuda. *Rethinking the Holocaust*. New Haven: Yale University Press,
2001.

Buber, Martin. *I and Thou*. Translated by Ronald Gregor Smith. New York:
Collier Books, 1958.

Dinnerstein, Leonard. *Antisemitism in America*. New York: Oxford University
Press, 1994.

Ellis, Mark. *Beyond Innocence and Redemption: Confronting the Holocaust and
Israeli Power*. New York: Harper & Row, 1990.

Fackenheim, Emil. *God's Presence in History: Jewish Affirmations and Philosophical Reflections*. New York: Harper Torchbooks, 1972.

———. *The Jewish Return into History: Reflections in the Age of Auschwitz and
a New Jerusalem*. New York: Schocken Books, 1978.

———. *To Mend the World: Foundations of Future Jewish Thought*.
Bloomington: Indiana University Press, 1994.

Fasching, Darrell J. *Narrative Theology after Auschwitz*. Minneapolis: Fortress
Press, 1992.

Haas, Peter J. *Morality after Auschwitz: The Radical Challenge of the Nazi Ethic*.
Philadelphia: Fortress Press, 1988.

Hertzberg, Arthur, ed. *The Zionist Idea*. New York: Atheneum Books, 1973.

hooks, bell. *Teaching to Transgress: Education as the Practice of Freedom*. New
York: Routledge, 1994.

Khalidi, Walid. *Palestine Reborn*. New York: I. B. Taurus, 1992.

Knight, Henry F. *Confessing Christ in a Post-Holocaust World: A Midrashic Experiment*. Westport, Conn.: Greenwood Press, 2000.

Kushner, Tony, and Alisa Solomon, eds. *Wrestling with Zion: Progressive
Jewish-American Responses to the Israeli-Palestinian Conflict*. New York:
Grove Press, 2003.

Lerner, Michael. *Jewish Renewal: A Path to Healing and Transformation*. New
York: G. P. Putnam's Sons, 1994.

Levi, Primo. *The Drowned and the Saved.* Translated by Raymond Rosenthal. New York: Random House, 1989.

Levinas, Emmanuel. *Difficult Freedom: Essays on Judaism.* Translated by Sean Hand. Baltimore, Md.: Johns Hopkins University Press, 1990.

———. *Nine Talmudic Readings.* Translated by Annette Aronowicz. Bloomington: Indiana University Press, 1990.

———. *Totality and Infinity: An Essay in Exteriority.* Translated by Alphonso Lingis. Pittsburgh: Duquesne University Press, 1969.

Morris, Benny. *Righteous Victims: A History of the Zionist-Arab Conflict, 1881-2001.* New York: Vintage Books, 2001.

Neher, André. *They Made Their Souls Anew.* Translated by David Maisel. Albany: State University of New York Press, 1990.

Patterson, David, and John K. Roth, eds. *After-Words: Post-Holocaust Struggles with Forgiveness, Reconciliation, Justice.* Seattle: University of Washington Press, 2004.

Pryce-Jones, David. *The Closed Circle: An Interpretation of the Arabs.* New York: Harper & Row, 1989.

Rosenbaum, Ron, ed. *Those Who Forget the Past: The Question of Anti-Semitism.* New York: Random House, 2004.

Ross, Dennis. *The Missing Peace: The Inside Story of the Fight for Middle East Peace.* New York: Farrar, Straus & Giroux, 2004.

Roth, John K. *Ethics during and after the Holocaust: In the Shadow of Birkenau.* New York: Palgrave Macmillan, 2005.

Rubenstein, Richard L., and John K. Roth. *Approaches to Auschwitz: The Holocaust and Its Legacy.* Rev. ed. Louisville, Ky.: Westminster John Knox Press, 2003.

Schwartz, Regina M. *The Curse of Cain: The Violent Legacy of Monotheism.* Chicago: University of Chicago Press, 1997.

Shipler, David K. *Arab and Jew: Wounded Spirits in a Promised Land.* New York: Times Books, 1986.

Soloveitchik, Joseph. *Fate and Destiny: From Holocaust to the State of Israel.* Hoboken, N.J.: Ktav, 2000.

Williamson, Clark. *A Guest in the House of Israel: Post-Holocaust Church Theology.* Louisville, Ky.: Westminster John Knox Press, 1993.

Woodruff, Paul, and Harry A. Wilmer, eds. *Facing Evil: Confronting the Dreadful Power behind Genocide, Terrorism, and Cruelty.* LaSalle, Ill.: Open Court, 2001.

Ye'or, Bat. *Islam and Dhimmitude: Where Civilizations Collide.* Madison, N.J.: Fairleigh Dickinson University Press, 2002.

About the Editors and Contributors

Editors

Leonard Grob is professor emeritus of philosophy at Fairleigh Dickinson University, Teaneck, New Jersey. He has published numerous articles dealing with the thought of Martin Buber and Emmanuel Levinas and is the coeditor of two anthologies: *Education for Peace: Testimonies from World Religions* (Orbis Books, 1987) and *Women's and Men's Liberation: Testimonies of Spirit* (Greenwood Press, 1991). Grob is the author of a memoir, "Good-bye Father: A Journey to the USSR," published in *Judaism* (Spring 1990), which describes his roots journey to Ukraine in 1989. His experience in uncovering the history of the destruction of his father's family during the Holocaust led him to the field of Holocaust studies. Within this field, Grob has authored articles and book chapters on topics such as post-Holocaust education, ethics after the Holocaust, post-Holocaust theodicy, and philosophical reflections on rescuers. Since 1996 he has served as coorganizer, along with Henry Knight, of the biennial Stephen S. Weinstein Holocaust Symposium (formerly the Pastora Goldner Holocaust Symposium), in Wroxton, England. Grob has also been involved in projects devoted to encouraging Israeli-Palestinian dialogue. He is the coeditor of *Teen Voices from the Holy Land: Who Am I to You?* (Prometheus Books, 2007), a volume of Israeli and Palestinian children's narratives.

John K. Roth is the Edward J. Sexton Professor Emeritus of Philosophy and the founding director of the Center for the Study of the Holocaust, Genocide, and Human Rights at Claremont McKenna College, Claremont, California, where he taught from 1966 to 2006. In addition to service on the U.S. Holocaust Memorial Council and on the editorial board for the journal *Holocaust and Genocide Studies,* he has published hundreds of articles and reviews and authored, coauthored, or edited more than forty books, including, most recently, *Genocide and Human Rights: A Philosophical Guide* (Palgrave Macmillan, 2005), *Gray Zones: Ambiguity and Compromise in the Holocaust and Its Aftermath* (Berghahn Books, 2005), and *Ethics during and after the Holocaust: In the Shadow of Birkenau* (Palgrave Macmillan, 2005). Roth has been visiting professor of Holocaust studies at the University of Haifa, Israel, and his Holocaust-related research appointments have included a 2001 Koerner Visiting Fellowship at the Oxford Centre for Hebrew and Jewish Studies in England, as well as a 2004-5 appointment as the Ina Levine Invitational Scholar at the Center for Advanced Holocaust Studies, U.S. Holocaust Memorial Museum, Washington, D.C. In 1988 Roth was named U.S. National Professor of the Year by the Council for Advancement and Support of Education and the Carnegie Foundation for the Advancement of Teaching.

Contributors

Rachel N. Baum is a senior lecturer and coordinator of Hebrew studies at the University of Wisconsin–Milwaukee, where she teaches courses on Holocaust literature and film, post-Holocaust theology, Jewish culture, and interfaith dialogue. Baum was named an Affiliated Scholar as part of UW-Milwaukee's Difficult Dialogues project, funded by the Ford Foundation; her work with the project centers on religious pluralism and expression at the university. She has also organized a conference at the University of Wisconsin–Milwaukee for both college teachers and K-12 educators, and she has worked with groups such as Milwaukee's Holocaust Education and Resource Center to promote teaching about the Holocaust throughout the state of Wisconsin. Baum's research and published essays on the Holocaust concentrate on pedagogy, the role of the emotions in Holocaust memory, and post-Holocaust Jewish identity.

David Blumenthal is the Jay and Leslie Cohen Professor of Judaic Studies at Emory University, Atlanta, Georgia. He is the author or editor of many books, including *Understanding Jewish Mysticism: A Source Reader* (Ktav,

1978-82), *Facing the Abusing God: A Theology of Protest* (Westminster/John Knox Press, 1993), *The Banality of Good and Evil: Moral Lessons from the Shoah and Jewish Tradition* (Georgetown University Press, 1999), *God at the Center: Meditations on Jewish Spirituality* (Jason Aronson, 1994), and *Philosophic Mysticism: Lessons in Rational Religion* (Bar-Ilan University Press, 2006). Blumenthal is also the author of numerous articles on subjects as diverse as medieval Jewish mysticism and philosophy, the Shoah, medieval Islam, and contemporary Jewish spirituality.

Margaret Brearley lectured on medieval and Renaissance German literature for many years at the University of Birmingham, England. She took early retirement from her academic post at Birmingham to establish and direct the West Midlands Israel Information Centre. From 1986 to 1996 she held academic posts at the Centre for Judaism and Jewish-Christian Relations at Selly Oak College, Birmingham, and at the Institute of Jewish Affairs, London. Brearley has lectured throughout Britain and abroad on Zionism, Judaism, terrorism, ideological sources of the Shoah, genocide, Roma/Gypsies, the history of antisemitism, and Jewish-Christian relations. Her publications include numerous research papers in such journals as *Patterns of Prejudice*, *Christian-Jewish Affairs*, and *American Journal of Behavioral Sciences*, as well as chapters in academic books, among them *Genocide in Rwanda: Complicity of the Churches* (Paragon House, 2004) and *Fire in the Ashes: God, Evil, and the Holocaust* (University of Washington Press, 2005). Brearley has served the Archbishops' Council as honorary adviser on the Holocaust.

Britta Frede-Wenger received her Ph.D. in Catholic theology at the University of Tübingen, Germany, in 2004 with a dissertation on the post-Holocaust Jewish thought of Emil L. Fackenheim. This work, the first German-language monograph on Fackenheim's thought, was awarded the Promotionspreis "Religion und Ethik" (2. Preis), issued by the Interdisciplinary Forum on Religion at the University of Erfurt, Germany. Frede-Wenger has worked as an academic assistant to the Catholic theological faculty in Tübingen, as well as for the Akademie der Diözese Rottenburg-Stuttgart. Her recent publications include a coedited volume *Neuer Antisemitismus? Eine Herausforderung für den interreligösen Dialog* (New Antisemitism? A Challenge for Interreligious Dialogue) (Frank & Timme, 2006).

Myrna Goldenberg, professor emerita from Montgomery College, Montgomery Country, Maryland, was the Ida E. King Distinguished Visiting Scholar of Holocaust Studies at the Richard Stockton College of New Jersey in 2005-6. She has published seminal articles on women and the Holocaust and coedited, with Elizabeth Baer, *Experience and Expression: Women, the Nazis, and the Holocaust* (Wayne State University Press, 2003); and, with Rochelle L. Millen, *Testimony, Tensions, and Tikkun: Teaching the Holocaust in Colleges and Universities* (University of Washington Press, 2007). She has also published numerous reviews and articles on curriculum transformation, American Jewish women's literature and history, and university teaching. Goldenberg has been an editor of and frequent contributor to *Potomac Review: A Journal of Arts and Humanities, Women Today, Belles Lettres,* and *Community College Humanities Review.* Her current research focuses on hunger and starvation as a weapon in Hitler's war against the Jews and on American Jewish women's Holocaust poetry.

Peter J. Haas is an ordained Reform rabbi who also served as an active-duty chaplain in the United States Army. From 1980 until 1999 he taught at Vanderbilt University, Nashville, Tennessee. Currently, he is the Abba Hillel Silver Professor of Jewish Studies at Case Western Reserve University, Cleveland, Ohio, where he directs the Samuel Rosenthal Center for Judaic Studies. His articles and books, including *Morality after Auschwitz: The Radical Challenge of the Nazi Ethic* (Fortress Press, 1988) and *Human Rights and the World's Major Religions* (Greenwood Press, 2005), focus on moral discourse, Jewish and Christian thought after the Holocaust, and human rights. He has lectured in the United States, Germany, Italy, Belgium, and Israel.

Henry F. Knight directs the Cohen Center for Holocaust Studies at Keene State College, Keene, New Hampshire, where he teaches in the program of Holocaust and genocide studies. A United Methodist minister and post-Holocaust Christian theologian, he was formerly on the faculty of the University of Tulsa, where he served for twelve years as university chaplain and associate professor of religion. Knight also served from 1979 to 1991 as chaplain and associate professor of religion at Baldwin-Wallace College in Berea, Ohio. He is cochair of the biennial Steven S. Weinstein Holocaust Symposium (formerly the Pastora Goldner Holocaust Symposium), which he founded with Leonard Grob of Fairleigh Dickinson University in 1996. Knight is the author of *Celebrating Holy Week in a Post-Holocaust World*

(Westminster John Knox Press, 2005), *Confessing Christ in a Post-Holocaust World* (Greenwood Press, 2000), and coeditor with Marcia Sachs Littell of *The Uses and Abuses of Knowledge* (University Press of America, 1997).

Hubert Locke is dean emeritus of the Daniel Evans Graduate School of Public Affairs at the University of Washington, where he held the John and Marguerite Corbally Professorship in Public Service. He has been a visiting professor in Holocaust studies at Whitman College, Walla Walla, Washington, and the Richard Stockton College of New Jersey, Pomona, New Jersey. In addition, he serves on the Church Relations Committee of the U.S. Holocaust Memorial Museum, Washington, D.C. Locke is author or editor of numerous books, including *Exile in the Fatherland: Martin Niemöller's Letters from Moabit Prison* (Eerdmans, 1986), *Learning from History: A Black Christian's Perspective on the Holocaust* (Greenwood Press, 2000), *Holocaust and Church Struggle: Religion, Power, and the Politics of Resistance* (University Press of America, 1996), and *Searching for God in Godforsaken Times and Places: Reflections on the Holocaust, Racism, and Death* (Eerdmans, 2003).

David Patterson holds the Bornblum Chair in Judaic Studies at the University of Memphis, Memphis, Tennessee, where he directs the university's Bornblum Judaic Studies Program. A winner of the Koret Jewish Book Award, he has published more than 125 articles and book chapters on philosophy, literature, Judaism, and Holocaust studies, as well as more than two dozen books. Patterson's writings have been anthologized in *Yom Kippur Readings* (Jewish Lights Publishing, 2005), *Holocaust Theology* (New York University Press, 2002), and *The Holocaust: Readings and Interpretations* (McGraw-Hill, 2001). His recent works include *Wrestling with the Angel: Toward a Jewish Understanding of the Nazi Assault on the Name* (Paragon House, 2006) and *Open Wounds: The Crisis of Jewish Thought in the Aftermath of Auschwitz* (University of Washington Press, 2006). He is also the editor and translator of the English edition of *The Complete Black Book of Russian Jewry* (Transaction Publishers, 2002) and a major contributor to and coeditor of the *Encyclopedia of Holocaust Literature* (Oryx Press, 2002). In addition, with John K. Roth, he edits the University of Washington Press series on post-Holocaust studies.

Didier Pollefeyt is professor of pastoral theology and theology of Jewish-Christian relations, chair of the Center for Teacher Education in Religion, and director of the Centre for Peace Ethics in the Faculty of Theology at Katholieke Universiteit, Leuven, Belgium. He also chairs the Institutum Iudaicum, Interuniversity Center for Judaism Studies, Belgium. In addition to his many articles on post-Holocaust ethics and theology, Pollefeyt's publications include the edited volumes *Jews and Christians, Rivals or Partners for the Kingdom of God? In Search of an Alternative for the Theology of Substitution* (Peeters, 1997), *Anti-Judaism and the Fourth Gospel* (Westminster John Knox Press, 2001), *Incredible Forgiveness: Christian Ethics between Fanaticism and Reconciliation* (Peeters, 2004), and *Hermeneutics and Religious Education* (Peeters, 2004).

Amy H. Shapiro is professor of philosophy and humanities at Alverno College, Milwaukee, Wisconsin, where she has also served as coordinator of the Department of Philosophy. For six years she directed the Holocaust Education and Resource Center for the Milwaukee Coalition for Jewish Learning. She has written on various Holocaust-related and feminist issues and often employs nontraditional expressions of philosophical ideas through writing fiction and poetry. Shapiro has also given numerous workshops and courses on the history of the Holocaust and on pedagogical issues involved in Holocaust education.

Index